Studies of the campaigns of the 1775–1783 American War for Independence often suffer from a lack of understanding of the operational aspects of the armies involved. This collection of essays looks at many facets of military operations in America, showing how the armies (British, French, Spanish, German auxiliaries, and the nascent Continental Army) involved adapted their recruitment, training, tactics, and logistics to the specific challenges of this war. The European forces adapted – much more readily than they are given credit for – to the needs of this particular conflict. The British Army adopted a doctrine of open-order light infantry tactics and raised large numbers of Loyalist troops in the theatre of war. The British government obtained the assistance of regiments from several German states, established military organizations that relied heavily on specialized skirmishing troops – jäger – and chasseur companies composed of picked men after the fashion of the British light infantry. The French government sent an expeditionary force from its regular army, while Spain largely employed colonial troops from its North American holdings; each of these armies faced significant logistical challenges while mounting major campaigns. Not least, of course, the American colonies rose to the monumental task of recruiting, training, and supplying an army created specifically for the conflict.

This collection of essays examines various aspects of the problems faced by each of these forces, and the solutions that they achieved – British training of regulars and raising of Loyalist militia, German adaptation of tactics, French and Spanish logistics and campaigning, and American recruiting and conscription. The authors featured have distinguished themselves by their use of primary sources to re-examine aspects of the period's armies long obscured by assumptions or inaccurate generalizations. Throughout their writings conventional wisdom is challenged, and established assumptions are dispelled by well-documented evidence, showing the real strengths and weaknesses of wide array of professional and part-time military organizations involved in this world-changing war.

Don N. Hagist is the managing editor of the *Journal of the American Revolution* (http://allthingsliberty.com) and author of several books focusing on common soldiers during the American War for Independence.

Waging War in America 1775–1783

Operational Challenges of Five Armies During the American Revolution

Edited by Don. N. Hagist

 Helion & Company

Helion & Company Limited
Unit 8 Amherst Business Centre
Budbrooke Road
Warwick
CV34 5WE
England
Tel. 01926 499619
Email: info@helion.co.uk
Website: www.helion.co.uk
Twitter: @helionbooks
Visit our blog at http://blog.helion.co.uk/

Published by Helion & Company 2023
Designed and typeset by Mach 3 Solutions (www.mach3solutions.co.uk)
Cover designed by Paul Hewitt, Battlefield Design (www.battlefield-design.co.uk)

Text © Individual contributors 2023
Cover: Original unsigned watercolor, line of British troops stretching into the distance across a featureless landscape. (Anne S.K. Brown Military Collection)
Illustrations © as individually credited
Maps by George Anderson © Helion & Company 2023

ISBN 978-1-804513-46-0

British Library Cataloguing-in-Publication Data.
A catalogue record for this book is available from the British Library.

For details of other military history titles published by Helion & Company Limited, contact the above address, or visit our website: http://www.helion.co.uk

We always welcome receiving book proposals from prospective authors.

Contents

List of Contributors

Dr Paul Knight is a major in the British Army's Army Reserve, was awarded a PhD in History from the University of Liverpool in 2004 and is a Fellow of the Royal Historical Society. His areas of research interest are the British Army in the First and Second World Wars as well as the American War of Independence. He has a particular focus on the tactical and doctrinal aspects of those wars. He is currently employed in Historical Analysis at the British Army's Land Warfare Centre.

Dr Alexander S. Burns is an Assistant Professor of History at Franciscan University of Steubenville. Alex studies North America and Military Europe in the eighteenth century. He completed his PhD under the supervision of Katherine B. Aaslestad at West Virginia University in 2021. His doctoral dissertation was entitled, '"The Entire Army Says Hello": Common Soldiers' Experiences, Localism, and Army Reform in Britain and Prussia, 1739-1789.' Alex was honored to edit Christopher Duffy's festschrift, *The Changing Face of Old Regime Warfare: Essays in Honour of Christopher Duffy* (Helion, 2022). His next book, *Infantry in Battle, 1733-1783*, will be published by Helion in 2024.

Dr Krysten Blackstone is a Lecturer in International and Military History at the University of Salford, where she has been since 2022. She completed her undergraduate, MSc and PhD at the University of Edinburgh. She is a social and military historian of Early America, and her current work examines the morale of the Continental Army during the Revolutionary War, 1775–1783. Her research is concerned with enlisted soldiers and utilises soldiers' narratives of the conflict, primarily diaries, to illuminate the diversity of soldiers' lived experiences. She also works on the book reviews team for the *Journal of American Studies*.

Todd Braisted is an author and independent researcher specializing in Loyalist studies during the American Revolution. He has published over 40 books and journal articles on a variety of period subjects, including the 2016 book *Grand Forage 1778*. Over the past four decades, he has served as president of the Bergen County Historical Society and the Brigade of the American Revolution and is a Fellow in the Company of Military Historians. He likewise serves as a history advisor to Crossroads of the American Revolution, and on the Advisory Council of Revolution NJ. He has lectured extensively on Loyalists and other subjects across the United States and Canada.

Dr Robbie MacNiven is an author and historian from the highlands of Scotland. He has a War Studies MLitt from the University of Glasgow and a PhD in American Revolutionary War massacres from the University of Edinburgh. His hobbies include historical re-enacting, wargaming and football.

John U. Rees has been writing for over 30 years on the experiences and material culture of common soldiers and women in the armies of the American Revolution. Subjects include military foods, soldiers' belongings and burden, army wagons and watercraft, campaign shelters, and battle and campaign studies; many of his works are available online. John's first book was *'They Were Good Soldiers': African Americans Serving in the Continental Army, 1775-1783* (Helion, 2019); he is currently working on his second, dealing with black soldiers in North America's founding wars, 1754–1865, covering British, Spanish, French, German, and American forces.

Joshua Provan is a writer, presenter, and artist from the UK, who specialises in early modern British colonial history. He regularly appears as an expert guest on popular history podcasts and is the author of three books on subjects ranging from the British in Japan, to the Second Maratha War, and most recently, the Siege of Pensacola.

Dr Robert A. Selig holds a PhD in history from the Universität Würzburg in Germany. He is a specialist on the role of French forces under the comte de Rochambeau during the American War of Independence and serves as project historian for the Washington-Rochambeau Revolutionary Route National Historic Trail. His publications include *Hussars in Lebanon!* (2004) and some 150 articles in American, German, and French scholarly and popular history magazines as well as chapters in books and anthologies. Honours and awards include the French *Ordre national du Mérite* (2022), *La Médaille d'Or des Valeurs Francophones* of La Renaissance Française (2019), the Erick Kurz Memorial Award of the Steuben Society of America (2015), and the Distinguished Patriot Award, National Society SAR (2012).

Don N. Hagist is managing editor of *Journal of the American Revolution* (allthingsliberty.com). His historical studies focus on presenting an accurate picture of individual soldiers and their families, especially those of the British Army who served in America. This research is done using exclusively primary sources, including regimental muster rolls, personal accounts, pension records, orderly books, and a wide range of other archival materials. His most recent books are, *Noble Volunteers: the British Soldiers who fought the American Revolution* (Westholme, 2020), *The Revolution's Last Men: The Soldiers behind the Photographs* (Westholme, 2015) and *These Distinguished Corps: British Grenadier and Light Infantry Battalions in the American Revolution* (Helion, 2022). Don is an engineer for a major medical device manufacturer.

Introduction

It is easy to simplify warfare into a conflict between two nations and reduce a military campaign into the operations of two armies, each with a clearly defined organization and pre-existing doctrine governing its employment. The reality is seldom so simple, and the American War of Independence characterizes the complexity often present even in a war with a seemingly straightforward cause. At times there were soldiers from Great Britain, France, Spain, several German states, and the nascent United States – including both colonists and Native Americans – all on the ground at the same time. Each of these nations and states had their own methods of organizing, managing, and deploying their regiments and corps. Add to this the diversity of organizations – regulars, militias, provincials, irregulars – and the challenges of waging this war become evident.

The concept for this book arose from Helion & Company's annual 'From Reason to Revolution' conference in 2022. The theme was 'For the Destiny of a Continent: Warfare in North American 1754-1815'; five of the papers presented dealt with the American War of Independence. Rather than focus on strategy, personalities or specific battles, each presenter looked at factors associated with adaptation to the specific conditions of the conflict. This book expands on that theme, including four of the conference papers and five additional essays, examining just a few of the challenges faced by five of the nations involved in the American War.

Only recently has literature on the conflict begun to give proper credit to the preparations and adaptation of British regiments to American conditions, which led to generally superb battlefield performance in campaigns that were planned without appreciation for how pervasive the spirit of revolution was in America. Paul Knight looks at the doctrine of skirmishing and fast, open order manoeuvre adopted by British infantry regiments in England and Ireland in the first half of the 1770s, laying the foundation for fighting in America. Todd Braisted examines the companies and regiments of militia raised in the City of New York, the largest American garrison during the war. Alexander S. Burns shows that troops from German states, brought into the war to augment Britain's army and often criticized for being unable to adapt their European training to American conditions, did in fact implement their own skirmishing doctrine.

On the American side, the *rage militaire* that swept the colonies after the outbreak of war began to wane as the conflict escalated and dragged on for several years. Struggling to maintain manpower quotas, colonies turned to conscription. John U. Rees presents a detailed study of the conscription system in New Jersey, and the movement of men through county militias, state regiments and continental regiments. Robbie MacNiven details one campaign on the American western frontier where the war was about territory rather than

viii

independence, and savage brutality was the way of war. And in an army that was plagued by mutiny more than any other of the era, Krysten Blackstone reveals mutiny to have been a form of protest rather than insurrection.

Crucial support for the American cause came from France, first clandestinely in the form of money and material, then with direct participation of the French army and navy. Robert A. Selig looks inside the much-heralded French expeditionary force that arrived in North America in 1780, revealing the many difficulties these European soldiers faced in establishing harmonious relations with a new ally and operating in unfamiliar land amid an untrusting population. And Joshua Provan examines the challenges faced by America's oft-forgotten ally Spain in conducting a masterful campaign that wrested the Gulf Coast from British control.

Using primary sources, the accounts and recollections of those who saw and experienced the American War of Independence, these authors bring forth aspects of warfare easily overlooked. Between the planning and personalities, and the campaigns and battles, were the mechanics and machinations of keeping armies in the field, campaigning in far-flung places, maintaining discipline in inherently chaotic situations. This is the pragmatic part of waging war, the complex process of turning intentions into outcomes. This is the reality of waging war in America.

1

British Army Pre-War Training Objectives and their Suitability for Operations, 1775–1777

Paul Knight

Introduction

The 1772 inspection return for the 47th Regiment of Foot concluded with the following remark under the heading of General Observations: 'This Regiment Performed all their Exercises, and Manoeuvres, with the greatest Exactness & Attention. And is a Very Fine Regiment and Fit for Service.'[1]

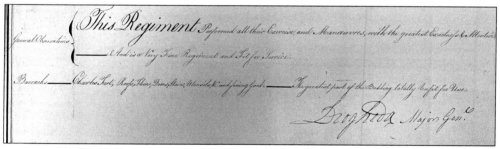

47th Foot 'Fit For Service', Ireland, 1772. Detail from WO 27/26. (The National Archives)

The phrase 'Fit for Service' appears regularly in inspection returns from this era, so much so that it became the title for J.A. Houlding's excellent study of the British Army in the eighteenth century: *Fit For Service: Training of the British Army 1715-95*.[2]

The significance of the General Observations in the 47th's 1772 inspection return was that early in 1773, the regiment deployed to New Jersey in North America, and subsequently

---

1   The National Archives (TNA): WO 27/26: Ireland 1772, in P. Knight, *A Very Fine Regiment: the 47th Foot during the American War of Independence, 1773-1783* (Warwick: Helion, 2022).

2   J.A. Houlding, *Fit for Service: Training of the British Army, 1715-95* (Oxford: Oxford University Press, 1981).

to New York and eventually Boston; this is the last known inspection return on the 47th for a decade. Also deploying to North America in 1773 was the 23rd (Royal Welch) Fuzileers. This regiment received an even more glowing report:

> This Regiment is very Fit for Service; Very well Disciplined & Unexceptionably good. Executed all their business, Exercised, Firings and Manoeuvres with great exactness, & are a very fine Battalion & in good order, greatly to the Credit of the Commanding Officer and the Regiment.[3]

23rd Royal Welch Fuzlieers 'Fit For Service', Britain, 1772. Detail from WO 27/24. (The National Archives)

The General Observations show that both of these regiments evidently met the standard of training expected, but this was a subjective assessment of the regiment's performance, based on a range of observations and data recorded in the inspection return. By studying a large number of inspection returns from the same period as those of the 23rd and 47th Foot, it is possible to draw conclusions about what 'Fit for Service' meant as an indication of each regiment's training regime, in relation to other regiments in the years leading up to the American War of Independence.

A study of inspection returns for 20 regiments reveals that a regiment's level of training effectiveness was based on three factors: recent military operations, the nature of the training undertaken, and the location where that training was undertaken. Some regiments had relevant operational experience in North America from the French and Indian War, while others had operational experience from Germany, for example, which was not directly applicable to the American War of Independence. Still others served in garrisons and so did not gain relevant experiences. The nature of the actual training undertaken is recorded in the inspection returns. It is also apparent that the training undertaken in Ireland was more robust than that undertaken in Britain.

It was not only regiments that had varying levels of relevant experience. The same could be said of the general officers. The generals who served in the opening years of the American War of Independence had experience from the French and Indian War, noticeably Guy Carleton, Thomas Gage and William Howe. They were replaced by generals with European experience, such as John Burgoyne, Henry Clinton and Charles Cornwallis. While they were undoubtedly knowledgeable, their experience was not necessarily relevant to warfare in the Americas.

In this study, only a General Observation which specifically states 'Fit for Service' is taken as being so; where it is not specified or where there is a caveat (for example, 'will be …'), it

---

3   TNA: WO 27/24: Britain 1772.

is assumed that the regiment was not 'Fit for Service.' This picture is confused somewhat by some General Observations which say 'Fit for Service' while also stating that, in some respects, the regiment had not reached the required standard. An example of this is the 20th Foot which, although 'Fit for Service', had a light infantry company which was not fully trained.[4]

The National Archives War Office 27 Series

The WO 27 Series contains regimental annual inspection returns conducted in the British Isles (and also Gibraltar, but they have not been included in this study). They are categorised as British or Irish, and by year. For the purposes of this study, they were examined up to and including 1774, the last year of peace. From 1775 onwards, it is anticipated that the impact of conflict in North America would be reflected in the Army's training regime as it transitioned from peacetime to wartime conditions.

The inspection returns consist of a number of data sources which can be divided into three categories:

1. Personnel. This includes a range of data on the officers and other ranks, collated in different formats, but focusing on similar aspects like age, length of service, height and nationality.
2. Equipment. Covering the condition of weapons, accoutrements, uniforms, and general appearance, highlighting deviations from the 1768 Clothing Warrant that prescribed the uniform in general, and noting missing items.
3. Training. Consisting of three elements:
    a) Manual of Arms. The performance of a specified series of drills conducted on the spot, including loading and firing, changing arms positions and turning.
    b) Movements, Evolutions, Firings and Manoeuvres. This has the potential to be the most detailed and demanding part of the whole report, often including multiple battalions conducting small divisional exercises with artillery and cavalry in support or playing the enemy. This appears to be the most important factor in influencing the General Observations, which often make reference to this section.
    c) General Observations. As shown above in the examples of the 23rd and 47th Foot in 1772.

In 1772, the average soldier of the 47th Foot was as likely to be Irish as English (and Welsh), about 45 percent each; young, under 24 years of age; and with just two years' service. The lack of service is likely to have been due to expansions of the regiment's establishment, including the re-establishment (or in the case of some regiments, the establishment for the first time) of a light infantry company. There was a spike in soldiers whose length of

---

4   TNA: WO 27/30: Britain 1774.

service coincided with the regiment's return from North America in 1764. There were also 20 percent of the soldiers whose length of service started before 1764, indicating that these were French and Indian War veterans.[5] Training was a regimental responsibility, and it would be to experienced soldiers such as these that commanding officers would turn for the training needs of the recruits. The importance of long service soldiers, and in particular senior non-commissioned officers in the management of a regiment, both in peacetime training and in operations, has recently been explored by J.A. Houlding.[6]

Similar patterns are found in other regiments. The 35th Foot, for example, was inspected in Bristol in 1771, when it was found to be 'a very good Regiment, & fit for Service, Great care has been taken in Recruiting and Disciplining the Men. A year or two when they have Spread more may make this one of the best Marching Regiments in the Service.' After nine years' service in North America, including Fort William Henry, Louisbourg, Quebec, Montreal, Martinique, Havana and Florida, the regiment returned to England in 1765. In 1771, 102 out of 410 soldiers (25 percent) were recruited in 1765, that is, upon the regiment's return to England. A further 84 (20 percent) had sufficient length of service to be French and Indian War veterans.[7] This same percentage of veterans is found in the 47th Foot the following year.

Training for A War and The War

If we are to take 'Fit for Service' as being the benchmark of military effectiveness, what does it mean for a British Army regiment and how suitable was it for the conflict that they would become embroiled in? It must be remembered that in the late 1760s and early 1770s, there was no intention for the British Army to fight its fellow countrymen across the Atlantic. A much more realistic prospect was that the next war would be a peer-on-peer conflict in Continental Europe. The experience of the 'long' eighteenth century and the political crises which could have escalated into war (for example, over Corsica and the Falkland Islands against France and Spain respectively) would support this assumption.

This means that the British Army's training objectives would be for 'A War,' that is a generic conflict against an unknown opponent. Only when a conflict had broken out would the army be able to adjust its training to those conditions – 'The War.' Carl von Clausewitz, although writing about a later war, explored the transition from the certainties of training for a conceptual war to the unforeseen difficulties of a real war.[8] Only experience can fully prepare the soldier, regiment, and general for this.

---

5   TNA: WO 27/26: Ireland 1772.
6   J. A. Houlding, 'The Commissioning of Non-Commissioned Officers, 1725-1792,' *Journal of the Society for Army Historical Research*, vol.98, no.395 (Winter 2020), pp.348–361, esp. p.361.
7   TNA: WO 27/21: Britain 1771. In 1774, the 24th Foot was noted as having 29 serving with 20 years' service. The 24th had served in Europe in the previous war, WO 27/32: Ireland 1774.
8   Houlding, *Fit For Service*, pp.2–3.

General Observations as Reliable Observations?

Are the General Observations reliable guides for the effectiveness of a regiment? The three General Observations given above (for the 23rd, 35th and 47th Regiments) were certainly glowing. In 1772, however, the 9th Foot was reported on thus: 'This Regiment is really a Very Bad One. Not withstanding they Performed the Firings Well, and marched Well, By the Plan laid down by the Colonel must Certainly improve. At Present not fit for Service.'[9]

From this report, it is clear that very harsh and critical General Observations could be made. To be fair to the 9th, they had been serving overseas for a decade in Havana, Cuba, and then Saint Augustine, Florida, before returning to Ireland. The regiment was rebuilding after this arduous period of service, and this is at least reflected in the General Observation.

We find a similar General Observation for the 47th in 1767: 'This Regiment is well Clothed, well appointed, and are greatly improved this last year, being almost New Men, Since they came from America. Completed.'[10]

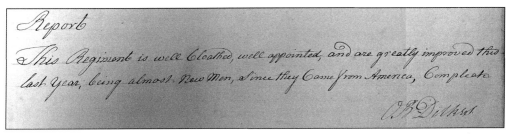

47th Foot, Ireland, 1767. Definitely room for improvement, but after over a decade overseas, mostly on operations, it is understandable. Detail from WO 27/11. (The National Archives)

Although it does not specifically say 'not fit for Service,' the absence of that phase is taken as indicative that the 47th was not at the required standard. Again, as with the 9th, the 47th had undertaken an extended period of arduous overseas service, in this case 13 years in Nova Scotia followed by the French and Indian War. On their return to Ireland in 1763, the 47th had evidently started recruiting and training – the 'New Men.' The inspection returns include a chart showing length of service. That for the 47th in 1772 shows a spike of soldiers with 8 years' service (42 out of 375, 11 percent), that were recruited around 1764.[11]

---

9   TNA: WO 27/26: Ireland 1772. Another similarly harsh comment, the 32nd Foot in 1773 was 'Totally unfit for Service', WO 27/27 Britain 1773.

10   TNA: WO 27/11: Ireland 1767. The 15th Foot went through a similar progression: 'being recently returned from America' (1770), 'will be a good regiment in time' (1771), and 'Fit For Service' (1772 and 1773). WO 27/18 Britain 1770; WO 27/21 Britain 1771; WO 27/24 Britain 1772; WO 27/27 Britain 1773.

11   TNA: WO 27/26: Ireland 1772.

Movements, Evolutions, Firings and Manoeuvres

For its inspection, each regiment went through a series of manoeuvres to illustrate its military effectiveness. The choice of manoeuvres is indicative of what commanding officers considered their regiment could perform, and also what was likely to be required in wartime. Consequently, there is no evidence of a prescribed set of tasks to be completed. An abbreviation of the 47th's manoeuvres in 1772 is:

- Received the general.
- Performed the manual exercise.
- Fired by subdivisions from right to left.
- Advanced by grand divisions, wings and battalion.
- Retired by grand divisions in Indian file; the light infantry company covered the retreat, received and attacked the column.
- Formed columns to the right by grand divisions; the light infantry company protecting it while it formed, and protected the flanks when formed.
- Advanced and retreated in column, formed battalion and fired by subdivisions.
- Each wing formed a column from the right, advanced, retreated and fired in column.
- Formed battalion and fired by subdivisions.
- Formed a solid column from the centre, grenadiers covered the head, light infantry covered the rear, fired from different faces and charged from centre divisions.
- Formed a reserve of colours, formed battalion, and fired by grand divisions.
- Passed the bridge, light infantry company lining the banks of the river, fired and charged over the bridge.
- Formed battalion, fired by subdivisions.
- Repassed the bridge, fired by grand divisions, and reduced to subdivisions.
- Formed battalion and fired by subdivisions.
- Wings wheeled on the centre to defend the flanks, fired twice by subdivisions from the centre of each wing.
- Formed battalion and fired once by wings.
- Formed the oblong square, marched and retreated.
- Formed battalion.
- Advanced by wings.
- Formed battalion.
- Changed front to the right and fired by subdivisions.
- Retreated from the left by grand divisions by files and formed battalion by the left.
- Wheeled to the right about upon the centre and fired by subdivisions.
- Retreated from the right by subdivisions by files and formed battalion on the right.
- Formed the oblong square (battalion marched by files).
- Formed battalion on the long march.
- Formed square, battalion marched by files.
- Formed solid column; grenadiers covered head; light infantry covered rear.
- Formed battalion on the march.
- Formed battalion on its first front.
- Fired and retreated by subdivisions, alternately twice.

- Formed battalion to the right.
- Formed battalion to its first front.
- Fired a volley and charged.
  'The whole performed in double quick time.'

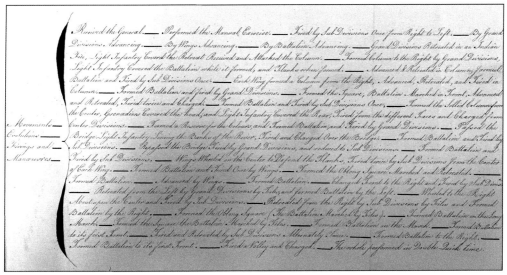

The demanding manoeuvres undertaken by the 47th Foot, Ireland, 1772. Detail from WO 27/26.
(The National Archives)

This shows a regiment proficient in firing, advancing and retiring in various combinations of companies and formations, from Indian (single) file to battalion. The grenadier company and light infantry company protected the main body during changes of formation, advancing and retiring, and were positioned on the flanks when not required. The regiment formed square against cavalry and conducted obstacle (river) crossings. The battalion was able to wheel by half-battalion wings, pivoting on the centre (so half the wing wheeled forwards and half wheeled backwards) to the flanks, which created two parallel lines firing to the left and right of the original position. The final act was a volley and bayonet charge, probably towards the inspecting general for maximum effect. This finale was typical.

The final comment, however, is unusual in the reports examined: 'The whole performed in Double Quick Time.' This indicates that these extensive manoeuvres were performed at a near run throughout. Although not specified, to conduct these manoeuvres and at this speed, the muskets would have been held at the 'trail arms' position. It is also most likely that the regiment formed up in open order. These manoeuvres were conducted on 13 June 1772; General George Townshend's *Rules and Orders for the Discipline of the Light Infantry Companies in His Majesty's Army in Ireland* had been issued on 15 May of that year, less than five weeks earlier. The order for the formation of light infantry companies for the regiments in Ireland had only been issued the previous September.[12] Townshend's *Instructions*

---

12   R.H.R., Smythies, *Historical Records of the 40th Regiment* (Devonport: Swiss, 1894), pp.547–548,

specified that light infantry companies were to be formed up 'two Deep with a space of Two Feet between the Files' and that when in a wood or 'upon any Service of a Secret Nature' they should 'carry [muskets] in a diagonal Position, with their hands on the swell of the firelock,' the 'trail arms' position.

Although Townshend's *Instructions* were for the light infantry company, not the whole battalion, this is likely to be the formation adopted by the 47th in order to conduct the manoeuvres described. The conceptual origins of Townshend's ideas derived from experiences gained during the French and Indian War, in which, as has been shown above, 20 percent of the 47th Foot is likely to have served. It appears that the 47th took the doctrine a step further and applied it to the whole regiment.[13] This looks like a regiment which took its training seriously, and capitalised on the extensive experience gained in the French and Indian War.

When the comparable report for the 23rd Fuzileers is read, a very different picture emerges. In contrast with the 47th's manoeuvres, the 23rd's were very few:

• Wheeled by companies to the right and left.
• Advanced by files from the right by grand divisions.
• Retired from the centre of wings by files.
• Advanced by files from the right of companies.
• Battalion advanced and fired by companies from the centre to the flanks.
• Advanced and retired by files from the centre of the battalion.
• Wheeled on the centre to the right and left.
• Flank grand divisions covered the flanks and fired by files.
• Formed two deep.
• Formed two lines of platoons and fired advancing and retreating.
• Formed three deep.
• Fired a volley and charged.[14]

Initially, it was assumed that the 23rd and 47th were comparably trained regiments. Both received very complimentary General Observations in 1772 and both were selected for what could be a decade-long deployment into a politically charged environment. It is clear, though, that the manoeuvres which the 23rd performed to achieve that General Observation (which, if anything, was more flattering than that received by the 47th) were significantly less complex than those performed by the 47th. Is this indicative of different training and assessment regimes in Britain and Ireland? It is difficult to compare like-with-like when the reports are prose; a 'tick box' exercise with a grade of A to E, for example, would have been far easier to use for objective comparisons. Only three regiments moved from Britain to

---

549–552.
13   See also, S.M. Baule, *Protecting the Empire's Frontier* (Athens, OH: Ohio University Press, 2014), p.14. The 18th Foot in Philadelphia in 1767 while en route to posts on the frontier, gave a demonstration of 'bush fighting' in front of General Gage. This was before the reestablishment of light companies and the publication of doctrine in the early 1770s. This regiment had served in Ireland during the Seven Years War and gained no relevant operational experience.
14   TNA: WO 27/24: Britain 1772.

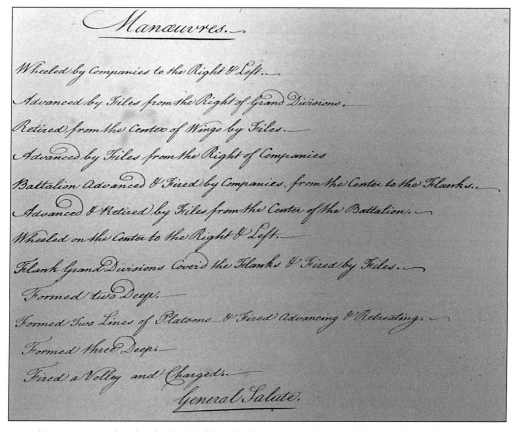

Manoeuvres undertaken by the 23rd Royal Welch Fuzileers, Britain, 1772. Detail from WO 27/24.
(The National Archives)

Ireland in the period under study, and none moved in the opposite direction. One of these was the 15th Foot. Assuming that their effectiveness was consistent, do their manoeuvres indicate a different reporting regime?

In 1773 at Inverness the 15th performed the following manoeuvres, as described in their inspection return:

> The advance and Retreat firing as usual.
> Their manoeuvres consisted of advancing and Retreating in files by Companies from Right and Left, by wings from the Centre of each Retreating by Grand Divisions two deep, forming the Square by Files, Retreating by Grand Divisions from the Right in a rank entire Passing and Repassing the defile. The several manoeuvres covered by the Skirmishing of the Light Infantry, and fire of the battalion.

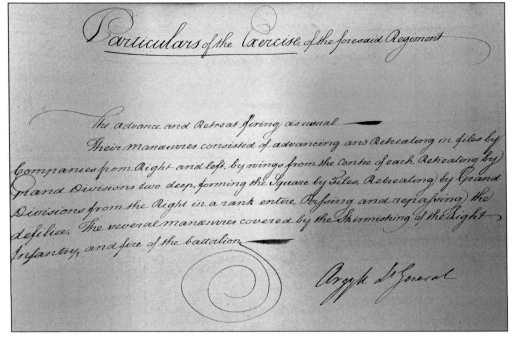

15th Foot's 1773 manoeuvres in Britain to be passed 'Fit For Service'. Detail from WO 27/27.
(The National Archives)

For this, the 15th was considered 'A well trained regiment and is fit for service.'[15]
The following year, at Athlone, the 15th performed the following:

> Received the General. Marched Past by Grand divisions. General Salute. Manual
> Exercise. Advancing Firing. By Sub divisions from Flanks to Centre. By Grand divi-
> sion from Flanks to Centre. By Wings. Retreating. By Sub divisions from Centre to
> Flanks. By Grand divisions from Centre to Flanks. By Grand divisions Right and
> Left. Evolutions. Advance by Sub divisions from right by Files. Retreat by Grand
> divisions from Left by Files. Right Hand Companies Fire. Retreat by Sub divi-
> sions from Left. Left Hand Companies Fire. Advance Form Columns from Centre
> Grand divisions. Retreat from Columns from Centre of Right. Form two Lines. Fire
> Advancing and Retreating. Form the Oblong Square. Fire by Sub divisions. Change
> Front. Volley and Charge. General Salute.

---

15   TNA: WO 27/27: Britain 1773.

15th Foot's more extensive manoeuvres conducted in Ireland in 1774. Detail from WO 27/32.
(The National Archives)

For these efforts:

> This Regiment showed great Attention and a good deal of Steadiness. Went through
> its Business well Particularly the Firings. And is fit for Service.[16]

From a stylistic point of view, the British report was written in prose, although lacking in
punctuation. The Irish report used long dashes which have been transcribed as full stops
here, and used a noticeably more succinct style, more akin to modern bullet points. It is
clear, however, that the 15th underwent a more rigorous inspection regime in Ireland in
1774 than in Britain the previous year.

Upper and Lower Range of Movements, Evolutions, Firings and Manoeuvres

Identifying the upper and lower range of 'Movements, Evolutions, Firings and Manoeuvres'
required for a regiment to be classed 'Fit for Service' would allow other regiments to be
ranked within the range.

The most unimpressive has to be the 3rd Foot, reviewed at Ripon in 1773, for whom,
under Firings & Manoeuvres, is a single word: 'None.'[17]

---

16   TNA: WO 27/32: Ireland 1774.
17   TNA: WO 27/27: Britain 1773.

The regiment which many modern authors consider to be the best trained and drilled was the 33rd Foot.[18] At Derby in 1770, the inspection return General Observations included the lines: 'from every circumstance relative to it, it may be expected that in two year's no Regiment shall exceed it in any Respect.'[19]

This is a statement which, in the context of all the General Observations of all the regiments examined, is so far outside the range of expected comments as to suggest over-reporting. Other regiments may have a prediction of improving or being 'Fit for Service' in the next few years, as with the 35th Foot. Perhaps tellingly, this prediction was not repeated in 1772. At Plymouth in 1773, the 33rd received a General Observation which was much more within the expected range: 'The Regiment is fit for immediate Service, and in every Respect a very fine Corps.'

The manoeuvres performed were extensive. They were written in detailed prose describing the terrain in far greater detail than was normal, for example 'Marches a considerable way… over very difficult Country… through Craggy Rocks & Brush wood… on a Steep & craggy declivity by the Sea Shore.' Such detail is not to be found in the other manoeuvres reviewed. Terrain details are normally limited to those specifically relevant to the tasks being undertaken (bridge, woods, defile) or, on one occasion, 'sand hills' reported for the 37th Foot. As with the General Observation of 1770, the florid style in which the 1773 manoeuvres were reported give the impression of over-reporting. They are summarised thus:

- Retreated in files by companies.
- Changed front to the right.
- Wheeled to the right by companies.
- Marched in column by companies from the right.
- Formed battalion.
- Advanced in Indian file.
- Formed battalion.
- Changed front to the left.
- Advanced in line 'as fast as the great difficulty of the ground would permit.'
- Grenadier and light infantry companies formed the advanced guard.
- Passed a defile in column of files from the centre.
- Advanced guard attacked.
- Column continued advance.
- Formed grand divisions.
- Formed two lines.
- First line supported grenadiers who had seized some high ground.
- Second line seized any unoccupied 'advantageous ground.'
- Battalion formed to the left two deep.
- Oblique fire.
- Formed three deep.

18   R. MacNiven, *The Pattern: the 33rd Regiment and the British Infantry Experience During the American Revolution, 1770-1783* (Warwick: Helion, 2023); R. Middleton, *Cornwallis: Soldier and Statesman in a Revolutionary World* (New Haven: Yale University Press, 2022), pp.18-19.
19   TNA: WO 27/18: Britain 1770.

- Charged.
- Formed wings, each with an advance guard.
- Each wing advanced on the same position, the advance guards firing on each other and the wings manoeuvres for advantage.
- Several sentences describing the two wings manoeuvring against each other.
- Commanding officer of the left wing returned to the attack.
- Right wing retired, firing by divisions from the flanks to the centre.
- Commanding officer of the left wing sent a detachment to the right to turn the left wing's flank, but this was countered.
- Left wing retired from the field.[20]

The manoeuvre phase of this inspection return shows some imagination in the scenarios in which manoeuvres were performed. The manoeuvres themselves do not show any variation from the range expected. The deployment of the regiment into two wings to exercise against each other is unusual as the majority of British inspection returns consisted of single battalions exercising as a single unit. However, the 33rd were not the only regiment to undertake innovative or imaginative training within the confines of being inspected in isolation. The same year and also in Britain, the 37th formed a 'Phalanx,' and 'fir'd irregularly' twelve deep, followed by forming a line of battle 'as practiced at the Battle of Culloden,' all of which are unexpected manoeuvres. An enemy was provided by the 66th Foot's light infantry company, who they exercised against in 'sand hills' and were forced to the shore.[21]

Different Inspection Regimes?

There is the impression, then, that there were different inspection regimes between Britain and Ireland. The inspecting generals did not cross the Irish Sea. Charles, Earl of Drogheda, for example, who inspected the 47th in 1772, only inspected in Ireland, while John Irwin, who provided the very short review of the 3rd Foot in 1773, only inspected in Britain. Some inspecting generals even appear to have a region within Britain or Ireland in which they operated.

In Britain, inspections were almost always of a single battalion, whereas in Ireland, while the single battalion inspection was common, so were inspections of small divisional-sized formations. These small divisional exercises are important because they could include cavalry and artillery, in support and as enemy, which provided battlefield inoculation for troops who had never been in battle before. They also allowed for much more complicated manoeuvres to be conducted and to train officers in the command of formations. Finally, and perhaps most importantly, the British Army did not fight battles as individual battalions, but as brigades and divisions.

Although the author has found no evidence of the inspection criteria, there is a distinct impression that regiments in Ireland were being inspected at (and, by implication, trained

---

20   TNA: WO 27/27: Britain 1773.
21   TNA: WO 27/27: Britain 1773.

to operate at) a far higher standard – to that of a warfighting division. The inspections of regiments in Britain give the impression of being a gendarmerie to support the civil powers, trained to a lower standard.

It would be wrong to assume that this inspection process was entirely limited to one country or the other. Major General William Howe was an inspecting general in Britain and in 1774 inspected the 3rd Foot, whose manoeuvres were performed well as a single battalion, but without any great complexity. Yet, two years previously, his own regiment, the 46th, had been inspected in one of the smaller (only four regiments) divisional inspections in Dublin. We must assume that Howe received a copy of his regiment's report. If that is the case, then he would have been very much aware that his own regiment was being subject to a far more stringent inspection regime than the one he was participating in.[22]

Pre-Deployment Training of the Canada Army regiments, 1774

During 1776 and 1777, seven British Army regiments drove American rebels from before the walls of Quebec City through a series of spectacular tactical and operational victories until forced to capitulate at Saratoga through a failure of British strategic planning. Six of these regiments deployed directly from Britain and Ireland, disembarking at Quebec City and almost immediately undertaking combat operations. The seventh regiment was the 47th, who deployed to Quebec City following the evacuation of Boston.

What does the 1774 inspection regime tell us about the level of readiness of this army? First, we need to identify the regiments and where they were inspected:

- 9th Foot – Waterford, Ireland.
- 20th Foot – Exeter, Britain but posted to Ireland later in the year.
- 21st Foot – Chatham, Britain.
- 24th Foot – Phoenix Park, Dublin, Ireland (July).
- 53rd Foot – Phoenix Park, Dublin, Ireland (July).
- 62nd Foot – Phoenix Park, Dublin, Ireland (May).[23]

Of these, three regiments were inspected singly, and three as part of two divisional exercises at Phoenix Park.

- 9th Foot – a basic report without any complex manoeuvres, was described as a 'pretty good Body of men' but still not 'Fit for Service.' The only reference to grenadier or light infantry companies is 'The Light Infantry of this Regiment was drawn up on the flanks as Grenadiers.'
- 20th Foot – 'Fit for immediate service' but with a number of caveats which would suggest the regiment was not really ready for immediate service:
    * Firings. Loads slow, presents too high, without aim.

---

22   3rd Foot, TNA: WO 27/30: Britain 1774; 46th Foot, TNA: WO 27/26: Ireland 1772.
23   TNA: WO 27/30: Britain 1774; WO 27/32: Ireland 1774.

* Light infantry company active, 'but not completely trained.' Still wore white accoutrements, although a black set had been ordered.
* Manoeuvres. 'Not performed with sufficient alacrity.'
* Clothing fitted with a shoulder strap on the right shoulder for carrying the waistbelt.
* 'Not highly trained nor perfectly silent under arms.'
* 'The files open but not sufficiently to prevent crowding in some of the Movements in Battalion.'

- 21st Foot – 'will be a very serviceable Regiment,' but a basic report, no mention of the grenadier or light infantry companies, and no evidence of any manoeuvres over obstacles.

For those regiments inspected at Phoenix Park, it was a very different picture. In May, the 62nd Foot was inspected alongside five other regiments, all of which would serve in North America although in different theatres.[24] The regiments were formed in two lines, which has been interpreted as being brigades, with artillery in support and with the 18th Light Dragoons as enemy. The line advanced, with the light infantry companies skirmishing forward and the grenadier companies in support. It is unclear whether these companies were supporting their individual regiments, or formed composite light infantry and grenadier battalions. Later, both the light infantry and grenadiers advanced into woods in pursuit of the enemy; it is most likely that they were acting as two composite battalions.

There was also an episode when the first line withdrew in the face of the enemy cavalry and was 'driven Pell Mell … upon Rear Line.' This was a rearwards passage of lines, whereby the first line, acting as if broken by the enemy's actions, retired through the second line to reform in a safe area, protected by the second line. This had to be conducted in such a manner as not to break the cohesion of the second line; otherwise the second line becomes vulnerable to collapse in the face of the enemy's attack, resulting in a general rout.

Finally, there was a volley firing six deep. How this was conducted is not specified. If each line was formed three deep, then the rear line closing up on the front line would create a formation six deep. Although not an orthodox manoeuvre, it illustrates a degree of tolerance for doctrinal flexibility.

In July, the 24th and 53rd exercised alongside four other regiments, and again, all the regiments would serve in North America.[25] On this occasion, the manoeuvres were significantly different from those in May. The regiments wheeled to the right by grand divisions in quick time. The light infantry companies formed on the right of the grenadier companies. Being placed on the right was usually the post of honour for the grenadier companies, so this was an unusual arrangement. The grenadier and light infantry companies are recorded as covering the van and flanks of a column as it advanced and then retired. They also performed bridge crossing and forming square against cavalry. On this occasion there was no enemy. It is also not clear that the six regiments were structured as two brigades; the implication is that they were acting as a single formation. Again, the organisation of the

---

24   These were the 22nd, 42nd, 54th, 55th and 63rd Foot.
25   These were the 35th, 40th, 49th and 54th Foot.

grenadier and light infantry companies is not specified, but it appears that they were acting as two composite battalions, as with the May exercise.

It is clear from this small selection of regiments that there was no one training regime or training standard across the British Army. Of the three regiments which were inspected individually, only one was 'Fit for Service, and even there, there were significant concerns about the overall standard of its training. The three regiments inspected at Phoenix Park clearly underwent a much more rigorous inspection regime, but there were differences between May and July.

With this evidence, we cannot generalise about the capabilities of regiments when they disembarked in an operational theatre. Yet despite that, when faced by the realities of combat and the arduous campaigning of North America with woodland fighting and amphibious operations, none of these regiments failed to perform to the standard required.

Roger Lamb and Light Infantry Training

A great deal has been written about the performance of British light infantry in the American War of Independence, which is understandable given the predominance of the 'American Scramble' and a natural tendency to seek out the 'special' over the 'routine' of military activities. One of the questions being examined here is how training was disseminated through the British Army? In the case of light infantry training, it is accepted that there was a hiatus of almost a decade between the end of the French and Indian Wars and the re-introduction of the light infantry companies in Britain in 1770 and in Ireland in 1771. This assumes, of course, that the regiment had had a light infantry company in the previous war.

Corporal Roger Lamb of the 9th Foot is the most instantly recognisable British Army diarist from the ranks of the war and is generally accepted as being a reliable source, despite writing 35 years after some of the events he describes. One of the incidents he recounts is the arrival of the 33rd Foot to teach light infantry tactics to the Dublin garrison, and how he was promoted to corporal and sent to receive instruction

> … in the new exercise which shortly before had been introduced by General Sir William Howe. It consisted of a set of manoeuvres for light infantry, and was ordered by His Majesty to be practiced by the different regiments. To make trial of this excellent mode of discipline for light troops, and render it general without delay, seven companies were assembled at Salisbury in the summer of 1774. His Majesty himself went to Salisbury to see them [at a demonstration at Richmond Park, near London], and was much pleased with their utility, and the manner of their execution. The manoeuvres were chiefly intended for woody and intricate districts, with which North America abounds, where an army cannot act in line. The light infantry manoeuvres made use of [at the time of writing] are different from, those of Sir William Howe, which were done from centre of battalions, grand divisions, and sub-divisions, by double Indian files.[26]

---

26   Don N. Hagist, *Roger Lamb's American Revolution: A British Soldier's Story* (Yardley, PA: Westholme,

There were two sets of light infantry doctrine extant in 1775:

- Townshend's *Rules and Orders for the Discipline of the Light Infantry Companies in His Majesty's Army in Ireland* (1772).[27]
- Howe's *Discipline Established by Major General Howe for Light Infantry in Battalion* (1774).

The 1764 Manual of Arms provided details of some manoeuvres, but did not cover tactics, while both Townshend and Howe provided some examples of tactics.

Townshend's *Instructions* were aimed at the recruitment and training of a light infantry company. These companies had only been established the previous year in Ireland. Most of his writing suggests that these companies would operate singly, in support of the battalion, although he did recognise that a composite light infantry battalion might be formed: 'When a Corps of Light Infantry is composed of Companies from different Regiments they must do Duty by Companies with their own officers.'

He included orders that they should be formed up two deep, at two feet spacings, and should 'run up briskly' with their muskets at the trail. They were to operate in files, with one man protecting the other while they fired and re-loaded, making use of obstacles for cover. The instructions warned that combat may become 'personal between Man and Man.'

Howe's *Discipline* is part drill manual and part exercise as a composite light battalion, when trialled at Salisbury and later shown to the king. This training was later applied to whole battalions, like the 20th and 33rd Foot. There were some differences between Howe and Townshend. Howe, for example, has three gradations of spacings: Order (two feet); Open Order (four feet); and Extended Order (10 feet).

Both Townshend and Howe were French and Indian War veterans, and it was from there that they received their doctrinal inspiration. Townshend had served as brigadier to Major General James Wolfe at Quebec in 1759, taking command of the later stages of the battle, and continued to serve in Quebec after Wolfe's death. Howe had commanded a composite light battalion for Wolfe at Quebec, where his second in command was Major John Hussey, of the 47th Foot. Was the drill manual part of Howe's *Discipline* new, as Lamb thought, or was it the re-issuing of drill taught to his light infantry battalion in 1759? Howe would later command a brigade during the advance on Montreal. Howe's elder brother, George, had trained his 55th Foot as a light infantry regiment, until his untimely death at Fort Carillon/Ticonderoga in 1758. Both of these authors had operational experience in North America and so had a shared heritage in light infantry tactics.

Lamb's comments on 'the new exercise … introduced by … Howe … for Light Infantry' are worth further examination against the background of his military experience in the summer of 1775. Firstly, Lamb had enlisted in August 1773 and was promoted to corporal early in 1775. By the time he was instructed in light infantry drill that summer, he had less than two years of military service. Clearly his education facilitated his rapid promotion, but such rapid promotion was probably enabled by a lack of competition in a regiment which

2022), pp.17–18.
27 Smythies, *Historical Records of the 40th Regiment*, pp.547–548.

was understrength. Secondly, Lamb had enlisted into a regiment, the 9th Foot, which was not 'Fit for Service.' In 1772, 'This Regiment is really a Very Bad One,' and the following year it was 'much Mended Since the Last Review ... Better against the Next.' The 1774 inspection was the first which Lamb would have participated in. This was conducted at Waterford and it was noted that there were 91 recruits. Lamb may well have been one of those recruits, but had he participated in the inspection, the 'Firings and Manoeuvres' he performed were, summarised:

- Drawn up three deep.
- Officers saluted.
- General salute.
- Manual exercise (described as well performed).
- Wheeled to the right by grand divisions.
- Marched by the general.
- Marched quick time and drew up on their former ground.
- Advanced in slow and quick time.
- Retreated in slow and quick time.
- Right about.
- Fired from the flanks to centre by subdivisions, by grand divisions chequered and by wings.
- Advanced in slow time.
- Fired by subdivisions from centre to flanks, by grand divisions and by wings.
- Formed on first ground.
- Manoeuvred in quick time.
- Formed a column from the right by grand divisions advancing.
- Formed battalion and fired by grand divisions from right to left.
- Formed a column from the left, by grand divisions, retreating.
- Formed battalion and fired by grand divisions from left to right.
- Formed a column from the centre, by companies advancing.
- Formed battalion and fired by companies from centre to flanks.
- Formed a column from the centre by companies retreating.
- Formed battalion and fired by companies from the centre to the flanks.
- Passed the bridge.
- Formed battalion and fired by companies from centre to flanks.
- Fired by companies from flanks to centre and repassed the bridge.
- Formed battalion and fired by companies from flanks to centre.
- Half wheeled to right by companies and changed front.
- Formed battalion and fired by companies from right to left.
- Formed 'potence'[28] and fired by companies from centre to flanks.
- Formed battalion.
- Left hand companies right about.

---

28   En Potence. Where a battalion in line advances or retires a company on the flank until perpendicular to the line, to provide flank protection. With thanks to Dr T. Whitfield for this explanation.

- Alternate firing by companies to front and rear, from flanks to centre.
- Left hand companies about.
- Passed the defile from the centre by files.
- Formed battalion and fired by companies from centre to flanks.
- Retreated from the right by grand divisions.
- Formed battalion to front and fired by grand division.
- Charged.
- Fired a volley.
- Open ranks.
- General salute.

These manoeuvres involved firing 26 rounds. The regiment was not yet 'Fit for Service,' being described as 'a pretty good Body of Men, pretty well dressed, Wants a great many men to Complete.' The only reference to the actions of the grenadier and light infantry companies was in the comments: 'The Light Infantry of this Regiment was drawn up on the flanks as Grenadiers.' These manoeuvres were more complex than those conducted by some regiments in Britain who were 'Fit for Service,' but were not overly complicated by the standards of the Irish Establishment. If this was the extent of Lamb's military training, then it is not surprising that he wrote so glowingly of undertaking light infantry training from a regiment freshly arrived from Britain, especially trained in light infantry tactics by General Howe, and who were 'Fit for Service.'[29]

It is also clear that light infantry tactics were already being implemented by regiments in Ireland. The 24th Foot in 1773, for example, had been criticised because 'the light infantry were drawn up three deep contrary to Orders.'[30] Townshend's *Instructions* specified two ranks. We have already seen how the May and July 1774 Phoenix Park exercises incorporated composite grenadier and light battalions, as Howe would demonstrate in September of that year. In 1772 the 47th Foot's manoeuvres were performed in double quick time and probably in open order, another feature of both Townshend and Howe, but pre-dating Howe. The idea of a corporate memory is an important one. In 1772, when the 47th sailed for New Jersey 20 percent of the regiment had sufficient length of service to have served in the French and Indian War. Lamb himself recounted that, when in combat for the first time in 1776, one of the older soldiers told him not to be alarmed by the noise of shot around him – those bullets had already passed him by.[31] As with the 47th, the 9th would have contained a pool of experienced soldiers to train and advise the newer men.

There is one final observation to be made about Lamb and Howe's light infantry manoeuvres, which is that Lamb never served directly under Howe, only indirectly through the instruction provided by the 33rd Foot. He later served two campaigning seasons in Quebec under Generals Carleton and Burgoyne. This was an operational theatre of 'woody and intricate districts.' Having evicted the rebels from Quebec in 1776, Carleton paused the pursuit while a fleet was constructed during which time further training was undertaken.

---

29   TNA: WO 27/26: Ireland 1772; WO 27/29: Ireland 1773; WO 27/32: Ireland 1774.
30   TNA: WO 27/29: Ireland 1773. See also 53rd Foot in the same year, and the 44th Foot the following year. WO 27/32: Ireland 1774.
31   Hagist, *Roger Lamb's American Revolution*, p.32.

Carleton, like Townsend and Howe, had served under Wolfe in 1759. He was also, coincidentally, the colonel of the 47th Foot. An anonymous 47th Foot light infantry company officer recorded the exploits of multiple light companies led by Captain James Henry Craig of the 47th during the campaign.[32] Surely, this summer of 1776 between Quebec and St. Johns, rather than the summer of 1775 around Dublin, was where Lamb learnt the 'manoeuvres for Light Infantry' which were 'chiefly intended for woody and intricate districts, with which North America abounds, where an army cannot act in line'?[33]

Training the Dublin Garrison in Light Infantry Tactics, 1775

Returning to the summer of 1775 and the training of the Dublin garrison in Howe's *Discipline*, who were the Dublin garrison to which Lamb refers? Lamb did not specify the other regiments. In June 1775 another Phoenix Park manoeuvre was held with six regiments, including the 9th and 33rd. Were these the regiments trained by the 33rd? If so, who where they and what was their operational experience from the French and Indian or Seven Years War?

- 9th Foot – Raids on the French Coast; Havana, 1762; garrison duty at St Augustine, Florida.
- 15th Foot – French and Indian War, St Lawrence, Quebec, 1759.
- 33rd Foot – Raids on the French Coast; Germany from 1760.
- 34th Foot – Raids on the French Coast; Havana, 1762; Florida.
- 37th Foot – Germany, Minden, 1759.
- 46th Foot – French and Indian War, Fort Carillon, Niagara, Montreal; Caribbean; Havana 1762.

What this brief survey shows is that, of the five regiments which we can assume were under instruction, all had extensive relevant operational experience. Two, the 15th and 46th, were French and Indian War veterans while two more had experience from the Caribbean and Florida (9th and 34th); the 46th actually having experience in both theatres. The published doctrine of both Townshend and Howe originated in these North American theatres where these regiments had operational experience. The only regiment not to have served across the Atlantic was the 37th Foot; this was a 'Minden regiment,' for which achievements the regiment could be justifiably proud. Also, the 46th Foot was Howe's own regiment. It would have been inconceivable that he had not sent a copy of his *Discipline* to his own regiment. Indeed, the regiment which was supposed to be instructing on American warfare was one

---

32   G.F.G. Stanley, *For Want of a Horse* (Sackville, NB: Tribune Press, 1961), for example, p.75: 'Three Companies of the Lt Infantry with the Canadian Volunteers under the Command of Captn Craig, of the 47th Regt.'

33   On 29 June 1776, General Carleton ordered regiments to train no more than 'Loading, Levelling, charging with Bayonets, and marching … changing front by Divisions, and by Files; suffering the Regiment to break and form … by a file from Right, Left or Centre: The Order of forming is to be two deep, and the Files 18 Inches asunder.' J. M. Hadden, *Hadden's Journal and Orderly Books* (Albany, NY: Joel Munsell's Sons, 1884), pp.197–198.

of the very few who had never served there and which was, arguably, the regiment with the least operational experience in the previous war.

What, then, was the 33rd Foot supposed to be teaching and to whom?

Adaptability to The War – The Opening Years of the American War of Independence

Flexibility is generally considered to be a key aspect in the learning experiences of armies. An object which flexes when pressure is applied to it, however, will revert to its original position once that pressure is released. There is no change, and no learning.

In contrast, adaptability implies the ability to adjust to new conditions, and to modify tactics and doctrine caused by those new conditions. In a disciplined, regimented and hierarchical organisation like the British Army of the eighteenth century, the ability for individual regiments to set their own training objectives seems, at first sight, to be anathema. Even for something as simple as fighting in two or three ranks, individual regiments adopted one or the other and in some cases even alternated between the two.[34] Officers and, as Houlding has recently argued, senior non-commissioned officers, were trusted to train their regiments in peacetime and lead them in wartime.[35] This implies that both officers and senior non-commissioned officers were themselves competent and knowledgeable in those forms of warfare.

The initial military operations around Boston, Massachusetts, were conducted in an environment not dissimilar to those in which the regiments had exercised in Britain and, in particular, Ireland. Eastern Massachusetts had been settled for over a century by British colonists. There were, in 1775, towns and cities, settled agricultural communities with arable land defined by field boundaries, bridges and roads, and areas of undeveloped woodland. During the Lexington and Concord raid, the main body consisted of a composite grenadier battalion and a composite light infantry battalion. The light infantry companies provided flank protection to the grenadiers, as was practiced at Phoenix Park. At Bunker Hill, composite grenadier and light infantry battalions were detached for the flanking move which was halted at the picket fence while the centre companies of their regiments conducted separate attacks. Again, this was not dissimilar to manoeuvres practiced at Phoenix Park.

There was one aspect of 1775 where the training failed, and that was the North Bridge outside of Concord. Bridge (and other obstacle) crossings had been practiced in peacetime yet at this critical juncture, cohesion was lost between the light infantry companies assigned to guard the bridge. It would be unfair to blame any one company for what occurred, but it is worth noting that the 10th Foot had been posted to Quebec a number of years previously and no known inspections had been carried out on it during the early 1770s. Furthermore, the regiment had only been involved in one, minor action (against a French raid on Carrickfergus in early 1760) since the Battle of Malplaquet in 1709. If possessing a core of veteran officers and non-commissioned officers for training recruits and stiffening

---

34   Both the 23rd and 33rd alternated between two and three ranks during an inspection; TNA: WO 27/24: Britain 1772, WO 27/27: Britain 1773.

35   Houlding, 'Commissioning of Non-Commissioned Officers.'

inexperienced soldiers in combat was a factor in regimental training, then the 10th Foot was not well provided for.

Turning to the Canada Army of 1776 and 1777 again, plus those posted to Quebec on garrison duties, like the 8th Foot,[36] these regiments showed remarkable adaptability. All were adept at close order tactics, as shown in the inspection returns. They also proved adept at amphibious operations on the Great Lakes and Lake Champlain, fighting in woods and forests, light infantry tactics for all companies rather than just the light infantry and grenadier companies, arctic warfare in the Canadian winters, and conducting operations in cooperation with indigenous forces. This suggests a degree of tactical adaptability not normally associated with the British Army of this period. This requires an institutional mindset which was adaptable, not rigid, and which is seen in the pre-war training exercises in Britain and especially Ireland.

Conclusion

At the outbreak of the American War of Independence, we cannot talk of a single British Army in terms of training regimes and effectiveness for operations. Training and effectiveness were variables influenced by a number of factors: The training regime of the commanding officer; whether on the British or Irish Establishment; previous relevant military experience; and the phase of the posting cycle.

Commanding officers were responsible for the training of their regiments. Even something as simple as whether to deploy in two or three ranks (or both) was variable. The commanding officers' previous experience influenced their training regimes.

While the training regime of a regiment in Britain could reach a very high standard, on average the inspection standard in Britain was significantly lower than that in Ireland. The differences between the Manoeuvres and the General Observations of the 23rd and 47th Foot in 1772, both despatched overseas on demanding tasks, shows the difference between the training and inspection regimes in Britain and Ireland. Similarly, the differences in the reports on the 15th Foot show a more demanding regime in Ireland. The range of 'Movements, Evolutions, Firings and Manoeuvres' required to be 'Fit for Service' in Britain is shown by the 3rd Foot in 1773 and 33rd Foot in 1774. In Ireland, in contrast, no regiment performed as little as the 3rd Foot to be classed 'Fit for Service,' and many performed more complicated manoeuvres than the 33rd Foot, especially those participating in the Phoenix Park manoeuvres.

Critically, only in Ireland were regiments inspected as a warfighting division. This may be the reason why the 33rd Foot was sent to Ireland to train the Dublin garrison on light infantry tactics, even though light infantry drills had been in general use for several years by that point. So, although the British Army is spoken of as a homogeneous whole, we should look at regiments as being trained under the British or Irish Establishments to gain an understanding of their level of pre-war training.

---

36   W.L. Potter, *Redcoats on the Frontier: A Study of the King's 8th Regiment in North America* (Unknown: privately published, 2003).

The level of relevant military experience for the American War of Independence (once it was clear that was where 'The War' was being fought) was critical in an era when there was no central repository of lessons. Corporate knowledge existed at the regimental level (officers and soldiers with sufficient relevant length of service) and at general officer level (which is identifiable as written peacetime doctrine and instructions in the field). All of this experience originated in the same conceptual space, the battlefields of North America during the previous war. While the generals issued doctrine, it was senior officers and (especially) the senior soldiers who actually conducted the training of the regiment. A regiment's (and to a lesser extent, general's) experience could be categorised as American, European or garrison.

American experience was obviously the most relevant, and was personalised in the form of key generals, noticeably Carleton, Howe and Townshend. As has been shown, the 35th and 47th Foot both had in their ranks 20 percent with sufficient length of service to have experience from the French and Indian War, and Roger Lamb provided anecdotal evidence for pre-war operational experience in the 9th Foot.

Regiments with operational experience from Europe during the Seven Years War, like the 23rd, 24th, 33rd and 37th Foot, can be expected to have had a core of seasoned veterans to 'stiffen' a group of young soldiers exposed to combat for the first time. On the other hand, they could not be expected to have had relevant operational experience for training for, and operating in, North America, especially when the operational theatre was away from developed agricultural regions.

Finally, there were regiments with no operational experience in the French and Indian or Seven Years War, including the 10th and 19th Foot, although both of these had peacetime service in North America before 1775.

The final factor which impacted a regiment's readiness for the conduct of operations was the posting cycle, that is, overseas deployments and the return to Britain. The 9th, 15th and 47th Foot all underwent this process in the period under review, meaning that they were engaged in recruiting and recruit training rather than in more complex military activities. Under normal peacetime conditions there would be sufficient time to rebuild and train to the required standard (15th and 47th Foot), but not all were so fortunate – the 9th Foot was still not 'Fit for Service' when it deployed to Quebec early in 1776.[37]

Bibliography

Primary Sources
The National Archives, Kew, UK (TNA)
    WO 27/11–32: Inspections, Britain and Ireland 1767–1774

Printed Primary Sources
Hadden, J.M., *Hadden's Journal and Orderly Books* (Albany, NY: Joel Munsell's Sons, 1884)
Stanley, G.F.G., *For Want of a Horse* (Sackville, NB: Tribune Press, 1961)

---

37   Houlding, *Fit For Service*, p.296.

Secondary Sources

Baule, S.M., *Protecting the Empire's Frontier* (Athens OH: Ohio University Press, 2014)

Hagist, D.N., *Roger Lamb's American Revolution: A British Soldier's Story* (Yardley, PA: Westholme, 2022)

Houlding, J.A., *Fit for Service: Training of the British Army, 1715-95* (Oxford: Oxford University Press, 1981)

Houlding, J.A., 'The Commissioning of Non-Commissioned Officers, 1725-1792', *Journal of the Society for Army Historical Research*, vol.98, no.395 (Winter 2020), pp.348–361

Knight, P., *A Very Fine Regiment: the 47th Foot during the American War of Independence, 1773-1783* (Warwick: Helion, 2022)

MacNiven, R., *The Pattern: the 33rd Regiment and the British Infantry Experience During the American Revolution, 1770-1783* (Warwick: Helion, 2023)

Middleton, R., *Cornwallis: Soldier and Statesman in a Revolutionary World* (New Haven: Yale University Press, 2022)

Potter, W.L., *Redcoats on the Frontier: A Study of the King's 8th Regiment in North America* (Unknown: privately published, 2003)

Smythies, R.H.R., *Historical Records of the 40th Regiment* (Devonport: Swiss, 1894)

2

'The Infantry Perform Honorable Service': 'Hessian' Tactics in the Context of Military Europe[1]

Alexander S. Burns

Misconceptions abound regarding the tactical background and performance of the German *Subsidientruppen* who served alongside the British in the American War of Independence. The popular perception is that they were greedy plundering mercenaries who lost to George Washington at Trenton as a result of being drunk at Christmas.[2] American and British perceptions, from the time of the war itself down to writings of modern historians, have painted these men as slow and ineffective, backward-looking troops who did not understand the flexibility of Revolutionary warfare. Defeats where the *Subsidientruppen* played a major role, like Bennington, Bemis Heights, Red Bank, and above all, Trenton, have done much to shape this narrative. This begs the question: were they good soldiers?

The 'Hessians' were in fact more flexible than has previously been shown, and in specific ways they adapted the martial culture of German Central Europe to a North American context. Too often, the American War of Independence is treated in splendid isolation from contemporary European practices. Following in the vein of Christopher Duffy, the *Subsidientruppen* must be assessed the context of military Europe: the transnational military elites of eighteenth-century Europe, and the collective martial culture that they created during this time.[3]

Colloquially in the United States, these German troops are remembered as 'Hessians.' In academic circles, German scholars have long abandoned 'Hessians' as a term for these soldiers.[4] While many of the 37,000 who served in America came from the provinces of

---

1 Portions of this chapter first appeared in *The Journal of the Seven Years War Association*. The author is grateful to editor of the *Journal*, Professor James R. McIntyre, for giving permission for their publication here.
2 The best discussion, in English, of plundering is still Rodney Atwood, *The Hessians: Mercenaries from Hessen-Kassel in the American Revolution* (Cambridge: Cambridge University Press, 1980), pp.171–184.
3 Alexander S. Burns, *The Changing Face of Old Regime Warfare: Essays in Honour of Christopher Duffy* (Warwick: Helion, 2022), p.50.
4 German scholars such as Stephan Huck have promoted the term *Subsidientruppen*, or in English:

Hessen-Kassel or Hessen-Hanau, others travelled from Ansbach-Bayreuth, Anhalt-Zerbst, Braunschweig-Wolfenbüttel, and Waldeck. These German soldiers accounted for almost one in three soldiers fighting on behalf of the British crown. Dr Friederike Baer's *Hessians: German Soldiers in the American Revolutionary War,* is the most recent scholarly survey of these troops.

'Hessians' in European Context: The Story of Four Regiments

What does it mean to be a good soldier? The question conjures up notions of loyalty, duty, and honour. In the middle third of the eighteenth century, most observers agreed that the Prussians, fresh from their victory in the Seven Years War, had produced some of the finest soldiers in Europe. In fact, many states adopted drill styles and even uniform modifications to appear more Prussian, a phenomenon often called Prussomania.[5] A large percentage of the north German protestant states, such as Hessen-Kassel and Braunschweig-Wolfenbüttel, armed and clothed their men in direct imitation of the Prussians. But as Christopher Duffy has rightly noted, few of these states managed to copy more than the outward veneer of 'Prussianness.'[6] What were the core aspects of being a successful infantryman, according to these Prussians: the martial culture with the most direct influence on the *Subsidientruppen*?

The positive traits which officers looked for included a strong work ethic, love for unit, region, and dynasty, synchronized movement with other soldiers in certain contexts, and above all, speed in loading the musket. Before proceeding, it will help to define each of these characteristics. In this context, a strong work ethic means a willingness to perform the manual exercise in an attentive and crisp manner, obey orders to the letter, and undergo hardship without complaint to superiors. Soldiers formed intense attachments to their individual units, local regions, and dynastic leaders.[7] Officers also valued synchronized movement, such as shouldering muskets or presenting muskets in unison, while performing manoeuvres in close order. While this uniformity of movement had little practical use on the battlefield, officers, particularly the 'Prussomaniacs' of the 1770s and 1780s, saw it as a benchmark for quality soldiers. Finally, and perhaps most importantly, military observers respected common soldiers who showed skill in quickly loading and firing their muskets. In practice drills, soldiers fired their muskets much more quickly than in battle. A shot every 20 seconds seems to have been the standard for highly drilled troops in combat conditions. When taken together, these traits helped military men judge the quality of infantry privates during the eighteenth century.

These characteristics can be seen by examining four units from armies in German Central Europe: Prussian infantry regiments No. 13 and No. 40 (Itzenplitz and Alt-Kreytzen) during the Seven Years War, and the Hessian von Bose Regiment and Braunschweig-Wolfenbüttel

---

subsidy troops. See Stephan Huck, *Soldaten gegen Nordamerika: Lebenswelten Braunschweiger Subsidientruppen im Amerikanischen Unabhängigkeitskrieg* (München: Oldenbourg Verlag, 2011).

5   Christopher Duffy, *The Military Life of Frederick the Great* (New York: Atheneum, 1986), p.247.
6   Christopher Duffy, *The Military Experience in the Age of Reason* (New York: Atheneum, 1988), p.25.
7   Alexander S. Burns, *'The Entire Army Says Hello': Common Soldiers' Experiences, Localism, and Army Reform in Britain and Prussia, 1739-1789* (PhD thesis, West Virginia University, 2021).

Prinz Friedrich Regiment during the American War of Independence. The regiments all came from north German Protestant states but had differing levels of quality. Frederick II 'the Great' of Prussia recognized that the men of No. 13 were rather exceptional, and that the men of No. 40 were rather mediocre. The von Bose Regiment was singled out particularly by the British as an effective Hessian unit. In the report of its commander, the Braunschweig Regiment Prinz Friedrich was rated as rather abysmal. This spectrum will clearly show the positive and negative aspects which officers and military observers witnessed in regiments of these Protestant German militaries.

Prussian Infantry Regiment No. 13, or, as it would have been called in the early Seven Years War, von Itzenplitz, set the standard for quality in the Prussian army from 1756 to 1758, or from the outbreak of the Seven Years War to the Battle of Hochkirch. In this period, Regiment von Itzenplitz fought in nearly all of the major battles of the central European theatre of the Seven Years War. Frederick II of Prussia showed great honour to this regiment in 1768 when he allowed it to form directly behind the *Garde* and Regiment No. 1 on parade. In addition, in his ranking of Prussian infantry regiments, Frederick ranked Regiment von Itzenplitz 'very good,' his highest category of praise. This particular regiment fought with distinction at the battles of Lobositz, Prague, Rossbach, Leuthen, and Hochkirch. What then, helped set Regiment von Itzenplitz apart?

The officers and men of the regiment showed an incredible work ethic. Non-commissioned officers strove to bring recruits to a high state of perfection, as evidenced by Ulrich Bräker's experiences as a private soldier in this regiment. Though originally a native of Switzerland, recruiting officers snatched Bräker into Prussian service. As a result, his writings describe attempts to desert and complaints about the Prussian service. Despite this, he often had positive things to say about the work ethic of the men around him. Other private soldiers offered to assist him in learning the arms drill. Bräker recalled that in his off hours he, 'practiced the arms-drill, read the Halle hymn book, and prayed.'[8] While Bräker seemed to resent the Prussians for supposedly dragooning him into their military, he portrayed common Prussian soldiers as a hardworking and cheerful lot.

The native Brandenburgers and Prussians in Regiment von Itzenplitz showed great love for their unit, their region, and their king. Bräker intimated that even years after his desertion from the Prussian army he still had some sense of unit pride, calling Itzenplitz 'a noble name.'[9] In the course of the Battle of Lobositz, Bräker reported that, 'Our native Prussians and Brandenburgers sprang upon the Pandurs like Furies,' and that, 'many a man, as I said before, jumped down much more nimbly than myself over one wall after another, to hasten to the help of his comrades.'[10] Here, like many soldiers throughout time, Bräker indicated that the primary motivating factor for the men of Regiment von Itzenplitz was helping their comrades. A sense of regional and unit loyalty existed even off the battlefield. While traveling to Berlin for the first time, Bräker conveyed, 'when we had passed the broad river the sergeants expressed great joy, for now we trod on Brandenburg soil.'[11] While this may not

---

8   Ulrich Bräker, *Lebensgeschichte Und Natürliche Ebenteuer Des Armen Mannes Im Tockenburg* (Zurich: Drell, Geßner, Füßli, 1789), p.124.
9   Bräker, *Lebensgeschichte,* p.141.
10   Bräker, *Lebensgeschichte,* pp.153–154.
11   Bräker, *Lebensgeschichte,* p.116.

be patriotism as such, native inhabitants of Brandenburg and Prussia drew on a sense of communal loyalty which translated into unit cohesion.

The men of Regiment von Itzenplitz also displayed a high degree of proficiency in their uniformity of movement. 'We ourselves, indeed, were always among the first in our places, and exerted ourselves bravely ... marching up and down poker-stiff, and continually practicing the arms-drill as quick as lightning.'[12] He also recounted that 'every day we went outside the city gates and fell to manoeuvring, advancing on the left and right, attacking, retiring, charging by platoons and by divisions, and whatever else that the god Mars teaches.'[13] However, they also knew when this drill-square synchronization needed to be abandoned. In both their attack on the Lobosch at the Battle of Lobositz, and the crossing of the Rocketnitzer Bach at the Battle of Prague, the unit had to abandon their reliance on close order tactics in order to move through rough terrain.

Bräker also recorded the attention his superiors gave to loading the musket quickly. One of his fellow soldiers, a man named Christian Zitterman, informed him, 'You'll soon get the knack of it', he said, 'but it's a question of doing it quickly. You must be able to do it like lightning!'[14] This attention, more to the speed than the process, would prove crucial for the Prussian army in combat. During the fierce fighting on the Lobosch hill at the Battle of Lobositz, Bräker reported that, 'I ... was quite beside myself with heat and excitement, and conscious of no fear or repugnance I loosed off nearly all my sixty cartridges without stopping, until my flintlock became almost red-hot and I had to carry it by the sling.'[15] While Bräker also admitted that he was sceptical about the accuracy of his fire, the first instinct for him in combat was not flight, but to loose off as many rounds in the shortest amount of time possible. This shows the success of the Prussian system of drill, even for a foreign soldier of questionable loyalty like Bräker.

In the early stages of the Seven Years War, Regiment von Itzenplitz proved that they were indeed exceptional soldiers. At the Battle of Lobositz, the regiment stormed the Lobsoch, and joined the spontaneous counterattack which helped swing the battle in Prussian favor. At Prague, the regiment joined Prinz Henri's decisive flank attack across the Rocketnitzer Bach.[16] Itzenplitz fought in the first line at Rossbach and formed part of the Prussian vanguard at Leuthen. This exceptional body of men met their end at the Battle of Hochkirch in 1758, where they lost 820 men in a disastrous attempt to retake Hochkirch village. With a service record like this, it is small wonder that Frederick II allowed No. 13 to form behind directly behind the *Garde* in reviews.[17]

If Regiment von Itzenplitz drew on exceptional soldiers, there were many other Prussian regiments who seemed to possess a more average body of men. Regiment von Alt-Kreytzen, or No. 40, also produced a private soldier writing from the ranks. Unlike Bräker, *Gemeine* Hoppe joined the ranks willingly, and did not desert at the first available opportunity. Also

12   Bräker, *Lebensgeschichte*, p.124.
13   Bräker, *Lebensgeschichte*, p.138.
14   Bräker, *Lebensgeschichte*, p.138.
15   Bräker, *Lebensgeschichte*, p.154.
16   Duffy, *The Military Life of Frederick the Great*, p.119.
17   Christopher Duffy, *The Army of Frederick the Great, 2nd Edition* (Chicago: Emperor's Press, 1996), p.330.

unlike Bräker, Hoppe seems to have been intensely loyal to the Prussian cause, despite being, in his own words, a foreigner. While he considered himself a foreigner, Hoppe hailed from the principality of Anhalt-Köthen, around 20 miles from Magdeburg. He described his experiences during the 1758 campaign season, after the Austrians had devastated the Alt-Kreytzen regiment at Kolin, and captured them at Schweidnitz. Hoppe's Alt-Kreytzen, then, consisted mainly of foreign soldiers brought in to fill the gaps from heavy losses.

A strong soldierly work ethic exudes from Hoppe's writing. The soldiers of Alt-Kreytzen drew an incredible amount of inspiration from the person of Frederick II of Prussia, whom Hoppe referred to simply as 'the King.' Thus, in terms of the four core traits of an eighteenth-century infantrymen, the men of Alt-Kreytzen seem to connect a strong work ethic with loyalty to the personage of the king. Hoppe related an anecdote where Frederick II passed by the regiment before the Battle of Zorndorf. 'He rode slowly passed each regiment and looked very gloomy, but nevertheless shouted a friendly, "Good Morning" to us. As he rode away, he asked, "Children, do you want to come along?" Everyone yelled, "Yes! Yes!"' In another passage, Hoppe recalled the effect which the presence of the King had on the troops: 'When we arrived before Küstrin, the King was already there with his army encamped, whom we joined. Everyone was cheerful and happy, and we forgot all our hardships and dangers once we knew that Fritz was with us.'[18] Hoppe connected the enthusiasm of the men of his regiment with the friendly, inspirational relationship it had with the king. Here, the work ethic of the men was inspired by its love for region and dynasty.

The strong work ethic of the Alt-Kreytzen regiment was nowhere more apparent than at their advance into the city of Küstrin during the Zorndorf campaign in 1758. Hoppe related the scene: 'The city itself had been transformed into a heap of rubble, and we hurried between the burning houses and mounted the walls. Now, a heavy cannonade started on both sides. The lads even poured the water out of their flasks and cooled down the gun barrels with rags so that we could return shot for shot.'[19] This willingness to assist artillerymen manning the fortifications shows the work ethic of the Alt-Kreytzen regiment. The men of this unit went on to assist gunners in the Battle of Zorndorf, again going beyond their training to achieve victory.

Gemeine Hoppe noted differences in the abilities of the Prussian regiment he joined and the Russian army he faced. When talking to Russian prisoners, Hoppe indicated that 'The Russian prisoners showed a great deal of admiration for the Prussians. They were proud of their own steadiness but admitted that they could not match the dexterity of the Prussians.'[20] However, while he remained proud of his regiment's abilities, a close reading of Hoppe's account shows some signs that he was less well trained than the Itzenplitz regiment. He noted that he was only trained for two months before joining the regiment at the front lines, less than the usual amount required to turn out a highly trained infantry soldier. While the men of the Alt-Kreytzen regiment seemed enthusiastic, their performance in battle implies that this regiment lacked in certain areas. During the heavy fighting at Zorndorf, Alt-Kreytzen, initially deployed in the second line, and faced near-capture by Russian heavy cavalry. They

---

18   Gemeine Hoppe, M. Lange (trans.), 'A Truthful Description of the Bloody Battle of Zorndorf', *Seven Years War Association Newsletter*, vol.1, no.5 (1983), p.8.
19   Hoppe, 'A Truthful Description,' p.8.
20   Hoppe, 'A Truthful Description,' p.11.

were often deployed in the second line and kept away from the main fighting. Thus, after their 1758 reconstitution, the men of the Alt-Kreytzen regiment remained competent, not exceptional, soldiers.

Moving to the American War of Independence, the Hessian Trümbach/von Bose Regiment (the name changed during the war when the commander changed) provides an example of an exceptionally adaptable Hessian regiment. Hailing from the Hessian state of Hessen-Kassel, during the course of the Seven Years War in Europe the regiment served with Prinz Ferdinand of Brunswick in the western European theatre. In the course of this war, the regiment served in a number of battles, such as Krefeld, Minden, Bergen, Emsdorf, Vellinghausen, and Wilhelmsthal. It served directly alongside Prussian troops at the combat of Langensalza. Although not performing poorly in any of these engagements, the regiment failed to win great distinction and fame in the course of the Seven Years War. Rather, they provided good, solid service.

For much of the American War of Independence, the then Trümbach Regiment was not heavily engaged. The regiment took part in the New York and New Jersey campaign of 1776 but was not among those that accompanied the main British army on campaign around Philadelphia in 1777. The regiment instead participated in attacks on Forts Clinton and Montgomery in October of that year. In 1780, the newly renamed von Bose Regiment was sent to the Southern theatre of war, where it served with the army led by Lieutenant General Charles, Earl Cornwallis on his campaigns in 1780 and 1781. Some authors claim that they fought in other battles such as Eutaw Springs. If so, it was only a company sized force or smaller, since the main regiment stayed with Cornwallis; it is also possible that authors confuse the von Rall/von Trümbach regiment with the von Trümbach/von Bose Regiment.

During the Southern Campaign in 1781, the average age in the regiment was 33, compared with the average age in the American army of 23, and in the British army of 28.[21] As a result, experienced men such as *Unteroffizier* Berthold Koch were prevalent in the regiment. Koch was born in 1742 (not recruited into the army that year, as Rodney Atwood claims), and joined the (then) Mansbach Regiment at 15, at the onset of the Seven Years War. During this time, he served in battles including Bergen.[22] The commander of the regiment in the 1781 campaign, *Major* Johann Christian du Buy, had joined the military at 14, and was now in his mid-forties. He was a veteran of 13 major battles in the European Seven Years War.[23]

The regiment fought its most famous action on 15 March 1781, the Battle of Guilford Courthouse. In the course of this battle, the von Bose Regiment, together with the British 1st battalion of the Brigade of Guards, broke through two lines of American defenders. Circumstantial evidence suggests that, by this point, the regiment had adopted the British standard style of advance during the War of Independence. *Unteroffizier* Berthold Koch

---

21   Lawrence E. Babits and Joshua B. Howard, *Long, Obstinate, and Bloody: The Battle of Guilford Courthouse* (Chapel Hill: University of North Carolina Press, 2009), p.89.

22   Atwood, *The Hessians,* p.41. The source Atwood cites makes the different claim: K. Rogge-Ludwig, *Mitteilungen an die mitglieder des Vereins für Hessische Geschichte und Landeskunde* (Kassel: Schönhoven, 1876), pp.1–2.

23   Atwood, *The Hessians,* p.138

noted that the regiment moved at a high rate of speed in this engagement.[24] *Major* du Buy reported to Hessian *Generalleutnant* Knyphausen:

> After quickly laying aside our tornisters and everything that could impede a soldier, the 71st and von Bose received orders to more forward and attack the enemy … We had not advanced more than 300 yards when we found a deep ditch in front of us, with tall banks and full of water. After crossing it with difficulty, we then came to a fenced wheat field; on the other side of this field 1500 continentals and militia were deployed in line … I formed the battalion into line with the greatest of speed and we ran to meet the enemy in tolerable order.[25]

It was then that the regiment, together with the 1st battalion of the Brigade of Guards, were drawn into a running firefight in the woods. *Major* du Buy and *Major* von Scheer first fought the Regiment back-to-back, and then led the regiment in two parts against the colonial enemy. *Unteroffizier* Koch recalled:

> … before we knew it, the enemy attacked us again in the rear. The regiment, therefore, had to divide into two parts. The second, command by Major Scheer, had to attack toward the rear, against the enemy who were behind us, and forced them once again to take flight … during this time, Colonel du Buy advanced with the first part of the regiment, and Major Scheer returned with the second part of the regiment and rejoined the first…[26]

As a result of this ingenuity, the von Bose Regiment won the praise of its army commander. In the aftermath of the Battle of Guilford Court House, Cornwallis praised von Bose, and listed them directly behind the Guards in his dispatches. Cornwallis believed, 'The Hessian Regiment von Bose deserves my warmest praises for its discipline, alacrity, and Courage, and does honour to Major Du Buy who commands it, and who is an Officer of superior merit.'[27]

The Braunschweig Regiment Prinz Friedrich differed substantially from the three regiments previously discussed. Prinz Friedrich hailed from a different state, the Duchy of Braunschweig-Wolfenbüttel. The officers and men of the Prinz Friedrich Regiment would nonetheless have applied the same standards of soldierly conduct, because they hailed from a north German state influenced by Prussian thinking. Prussia and Braunschweig shared more ties than most of the states of military Europe. The connectedness can be seen through religious and dynastic links, and also in a community of shared military men. The Prinz Friedrich Regiment served in the 1777 campaign led by Lieutenant General John Burgoyne during American War of Independence. During this conflict, the commanding general of

---

24   Berthold Koch, Bruce E. Burgoyne (trans.), *The Battle of Guilford Courthouse and the Siege and Surrender at Yorktown* (Greensboro: Guilford Courthouse National Park, 2014), p.8.
25   Hessisches Staatsarchiv, Marburg (HSa): Best. 4h Nr. 3101, Du Buy, Raports vom Oberst Lieut. du Buy Regts v. Bose zu der General Lieutenant v. Knyphausen.
26   Koch, *The Battle of Guilford Courthouse*, p.8.
27   The National Archives, UK (TNA): CO 5/184: ff.114–115.

the German forces with Burgoyne, *Generalmajor* Adolph Friedrich von Riedesel, noted some severe problems with the Prinz Friedrich regiment.

While inspecting the men upon their initial arrival in Canada, Riedesel found all the regiments under his command fit for service, except the Prinz Friedrich Regiment. In a report to the Duke of Braunschweig-Wolfenbüttel, Riedesel wrote, 'as regards the Prinz Friedrich Regiment I regret to say that I did not find it in the condition I desired, and which I had hoped for after the assurance given me by Lieutenant-Colonel Prätorius.'[28] Riedesel worried greatly about the performance of the Prinz Friedrich Regiment, and even made provisions to leave the regiment in Montreal if its quality did not improve.

Riedesel pulled few punches in his letter to *Oberstlieutenant* Praetorius, the regiment's commander. He opened, 'Major von Hille has probably already reported to you, that I saw your regiment drill in Quebec … in what a bad condition I found the Regiment Prinz Friedrich! I am convinced that as long as the regiment has existed, it has never drilled so badly as on the day I saw it.' He continued, 'I have to state to you with the utmost regret, that the Regiment Prinz Friedrich, which is under your command, is the one that is most backward, and that it can neither be compared to any of the other regiments in drill nor in marching.'[29] Riedesel was an experienced soldier. He had served as a hussar in the Seven Years War, and married the daughter of a Prussian general. His insights into the deficiencies of the Regiment Prinz Friedrich speak volumes about the qualities which commanding officers prized in eighteenth century infantrymen. [30]

Riedesel first took the regiment to task for their lack of work ethic. According to Riedesel's observations, during drill 'Most of the men rest their heads on the right shoulder, consequently, the left point on their hats is in a line with their guns. There is no life in their manual exercises.'[31] Riedesel instructed, 'they must be made to drill again, and if there is any laziness, you must have recourse to the stick.' Here, Riedesel instructed Prätorius to beat his men when they failed to perform to the correct standard. He also encouraged Prätorius to punish the officers who were 'not attentive or diligent.'[32] Riedesel found this lack of diligence in both officers and men inexcusable, as it was one of the expected norms for eighteenth century soldiers.

Riedesel also found the regiment unacceptable in the area of crisp and uniform movement. He informed Prätorius, 'After each exercise the men move their hands, knees and feet, touch their faces, or grasp their hats, and even look to the left. The regiment is never in step when advancing, the line wavers constantly, [and] the men bend their knees and stick out their heads.'[33] The lack of crisp movement in drill shocked Riedesel. While German officers did not expect this type of perfection on the battlefield, they required it in drill. Well drilled men worked well together, and above all, knew how to load and fire correctly.

---

28   Morristown National Historical Park, Lidgerwood Collection (MNHP): Hessian Documents of the American Revolution: Correspondence of General Riedesel, p.HZ-1 928 microfilm.
29   MNHP: Correspondence of General Riedesel, p.HZ-1 930.
30   Louise Hall Tharp, *The Baroness and the General* (Boston: Little, Brown and Co., 1962), p.23.
31   MNHP: Correspondence of General Riedesel, p.HZ-1 930.
32   MNHP: Correspondence of General Riedesel, p.HZ-1 932.
33   MNHP: Correspondence of General Riedesel, p.HZ-1 931.

Riedesel made his most damning accusations later in the letter. In his observation, the regiment's, 'running fire lasts a quarter of an hour.'[34] Most shockingly to Riedesel, 'they load their guns so slowly, that not of them has it resting firmly on his shoulder at 30 [seconds.] The platoons do not fire at the same time when advancing, and after the men have loaded they run back to the battalion line just as unevenly.'[35] German officers viewed rapid fire as the key to battlefield success, and hoped for their men to fire one shot every 20 seconds in battlefield conditions. That the Prinz Friedrich Regiment was unable to load one round in 30 seconds on the drill square speaks volumes as to the poor quality of this unit. This shocking inability horrified Riedesel, as he knew that the Regiment Prinz Friedrich would be combat ineffective.

Despite his scathing critique, Riedesel instructed Prätorius on how to retrain his unit. He believed that Prätorius had drawn his regiment together too early; the individual companies lacked sufficient training. Riedesel informed Prätorius, 'True, the companies have put in the usual amount of drills, but the faults have not been noted, and every exercise has not been corrected until the men did it as it should be done. You have drawn the battalion together too early, as this ought not to have been done until all the companies were equally efficient.' So, in a situation rather the opposite of the British army during the same period, Riedesel argued that training should be carried out on a smaller scale before occurring on the regimental level.

Riedesel sadly noted, 'You will have to commence again from the beginning, first in files and then in companies, to march, do manual exercises, load, and repeat this until all the companies are equally well drilled.' He exhorted Prätorius to 'make the maladroit and the ignorant step forward every time,' for punishment. The letter made clear that Riedesel no longer trusted Prätorius. He appointed another *Oberstlieutenant* Friedrich Baum of the Braunschweig Dragoon Regiment, to oversee the drilling of Regiment Prinz Friedrich. 'Baum … has received orders from me to see them drill frequently, and to tell you when he finds the companies so far advanced that you can draw the battalion together, and then you will unite all the companies.'[36] By placing the decision-making power in the hands of Baum, rather than Prätorius, Riedesel showed his lack of faith in Prätorius' judgment.

Riedesel continued,

> as soon as Lieutenant-Colonel Baum finds that the regiment drills well and reports it to me, you can cease drilling when [Baum] has given you permission, and then only drill once a week, so that the men do not forget what they have been taught. But until the regiment gets into proper condition, you must drill 4 times a week, and leave 2 days for resting.[37]

Riedesel closed his letter on a rather hopeful note, indicating that Prätorius would be able to achieve the outlined requirements. Regiment Prinz Friedrich did indeed join the invasion south into the rebellious colonies in 1777. However, after the capture of Fort Ticonderoga,

---

34   MNHP: Correspondence of General Riedesel, p.HZ-1 931.
35   MNHP: Correspondence of General Riedesel, p.HZ-1 931.
36   MNHP: Correspondence of General Riedesel, p.HZ-1 932.
37   MNHP: Correspondence of General Riedesel, p.932.

Regiment Prinz Friedrich remained as a garrison. Garrison regiments did not enjoy a high reputation in Germanic military circles and were often referred to as *Mauerscheisser*.[38] Thus, by choosing to leave Regiment Prinz Friedrich behind, Riedesel indicated it was still the least trustworthy of the regiments he had available. In an ironic twist, the American rebels subsequently captured Riedesel and his regiments, but since the Regiment Prinz Friedrich stayed at Fort Ticonderoga, they remained in British service, out of American hands. At times, it paid to be a poor soldier.

Regiment Prinz Friedrich redeemed their honour during Browne's Raid on Fort Ticonderoga in September 1777. In this battle, Regiment Prinz Friedrich defended the fort against a numerically superior force of rebels. The rebels overran and captured four companies of the 53rd Foot, a British unit stationed alongside Prinz Friedrich, but the rebels could not break into the German portion of the lines. A number of officers wrote to the Duke of Braunschweig-Wolfenbüttel, praising the regiment's quick reaction to the danger and steadfast defence of the works around Ticonderoga.

Hessian Adaptation: The Flanquer Skirmishing System

The *Subsidientruppen* from Hessen-Kassel used a specific style of skirmishing, inherited from their experiences during the Seven Years War. In his monograph discussing the battlefield aspects of the Hessians, Rodney Atwood devotes a couple of paragraphs to this style of fighting, introducing the reader to these concepts but leaving many of the details unexplored.[39] According to Atwood, the Hessians employed the terms *Pelotons* and *Flanquers* to describe skirmishers who operated ahead of the main body of the regiment, which remained closed up, arm to arm. These troops should not be confused with *jäger*: greencoated riflemen who screened German armies in the eighteenth century. The term *Pelotons*, from the French, gives us the English word Platoons. The skirmishers deployed were either volunteers or members of one platoon chosen to operate ahead of the main body. *Flanquers*, also from the French, denotes a group of men preceding ahead of the main body in order clear the way. This style of attack was used at the major victories of the Crown forces in 1776: The Battle of Long Island, the Battle of White Plains, and the Battle of Fort Washington. Atwood fails to note that the Hessians also attempted to use this skirmishing tactic during the surprise at Trenton.

By far the most well-documented example of skirmishing among the Hessian *Subsidientruppen* in North America was the Battle of Long Island. Here, on 27 August 1776, the Hessians were charged with pinning the enemy centre while the British marched in a wide outflanking movement. The British hoped that the Americans would be unable to move to meet this flanking threat. This battle provides a clearly documented case of the Hessians drawing integrated skirmishers from line infantry regiments. In order to break into the enemy positions, the Hessians used skirmishers in a way quite similar to later Napoleonic warfare. These soldiers were not *jäger*, although *jäger* were also employed.

---

38   Cathal J. Nolan, *Wars of the Age of Louis XIV, 1650-1715: An Encyclopedia of Global Warfare and Civilization* (Westport, CT: Greenwood Press, 2008), p.286.
39   Atwood, *The Hessians*, pp.82–83.

As the Hessians advanced on the rebel positions, groups of men were detached to clear the way ahead of the main body of the regiment. The Hessian commanding general does not appear to have issued any special orders for this to have happened, rather, it appears to have been the standard practice in this type of encounter. Usually a junior officer (often a lieutenant) was selected to command this skirmisher detachment.

In his diary, *Premier-Leutnant* Jakob Piel noted that, at the onset of the attack at Flatbush, 'Lieutenant Zoll with fifty volunteers was sent into the woods and exchanged shots with the rebels.'[40] Piel did not suggest that this practice of detaching volunteers was anything out of the ordinary. He used the term volunteers to describe these men, indicating that they were not part of a pre-formed group. The official journal of the Alt-Lossberg regiment records the event in similar terms.

Another young *Premier-Leutnant*, Karl Friedrich Rüffer of the Mirbach Regiment, described his role in the action: 'Lieutenant Schraitd was sent into the thicket with some eighty flanqers, which resulted in us taking some captives.'[41] He described the activity of his men by using the term *Flanquer*. The best English translation of this word is 'skirmisher.' Again, these were men drawn from the main body of the regiment, not dedicated light infantry.

Johann Heinrich von Bardeleben of the von Donop Regiment was also present and described the attack. In his opinion, 'Because of the landscape and the terrible hills, [the rebels] could not be attacked *en masse,* but only by groups. All the regiments at once sent out strong patrols, as strong as possible, in general, to attack the enemy.'[42] Bardeleben's description presents two problems for the interpretation that this attack was a regular practice. First, he indicated that the only reason the Hessians sent out skirmishers was 'because of the landscape,' and second, he referred to them as 'patrols,' not *Flanquers* or skirmishers.

While the Hessians were undoubtedly motivated by the rough nature of the terrain they had to attack, they would continue to use this formation, even when the position they were attacking was not in rough terrain. This occurred in particular at the Battle of Trenton. While Bardeleben specifically referred to patrols, most other Hessian officers, including *jäger* veteran Johann von Ewald and the Hessian commanding general, Leopold Philip von Heister, referred to this type of soldier as a *Flanquer*.[43] The Hessian use of *Flanquers* was extremely successful at the Battle of Long Island, and the Hessians were able to apply the appropriate amount of pressure, which allowed the British to devastate the rebel positions.

In his landmark study, *With Zeal and With Bayonets Only,* Matthew H. Spring has overturned the old notion that the British army in North America was slow and machinelike. Spring instead demonstrates that the redcoats adopted an open order, two-rank system relatively early in the war, by the command of General William Howe. Spring is overly

---

40 Jakob Piel and Andreas Wiederholdt, Bruce E. Burgoyne (trans.), *Defeat, Disaster and Dedication: The Diaries of the Hessian Officers Jakob Piel and Andreas Wiederhold* (Bowie, MD: Heritage Books, 1997), p.17.

41 August Schmidt and Karl Friedrich Rüffer, Bruce E. Burgoyne (trans.), *The Hesse-Cassel Mirbach Regiment in the American Revolution* (Bowie, MD: Heritage Books, 1998), p.54.

42 Johann Heinrich von Bardeleben et al., *The Diary of Lieutenant von Bardeleben and Other von Donop Regiment Documents* (Bowie, MD: Heritage Books, 1998), p.56.

43 Johann von Ewald, *Diary of the American War: A Hessian Journal* (New Haven: Yale University Press, 1979), p.85; HSa: 4h. 409 nr. 3, f.53.

critical of the German *Subsidientruppen* who fought alongside in North America, and, like the contemporary British commanders, repeatedly indicates that the Germans should have adopted an open order, two-rank system.[44] In Spring's account, the *Subsidientruppen* become a useful foil: the 'slow' Germans versus the adaptable British.[45]

There were reasons for this 'German slowness.' The overall Hessian commander, von Heister, was less than impressed with the British ideas.[46] In a report to Landgraf Friedrich II of Hesse-Kassel, von Heister described his thoughts on the skirmishing order which the Hessians used, and its comparison to the British system. 'Because of the steady fire of the Jäger, henceforth, the four Grenadier battalions, brigaded together with the English Grenadiers and Light Infantry, will obey the regulations of General Howe, to which the troops of the army submitted.'[47] Here, von Heister agreed that since his combined grenadier battalions were brigaded with the *jäger*, British grenadiers, and British light infantry, it would make sense for them to follow the new British open order system.[48]

However, von Heister refused to be swayed when it came to the infantry under his personal command. He went on to describe the system which the other troops of the Hessian army had been using, and would continue to use:

> However, the rest of the infantry perform honourable service, which is evident from the reports of more than a few regiments. The platoons of skirmishers peel out, at all times gives the best service; but the main battalions are always closed up arm in arm, following the skirmishers at a musket shot distance, unless the rough terrain forces them, at some times, to break ranks, which the reports show is happening rather often.[49]

For von Heister, this system provided the best of both worlds. These '*Pelotons zu Flanquers*' (or platoons of skirmishers, in the odd French/German hybrid of eighteenth-century military circles) prevented rebel riflemen or free ranging rebel musketeers from damaging the main battle line of the Hessian infantry battalions. These soldiers, according to von Heister, remained, 'closed up, arm in arm.' Thus, at Flatbush Pass in the Battle of Long Island, the Hessians definitely employed integrated skirmishers.

There is evidence to suggest that the Hessians used *Flanquers* at most of the major engagements of 1776. At the Battle of White Plains, the von Lossberg Regiment advanced through a burning wheat field, holding their cartridge boxes over their heads, while *Flanquers* covered the advance of the main body of the regiment.[50] Furthermore, at the attack on Fort Washington on 16 November, groups of grenadiers, *jäger* and infantry moved ahead of the main body of Hessians.[51] While no direct evidence exists that these soldiers were being used

---

44   Matthew H. Spring, *With Zeal and With Bayonets Only: The British Army on Campaign in North America, 1775-1783* (Norman: University of Oklahoma Press, 2008), pp.146–147.
45   Spring, *With Zeal and with Bayonets Only,* pp.143–149.
46   Atwood, *The Hessians,* p.82.
47   HSa: 4h.410 nr. 1 507, Heister zu Landgraf, 21 March, 1777.
48   HSa: 4h.410 nr. 1 507, Heister zu Landgraf, 21 March, 1777.
49   HSa: 4h.410 nr. 1 507, Heister zu Landgraf, 21 March, 1777.
50   David Smith, *New York 1776: The Continentals' First Battle* (Oxford: Osprey, 2008), p.78.
51   Von Ewald, *Diary of the American War,* p.15.

as *Flanquers,* the similarity of this organization to the groups of soldiers used at Flatbush pass and White Plains indicates that they may also have been in a skirmishing order. In addition, evidence exists that Hessians used skirmishers to cover battalions in very small-scale conflicts. On 15 November 1776 the Block Grenadier Regiment used skirmishers in a confrontation with a lone rebel regiment.[52]

On 26 December 1776, the rebel army under the command of George Washington attacked the Hessian garrison outpost at Trenton. In popular memory, the American army defeated the garrison by skill and surprise, because the Hessians had been drunk after a Christmas celebration. Historian David Hackett Fischer destroyed this myth in his landmark study of the battle, *Washington's Crossing.* In this book, Fischer clearly demonstrates that not a drop of liquor had been drunk before the battle, and that the Hessians were worn out from days of patrols in the snow and rain. Fischer displays that some 6,000 Americans, with a vast superiority in numbers and cannon, easily defeated the 1,400 Hessian defenders.[53]

If, then, the Hessians were sober and alert, did they deploy their integrated skirmishers? While this idea has been missed by most historians who have studied the battle, there is evidence to suggest that the Hessians did indeed attempt to use their skirmishers during the battle. This comes from a man of extensive military experience: *Leutnant* Christian Sobbe. While a *leutnant* was a junior officer, Sobbe had served for 19 years by the time he recorded his experiences, despite being only 33 years old. He enlisted in 1759, during the height of the Seven Years War. At that time, Sobbe had only reached 14 years of age, and had known no life but soldiering since that time.[54] This is undoubtedly the type of soldier which Christopher Duffy refers to in *Military Experience in the Age of Reason,* when he states, 'The Hessians were state mercenaries *par excellence,* and they contributed a military cast of mind and a great depth of experience.'[55]

Many details exist regarding the Battle of Trenton from the Hessian perspective because after the battle, in 1778, the Hessians established a court martial and took statements from every officer they could find who survived the battle. The son of *Generalleutnant* von Heister complied and published these statements, in 1787, in his work *Darstellung der Affaire von Trenton, 26 Dec. 1776,* or in English, 'Description of the Affair at Trenton.'

Leutnant Sobbe testified that near the end of the conflict, the von Knyphausen regiment attempted to escape from American capture by fleeing across a river. Sobbe indicates that the regiment employed skirmishers at this point in the battle. He states, 'the regiment had been driven into a marsh [the edge of the river], and stuck fast there, and the regiment had been halted.'[56] He continued, 'Captain von Biesenrodt had thereupon called out, "skirmishers to the fore."'[57] For Sobbe, this meant a personal instruction. As a lieutenant,

52   Bernhard A. Uhlendorf (ed.), *Revolution in America: Confidential Letters and Journals 1776-1784 of Adjutant General Major Baurmeister of the Hessian Forces,* (New Brunswick: Rutgers University Press, 1957), p.49.
53   David Hackett Fischer, *Washington's Crossing* (Oxford: Oxford University Press, 2004), pp.225–235, 392–395.
54   MNHP: Hessian Documents of the American Revolution: The Affair at Trenton, p.M.L.364.
55   Duffy, *The Military Experience in the Age of Reason,* p.22.
56   MNHP: The Affair at Trenton, p.M.L.375.
57   MNHP: The Affair at Trenton, p.M.L.375.

this order instructed him to 'run around the battalion in order to call out the skirmishers required, and to form them up.'[58] This allows historians to understand, with certainty, that the command to call out *Flanquers* came from the commander of the regiment, who was in this case *Hauptmann* von Biesenrodt, because his superior had been wounded. Once the command had been issued, lieutenants were responsible for gathering up the skirmishers.[59]

In addition, it was the responsibility of the lieutenants to lead the skirmishers forward. *Leutnant* Werner von Ferry of the von Knyphausen Regiment also described this moment in the battle when the Hessians attempted to use skirmishers. Von Ferry stated that, 'As the regiment reached the water, Captain von Biesenrodt had ordered, "skirmishers forward."'[60] On that command, von Ferry, 'Marched forward with the skirmishers up the hill.' Upon reaching the hill, Ferry noted that they encountered resistance: 'The skirmishers were fired on from the woods by the militia, and immediately … Lord Sterling and his brigade … had marched up on this same hill.'[61] Ferry indicated that, 'because the enemy were pressing … in such great strength,' he and the skirmishers 'had been forced to retire to the regiment.'[62] Von Ferry's testimony shows an operation of Hessian skirmishers from beginning to end: the order came to deploy, the men marched forward and encountered resistance, and when that resistance mounted, they returned to the shelter of the regiment.[63]

Not content to let his junior officers tell the story, *Hauptmann* von Biesenrodt also described his role in sending skirmishers forward. Biesenrodt stated that 'The skirmishers that I sent forward had begun to fire, but very few of the muskets would go off, owing to the heavy snow and rain.'[64] A little further on, Biesenrodt indicated, 'The enemy had pressed on in such great numbers,' that the skirmishers had been forced to retire. While his description ended there, Biesenrodt was later recalled to give further testimony, when he informed the court of the reasons for his decision to deploy skirmishers.[65]

In this second testimony, Biesenrodt gave insight into the thinking which led him to deploy skirmishers, and what his goal in doing so had been. As the von Knyphausen regiment was caught between the Americans and a marshy creek, he had been attempting to find a ford by which the men could escape. Thus, in his words, his 'intention had been cover the regiments crossing through the water with the skirmishers, and … to make with them also the rear guard.'[66] Sadly, Biesenrodt noted that this had been made 'impossible by the rapid approach of the overpowering enemy.'[67] From this testimony it is apparent that skirmishers could not only be used to cover the regiment during an attack, but also to cover a regiment during withdrawal.[68]

---

58   MNHP: The Affair at Trenton, p.M.L.375.
59   MNHP: The Affair at Trenton, p.M.L.375.
60   MNHP: The Affair at Trenton, p.M.L.444.
61   MNHP: The Affair at Trenton, p.M.L.444.
62   MNHP: The Affair at Trenton, p.M.L.444.
63   MNHP: The Affair at Trenton, p.M.L.444.
64   MNHP: The Affair at Trenton, p.M.L.456.
65   MNHP: The Affair at Trenton, p.M.L.456.
66   MNHP: The Affair at Trenton, p.M.L.481.
67   MNHP: The Affair at Trenton, p.M.L.481.
68   MNHP: The Affair at Trenton, p.M.L.481.

It does not appear that the Hessian *Subsidientruppen* were the only German troops to use skirmishers. The soldiers from Braunschweig-Wolfenbüttel, or Brunswick, also used skirmishers ahead of the main body, at least in training. In Quebec on 6 August 1776, the Brunswick commander, Baron von Riedesel performed a mock attack on a wood, 'with skirmishers in advance.'[69] While Matthew H. Spring has shown that the Braunschweigers did not adopt the open formations of the British during the American War of Independence, there is no evidence to suggest that Braunschweigers did not use *Flanquers* in the 1777 battles of Saratoga. At the Battle of Freeman's Farm, the main body of the Braunschweigers formed with 'closed ranks,' while the use of *Flanquers* might explain the ability of slow-moving German troops to deliver an 'unexpected fire.'[70]

The fact that the *Subsidientruppen* used skirmishers in some, but not all, of their battles in North America is clear beyond doubt. This has already been documented by other historians, if never with this amount of detail.[71] Not previously discussed is how this skirmishing developed. It does not appear in the 1767 Hessian infantry regulation, which still recommended *Heckenfeuer*: a controlled system of skirmishing utilized by the Prussians. Therefore, the use of *Flanquers* must have been part of a body of acquired knowledge, not present in the official drill manuals. In order to understand how this unwritten knowledge came to be used, we must search for similar developments in militaries during the most recent war the *Subsidientruppen* had participated in: The Seven Years War.

Three potential militaries might have transmitted their ideas about skirmishing to the Hessians during the Seven Years War; the British, the Prussians, or the French. The British served as part of a coalition force with the Hessians (as well as other western Germans) during that war. The Hessian drill manual and uniforms were both based on Prussian models, and many officers who served with the Hessians during the American War of Independence were Prussian. The French were the main antagonists of the Hessians during the Seven Years War. It is very possible that the Hessians witnessed useful tactical developments from the French and incorporated them into their own military thinking.

As far as potential influencers, the British are an excellent guess. They served with the Hessians during the Seven Years War and were quick to adopt a loose style of fire and movement during the American War of Independence. In addition, scholars have presented strong evidence to suggest that the British used a system of skirmishers, like that of the Hessians, in their peacetime manoeuvres of the 1770s.[72] But, upon closer examination, potential links between these two sets of skirmishers fall apart.

British peacetime manoeuvres in the 1770s demonstrated a system of skirmishers. However, these skirmishers were not, as in the Hessian system, deployed by and formed as a temporary screen in front of light infantry regiments. Rather, these men were drawn

---

69   Friederich Adolphus Riedesel, Max von Eelking (trans.), *Memoirs, and Letters and Journals, of Major General Riedesel, during His Residence in America*, (Albany, NY: J. Munsell, 1868), p.58.

70   Riedesel, *Memoirs*, p.204; MNHP: Hessian Documents of the American Revolution: Brunswick Order Book, 1776-83, p. H.Z. 307, microform.

71   Indeed, this style of fighting is not mentioned by Friederike Baer in her excellent new survey of the *Subsidientruppen*. Friederike Baer, *German Soldiers in the American Revolutionary War* (Oxford: Oxford University Press, 2022).

72   J.A. Houlding, *Fit for Service: The Training of the British Army, 1715-1795* (Oxford: Clarendon Press, 1981), pp.278–288, 304–306.

from the light infantry and grenadier companies. Both of these companies were frequently detached from the line regiments on campaign in North America.[73] By contrast the Hessian *Flanquers* who served at Flatbush and the other battles of 1776 were drawn from line regiments they covered. Thus, while the Hessians may have witnessed, or heard about the British use of skirmishers, their use of *Pelotons* of men from the line regiments implies that this idea had a different source.

The Origins of the *Flanquer* System

The Hessian use of skirmishers (not *jäger*, but integrated line skirmishers), is consistent with other connections between the Hessian and Prussian military systems. Atwood indicates that the Hessians copied their drill manual from the Prussians, which when it comes to speed of fire may well be right.[74] By the 1780s, Frederick the Great argued that *Frei-Infanterie* should be adept at taking cover 'behind trees … in houses … lie flat … shoot from behind stones … fire from behind the crest of a ridge.'[75] Frederick may or may not have intended to use *Frei-Infanterie* as skirmishers, depending on how one reads the 1783 *Instruction*.[76] However, another Prussian commander may well have used infantry skirmishers during the Seven Years War.[77]

At the Battle of Reichenbach on 16 August 1762, the Duke of Bevern employed infantry *Pelotons* as skirmishers, in order to disturb the Austrian advance. Two writers from the period noted this use of individual Prussian *Pelotons* as skirmishers, in order to delay the advance of the Austrian column under General Philipp Levin von Beck.

The first author to notice this strange use of the normally rigid Prussian infantry was Georg Friedrich Tempelhoff, who had served as a Prussian gunner during the war and translated and expanded the work of Henry Lloyd, a veteran of the Austrian forces.[78] Tempelhoff described the Duke of Bevern's use of these *Pelotons* at Reichenbach in the following way:

> Because the Duke was going to have a second engagement and could not draw from the forces already engaged without showing the enemy his weakness, he drew off a few platoons (*Pelotons*) and put them into the swampy area by the Schrober-Grund. These platoons fired on the enemy, and resisted during his march, in order to delay him as long as possible.[79]

Tempelhoff also noted the extreme number of causalities suffered by these platoons and the first battalion of the Margraf Heinrich Regiment.

73   Spring, *With Zeal and With Bayonets Only*, p.246.
74   Atwood, *The Hessians*, p.66.
75   Gustav Berthold Volz, *Die Werke Friedrichs des Grossen in deutscher Übersetzung*m (Berlin: Reimar Hobbing, 1913), p.300.
76   Duffy, *The Army of Frederick the Great*, p.138.
77   Atwood, *The Hessians*, p.83.
78   Christopher Duffy, *By Force of Arms* (Chicago: Emperor's Press, 2008), p.473.
79   George Friedrich Tempelhoff and Henry Lloyd, *Geschichte Des Siebenjährigen Krieges in Deutschland* (Berlin: Unger, 1801), vol.6, pp.149–150.

A single source, even one as respected as Tempelhoff, might not be enough to confirm the use of *Pelotons* as a delaying force at Reichenbach. However, another military authority, Hessian *jäger* Johann von Ewald, in the third volume of his work *Belehrungen über den Krieg: Besonders über den kleinen Krieg,* described the same type of occurrence at the Battle of Reichenbach. Ewald knew officers who had served in the Prussian army, and was himself a veteran of the Seven Years War in western Germany. He described the Duke of Bevern's reaction to the appearance of Beck's corps, saying:

> In this battle, the Prussian general was obliged (as a strong as a strong Austrian corps under General Beck bypassed the Prussian left, and had already maneuvered behind and above the Prussians, while the Prussian front was already engaged with the enemy,) to draw off single platoons of different battalions, and send them backwards to offer resistance to the enemies' lead elements. As a result of this, and also the appearance of the army of the king, the enemy was completely repulsed, which decided the fate of the battle and the whole campaign.[80]

From these two examples, it is not only clear that the Prussians used individual platoons in this battle, but also that this use was noted by other military authorities, including a Hessian *jäger* commander. This event marks part of the development of the skirmishing style used by the Hessians in the American War of Independence.

The Hessians did not, however, serve in the eastern German theatre where the Battle of Reichenbach occurred – they were busy fighting the French, in western Holy Roman Empire. Thus, while Hessian military thought was influenced to a great extent by the successes of the Prussian army, the Hessian military remained a distinct entity. In order to fully understand the development of the skirmish system employed by the Hessians in the American War of Independence, it is necessary to understand the use of light troops in the Seven Years War, and specifically how these troops were employed by the French.

Many authors, such as Reginald Savory, have described the rise of light troops within European armies in the Seven Years War, generally asserting that these troops played a minor role in set-piece battlefield encounters. There is evidence to suggest that the French may have begun using integrated line skirmishers, particularly towards the end of the Seven Years War, in small encounters. At the attempt on Lippstadt on 1 July 1759, the Comte de Melfort described his use of skirmishers in a small confrontation with Hanoverian troops.

In the battle, the French used skirmishers in an attempt to clear the way for an attack. In his letter, Melfort uses the term *Tirailluers* – the traditional French term for skirmishers which we commonly associate with the French Revolutionary Wars. A French dictionary from 1752 defines a 'Tirailleur' as 'one who skirmishes.'[81] Melfort's choice of this term, and the forces present at the battle, indicate that he is referred to line infantry skirmishers, not *chasseurs* or *volontaires*. Thus, according to the letter of the Comte de Melfort, both the French and the Hanoverians used skirmishers in this conflict.[82]

80   Johann von Ewald, *Belehrungen Über Den Krieg: Besonders Über Den Kleinen Krieg, Durch Beispiele Großer Helden Und Kluger Und Tapferer Männer* (Schleswig: Röhß, 1803), vol.III, p.321.
81   Annibale Antonini, *Dictionnaire françois, latin et italien* (Venice: François Pitteri, 1752), p.520.
82   Service Historique de la Défense, Vincennes, France (SHD): A1 3518: pièce 40, p.3.

The idea that the French employed skirmishers in the Seven Years War is confirmed by a letter from Victor-François, Duc de Broglie. In this letter, de Broglie confirms that in the winter of 1759–1760 French infantry regiments trained 50 men per battalion to operate as skirmishers.[83] The 1764 *Ordonnance du Roi*, which was likely written by de Broglie, instructed the French Infantry to use skirmishers:

> Nothing should prevent you, when on the advance or retreat, from detaching a half-section, and scattering these volunteers in front of the battalion, to make a feu de billebaude, and then retreat through the intervals behind the battalion when the enemy is very close.[84]

The French and western Germans both developed a plethora of light troops for use in the war of posts. In addition to this development of light troops, the use of integrated skirmishers appears to have been in the extremely early stages of development, and this development was noticed and emulated by the western German army facing the French, under Ferdinand of Brunswick.

In a letter describing the Battle of Bergen, fought on 13 April 1759, Ferdinand described the early stages of the action. He stated, 'I ordered our Grenadiers and Jägers to amuse the enemy, supported by detached platoons, so that our columns would have time to arrive.'[85] The three types of troops used in this delaying action correspond exactly to the three types of troops used at the Flatbush attack in 1776. It appears that the skirmishing system employed by the *Subsidientruppen* developed out of the Seven Years War in Europe, rather than North American experience.

Conclusion

Primarily influenced by Prussian and French military perspectives, German *Subsidientruppen* tried to combine the solidness of the Prussians and the flexibility of the French in their North American service. Commanders like Riedesel harped on the poor performance of units who were not spit-and-polish on the drill square, even as they experimented with novel skirmishing tactics.

For the 'Hessians,' being combat effective in North America meant at times adapting to the speed of the British, as the von Bose Regiment did at Guilford Courthouse. Usually, however, officers found their own system of skirmishing more than effective, combining the flexibility of the British open-order system with the staying power of compact linear formations in the Prussian style. The failures at Trenton, Red Bank, Bennington, and Bemis Heights should not hide the fact that the *Subsidientruppen* were an innovative and flexible

---

83   Jean Lambert Colin, *L'Infanterie Au XVIIIe Siècle. La Tactique* (Paris: Berger-Leverault, 1907), pp.76–77.
84   Anon., *Ordonnance du roi, pour régler l'exercice de l'infanterie. Du 20 mars 1764* (Paris: De L'Imperimerie Royal, 1764), pp.106–107.
85   Ferdinand Von. Westphalen, *Geschichte Der Feldzüge Des Herzogs Ferdinand von Braunschweig-Lüneburg* (Berlin: Verlag der König, 1872), vol. III, p.242.

force. During the American War of Independence, the *Subsidientruppen* used integrated skirmishers as a way of clearing the path for the main body of men in closed ranks or delaying an enemy force. Here, the seemingly slow and ineffective Hessians had anticipated one of the key developments of Napoleonic warfare: utilizing battalion-company men as skirmishers to screen close-order battalions.

This research has focused explicitly on the service of infantry regiments with the *Subsidientruppen*. They also brought specialist troops like *jäger*, admired by the British and feared by the Americans. In utilizing riflemen, skirmishers, grenadiers, and line infantry, the Hessian *Subsidientruppen* combined many of the ingredients that scholars associated with Napoleonic infantry warfare. Historians should understand the Hessians as a Janus-faced force: looking forward to Napoleonic warfare, not just backwards towards Frederician warfare.

Bibliography

Primary Sources
Hessisches Staatsarchiv Marburg, Marburg, Germany (HSa)
    Best. 4h
Morristown National Historical Park, Morristown, New Jersey (MNHP)
    Lidgerwood Collection, Hessian Documents of the American Revolution
Service Historique de la Défense, Vincennes, France (SHD)
    A1 3518
The National Archives, Kew, UK (TNA)
    CO 5/184, Military despatches and Miscellaneous

Printed Primary Sources
Anon., *Ordonnance du roi, pour régler l'exercice de l'infanterie. Du 20 mars 1764* (Paris: De L'Imperimerie Royal, 1764)
Antonini, Annibale, *Dictionnaire françois, latin et italien* (Venice: François Pitteri, 1752)
Bardeleben, Johann Heinrich von et al., *The Diary of Lieutenant von Bardeleben and Other von Donop Regiment Documents* (Bowie, MD: Heritage Books, 1998)
Bräker, Ulrich, *Lebensgeschichte Und Natürliche Ebenteuer Des Armen Mannes Im Tockenburg* (Zurich: Drell, Geßner , Füßli, 1789)
Ewald, Johann von, *Belehrungen Über Den Krieg: Besonders Über Den Kleinen Krieg, Durch Beispiele Großer Helden Und Kluger Und Tapferer Männer* (Schleswig: Röhß, 1803)
Ewald, Johann von, *Diary of the American War: A Hessian Journal* (New Haven: Yale University Press, 1979)
Hoppe, Gemeine, M. Lange (trans.), 'A Truthful Description of the Bloody Battle of Zorndorf,' *Seven Years War Association Newsletter* vol.1, no.5 (1983)
Koch, Berthold, Bruce E. Burgoyne (trans.), *The Battle of Guilford Courthouse and the Siege and Surrender at Yorktown* (Greensboro: Guilford Courthouse National Park: 2014)
Piel, Jakob and Andreas Wiederholdt, Bruce E. Burgoyne (trans.), *Defeat, Disaster and Dedication: The Diaries of the Hessian Officers Jakob Piel and Andreas Wiederhold* (Bowie, MD: Heritage Books, 1997)
Riedesel, Friederich Adolphus, Max von Eelking (trans.), *Memoirs, and Letters and Journals, of Major General Riedesel, during His Residence in America* (Albany: J. Munsell, 1868)
Schmidt, August and Karl Friedrich Rüffer, Bruce E. Burgoyne (trans.), *The Hesse-Cassel Mirbach Regiment in the American Revolution* (Bowie, MD: Heritage Books, 1998)
Uhlendorf, Bernhard A. (ed.), *Revolution in America: Confidential Letters and Journals 1776-1784 of Adjutant General Major Baurmeister of the Hessian Forces* (New Brunswick: Rutgers University Press, 1957)

Secondary Sources

Atwood, Rodney, *The Hessians: Mercenaries from Hessen-Kassel in the American Revolution* (Cambridge: Cambridge University Press, 1980)

Babits, Lawrence E. and Joshua B. Howard, *Long, Obstinate, and Bloody: The Battle of Guilford Courthouse* (Chapel Hill: University of North Carolina Press, 2009)

Baer, Friederike, *German Soldiers in the American Revolutionary War* (Oxford: Oxford University Press, 2022)

Burns, Alexander S., *The Changing Face of Old Regime Warfare: Essays in Honour of Christopher Duffy* (Warwick: Helion, 2022)

Burns, Alexander S., *'The Entire Army Says Hello': Common Soldiers' Experiences, Localism, and Army Reform in Britain and Prussia, 1739-1789* (PhD thesis, West Virginia University, 2021)

Colin, Jean Lambert, *L'Infanterie Au XVIIIe Siècle. La Tactique* (Paris: Berger-Leverault, 1907)

Duffy, Christopher, *By Force of Arms* (Chicago: Emperor's Press, 2008)

Duffy, Christopher, *The Army of Frederick the Great, 2nd Edition* (Chicago: Emperor's Press, 1996)

Duffy, Christopher, *The Military Experience in the Age of Reason* (New York: Atheneum, 1988)

Duffy, Christopher, *The Military Life of Frederick the Great* (New York: Atheneum, 1986)

Fischer, David Hackett, *Washington's Crossing* (Oxford: Oxford University Press, 2004)

Houlding, J. A., *Fit for Service: The Training of the British Army, 1715-1795* (Oxford: Clarendon Press, 1981)

Huck, Stephan, *Soldaten gegen Nordamerika: Lebenswelten Braunschweiger Subsidientruppen im Amerikanischen Unabhängigkeitskrieg* (München: Oldenbourg Verlag, 2011)

Nolan, Cathal J., *Wars of the Age of Louis XIV, 1650-1715: An Encyclopedia of Global Warfare and Civilization* (Westport, CT: Greenwood Press, 2008)

Rogge-Ludwig, K., *Mitteilungen an die mitglieder des Vereins für Hessische Geschichte und Landeskunde* (Kassel: Schönhoven, 1876)

Smith, David, *New York 1776: The Continentals' First Battle* (Oxford: Osprey, 2008)

Spring, Matthew H., *With Zeal and With Bayonets Only: The British Army on Campaign in North America, 1775-1783* (Norman: University of Oklahoma Press, 2008)

Tempelhoff, George Friedrich and Henry Lloyd, *Geschichte Des Siebenjährigen Krieges in Deutschland* (Berlin: Unger, 1801)

Tharp, Louise Hall, *The Baroness and the General* (Boston: Little, Brown and Co., 1962)

Volz, Gustav Berthold, *Die Werke Friedrichs des Grossen in deutscher Übersetzung*m (Berlin: Reimar Hobbing, 1913)

Westphalen, Ferdinand von, *Geschichte Der Feldzüge Des Herzogs Ferdinand von Braunschweig-Lüneburg* (Berlin: Verlag der König, 1872)

3

'See some of our Grievances Redressed': What Patterns of Mutiny Tell Us About Morale in the Continental Army

Krysten Blackstone

On New Year's Day 1781, encamped in Morristown, New Jersey, officers in the Continental Army sat in their tents enjoying a grand regimental dinner. The next day, a re-organisation of the Continental Army would go into effect and the officers would be redistributed. To ring in the new year, and say goodbye to parting friends, the officers partook in festivities throughout the night. Around 8:00 p.m. they heard a rousing HUZZAH from the soldiers outside. Concerned, they sent Lieutenant Enos Reeves to assess the situation. Soldiers on the right met the cry of soldiers from the left. Reeves noted that he 'found numbers in small groups whispering and busily running up and down the line.'[1] He would soon find out why.

The events of the next hour happened quickly. Someone fired a gun, followed quickly by a second shot and then a third. Officers rushed from their tents, abandoning festivities, only to find soldiers running from their own tents and forming lines. Around 1,500 enlisted men and non-commissioned officers gathered in revolt. Commissioned officers attempted to calm the men, but to no avail. Finally, overwhelming their officers, the soldiers successfully commandeered a cannon, forcing the remaining officers to retreat. The entirety of the Pennsylvania line, save two of its regiments, had mutinied. General Anthony Wayne and other high-ranking Continental officers attempted to squash the mutiny, but to no success. Mutineers' demands were simple: they wanted to be discharged immediately, paid their months of back pay, and have 'no aspersions cast against them for participating in the mutiny.'[2] Well organised, armed, and frustrated, the soldiers marched towards Philadelphia intent on laying their grievances against the army to Congress.

---

1   Enos Reeves 'Letterbook Extracts January 2–17, 1781,' 2 January 1781, in John Rhodehamel (ed.), *The American Revolution: Writings from the War of Independence, 1775–1783* (New York: Library of Congress, 2001).

2   Demands delivered in conjunction by the sergeants to General Wayne, 4 January 1781, 'Diary of the Revolt – Pennsylvania in the war of the revolution battalions and line 1775–1783,' John Blair Linn and

Mutiny was a protest that revealed soldiers' acknowledgement that they lacked the ability to endure war without a change in their present circumstances. Considering mutiny does not give a definitive measurement of morale by any means, but does expose quantifiable patterns of dissatisfaction, which contributes to our understanding of morale more generally. Soldiers' understandings of their place within the conflict and society, their value to the army, and individual rights manifested themselves in unique patterns during mutiny. Early in the war, mutinies were results of power struggles. Mutinies later in the war were typically the consequences of military authorities' failure to fulfil their contractual obligations to the soldiers. Perpetrators of mutiny used the protest to address grievances and force change within existing systems, rather than giving up on them entirely. As military authority and structures were defined throughout the war, mutinies shifted into a last resort for soldiers to protest and address their grievances. Mutiny demonstrated an acknowledgement that the problems within military life were hindering soldiers' ability to carry out their service, and was an attempt to resolve these from within existing systems. Instead of leaving the army, mutineers sought to highlight their grievances and, in doing so, attempted to fundamentally change military life.

Mutiny looms much larger than desertion in the historiography of the Continental Army, and eighteenth-century militaries more generally. The relative rareness of mutinies in European armies meant that those that did occur have been studied in detail. The inverse is true of the Continental Army, as the frequency with which mutiny occurred is unique. Peter Way conceptualised mutinies as early forms of labour strikes and the patterns of mutiny in the Continental Army arguably support that assertion.[3] Fundamentally, mutinies were a radical break with military policy, over issues such as poor living and working conditions, pay and insufficient provisions. Eric Hobsbawm characterises this action as a form of riotous collective bargaining.[4] Indeed, Joseph Plump Martin, in his famous narrative of the war, frequently referred to his service as labour and his fellow soldiers as labourers – deserving of 'their meat.'[5] Soldiers, after all, were employed by the military to provide a service, and their enlistment guaranteed them certain compensations. Charles Neimeyer argues that this was the 'moral economy' of soldierhood. In exchange for the temporary surrender of civil liberties in favour of military service, the army was obligated to pay wages and supply soldiers' basic needs.[6] Mutiny, then, served as a reminder to the Continental Army of what its soldiers were owed. When the terms agreed upon were not met, soldiers rebelled.

On the whole, individual mutinous actions demonstrated a soldier's rejection of their subordination – an unwillingness to accept and respect the hierarchy of military life.

William H. Egle (eds), *Pennsylvania archives* (Harrisburg: Clarence M. Busch, 1896) , 2d ser. vol.11, pp.633–634, and *Papers of the Continental Congress 1774-1789*, reel 170, vol.9, p.481, Washington, D.C., National Archives & Records Administration, 1962; National Archives microfilm publications; M0332.; Charles Patrick Neimeyer, *America Goes to War: A Social History of the Continental Army* (New York: New York University Press, 1996), p.149.

3   Peter Way, 'Rebellion of the Regulars: Working Soldiers and the Mutiny of 1763–1764,' *William and Mary Quarterly*, vol.57, no.4 (October, 2000), p.763.

4   E.J. Hobsbawm, 'The Machine Breakers,' *Past & Present*, vol.1, no.1 (February 1952), p. 59.

5   Joseph Plump Martin (ed. James Kirby Martin), *Ordinary Courage: The Revolutionary War Adventures of Joseph Plump Martin* (Chichester: Wiley Blackwell Publishing, 2013), p.99.

6   Neimeyer, *America Goes to War*, p.157

Although these actions happened and were punished accordingly, the mutiny with which this chapter is chiefly concerned involved collective actions. There was a key distinction within Continental Army policy between acting in a mutinous way, and participating or inciting a mutiny. Mutiny as an adjective was punished and treated differently to mutiny as a verb. Thomas Simes's dictionary defined perpetrators of mutiny as any actors who began, excited, caused or joined mutiny – similarly, anyone who knew about or was present for a mutiny and did not actively participate, but also did nothing to stop it or report it, was guilty.[7] This chapter uses mutiny to refer only to a group action, rather than an individual act of insubordination. Such subordination was commonplace within military life and highlighted dissatisfaction in its own way. Indeed, smaller individual instances of mutiny highlighted the dissatisfaction amongst soldiers that culminated in larger actions.[8] However, it functioned differently to collective mutiny. Individual soldiers who felt personally let down by the army, or the leadership within it, could desert or act out in an individual form of mutiny.[9] Mutiny as a protest against an army that was not fulfilling their end of the contract was most effective as a collective action.

Mutiny charges accounted for 5.8 percent of all court martials in the Continental Army during the Revolutionary War.[10] Fundamentally, mutiny was a defiance of the military system from within – a plea for change and recrimination for grievances. It is important to highlight that the line between mutiny and mere disobedience was relatively fluid. Many soldiers were charged with mutiny and found guilty only of disobedience.[11] For the purposes of this chapter, groups found guilty of disobedience will not be considered as mutinous. However, this does not negate the importance of their actions. Many of the issues these groups protested paralleled issues highlighted in larger subsequent mutinies. Mutinies rarely existed as singular incidents, unlike desertion, where an individual soldier's decision to leave cannot easily be attributed to any particular event because of the lack of documentary evidence that exists. Large mutinies were normally foreshadowed by smaller acts of disobedience and followed by other mutinies where soldiers complained about the same issues. Mutinies were often culminations of complaints the army failed to rectify – final desperate attempts for soldiers to have their concerns heard.

The threat of mutiny was consequently ever present in the Continental Army. Mere months after his appointment as Commander-in-Chief, George Washington began advising

7   Thomas Simes, *The Military Medley Containing the Most Necessary Rules and Directions for Attaining a Competent Knowledge of the Art: To Which is Added an Explanation of Military Terms, Alphabetically Digested* (London: n.p., 1768), entry for 'Mutiny'.
8   It should also be addressed that a number of mutinies were committed by militiamen exclusively, or militiamen participated within the ranks of the larger mutinies alongside enlisted soldiers. Although these men are not considered throughout the rest of this thesis, their participation and incitement of mutinies are significant. Unlike in cases of desertion, when the army punished militiamen differently because of the nature of their service, the army doled out punishments for mutiny without prejudice – militiamen were treated as if they were enlisted men.
9   Ilya Berkovich, *Motivation in War: The Experience of Common Soldiers in Old-Regime Europe* (Cambridge: Cambridge University Press, 2017), p.96.
10   John A. Nagy, *Rebellion in the Ranks: Mutinies of the American Revolution* (Westholme Publishing, 2016), p.xv.
11   See James C. Neagles, *Summer Soldiers: A Survey & Index of Revolutionary War Courts-Martial* (Salt Lake City: Ancestry Incorporated, 1986).

Congress that mutiny was imminent if the troops were not adequately supplied.[12] Concerns regarding mutiny even affected the civilian population. In July 1775, Abigail Adams wrote to her husband informing him that the townspeople had been ordered not to use white handkerchiefs because 'tis a signal of mutiny.'[13] Despite the consistent and looming potential for mutiny from the very beginning of the war, the nature and severity of mutinies grew annually. Soldiers' reliance on mutinies to redress their grievances directly relates to their cultural wariness of standing armies. Mutiny within the Continental Army acted as an unofficial system of checks and balances that the soldiers used to safeguard their rights as afforded to them by their contractual agreements.

This chapter is not intended to be an exhaustive study of mutiny perpetrated by the rank and file in the Continental Army, but rather to highlight the patterns in mutiny and evaluate what they reveal about morale. Mutiny was typically a last resort as a form of protest. Soldiers utilised petitions liberally throughout the war as a way to raise their grievances to officers and members of state governments.[14] Mutinies occurred within the Continental Army as early as 1775. Although there were no significant mutinies during the 1777–1778 campaign, there were at least four major mutinies in 1779. From 1779 onwards, mutinies occurred annually and with increasing severity. Three Continental Army lines revolted in 1780, which led to the famed Pennsylvania line mutiny of 1781, the largest mutiny of the Revolution. Each period of mutiny had distinct characteristics. As such, this chapter will view mutinies in three stages: early in the war, 1775 and 1776; the middle of the war, 1777–1779; and the end of the war, 1780–1781. Concerns raised during earlier mutinies never fully evaporated, and each grouping of mutinies built upon previous concerns. The events of 1781, unlike previous mutinies, were therefore a culmination of grievances, not merely an outbreak of them. The progression of mutinies demonstrates the growing consciousness within common soldiers in the Continental Army, that their service was valuable and could be leveraged.

Evaluating mutiny by year, rather than individual incident, does remove some of the characteristics unique to each circumstance. However, considering them chronologically highlights the growth and nuance mutinies gained throughout the eight years of war. The mutinies in 1781 were the culmination of a consistent pattern of rebellion. Mutinies early on in the war were primarily power struggles between the militia turned army and Continental Army leadership. Those in the middle focused more on grievances, but that is not to say that both issues were not at play throughout the entire war, or that the two issues functioned independently of one another. Mutiny is inherently a power struggle – a revolt against the status quo to effect a major change. In the early years, mutiny highlighted the limits and gaps in military authority, whereas later years highlighted limits within army structures to provide for soldiers. Just as the Continental Army developed alongside the progression of the war, so did soldiers' grievances and how they approached them.

The Continental Army was not the only army that suffered from soldiers mutinying. However, the extent to which it happened in the Continental Army was greater than in its

---

12   Philander D. Chase (ed.), *The Papers of George Washington, Revolutionary War Series, vol.2, 16 September 1775–31 December 1775* (Charlottesville: University Press of Virginia, 1987), pp.24–30.
13   Nagy, *Rebellion in the Ranks*, p.2
14   Ricardo Herrera, 'Self-Governance and the American Citizen as Soldier, 1775-1861,' *The Journal of Military History*, vol.63, no.1 (January 2001), p.48.

European counterparts. Ironically, notions of service as a contract were particularly important to the Continental Army's soldiers' understanding of their own citizenship. Due to the persistent difficulties the Continental Congress had supplying and paying soldiers, the Continental Army could not uphold its end of the contract significantly more often than the established and better organised armies of Europe. This, combined with soldiers understanding of their position in the war, 'conscious of their rights … liberties,' created an environment where mutinies flourished.[15] When mutinies occurred in European armies, they were almost always over backpay issues. Professional soldiers were significantly less likely to endure contract breaks than the Continental Army citizen-soldiers. The Swabian mutinies of 1757 highlighted an exceptional occurrence. The Württemberg Army suffered five mutinies and significant desertions within the space of a few months.[16] The two phenomena coalescing only happened once during the Revolutionary War but was much more common in Europe. Only in the winter of 1780 to 1781 could the same be said of the Continental Army. The winter of 1780 saw a spike in desertions, and, early in 1781, the largest mutiny of the war happened.

In the Continental Army, the soldiers who were likely to desert were not those who mutinied, and peaks in either action happened independently. This is in contrast to trends seen in contemporary, old-regime armies. Typically, in these armies, mutiny occurred simultaneously with large-scale desertion. Although contemporary European armies experienced comparative levels of desertion to the Continental Army, they saw significantly fewer mutinies, underscoring a key difference in the function of mutiny and desertion within the Continental Army and its European counterparts. As such, a study of mutiny within the Continental Army is particularly revealing regarding the various ways in which morale functioned and the determinants of morale in the Continental Army. When considered as acts of protest, mutiny and desertion also highlight soldiers' dedication to and understanding of Revolutionary ideals. The persistence of mutiny within the Continental Army reveals a rank-and-file that was aware of their importance to the war and aware of what was owed to them from their enlistment contracts. Soldiers understood they had certain rights and were due compensation as payment for a temporary abdication of their personal freedoms, in favour of military service for the public good. Enlisted men in the Continental Army used mutiny to express their dissatisfaction and advocate for what they believed the army owed them. Although both actions were against the Articles of War set out by the army, soldiers' utilisation of them as forms of protest demonstrated a clear inculcation of the revolutionary ideals.

Conceptually, it is important to understand mutinies simultaneously as direct challenges to authority figures and structures and breaches in military discipline. As Peter H. Wilson argues regarding the Swabian mutinies of 1757, the frequency of mutinies highlighted the army's inability and, in some cases, unwillingness, to enforce the harsh punishments dictated by military law regarding mutinies.[17] European armies were not sympathetic

---

15   Don Higginbotham, *The War for American Independence: Military Attitudes, Policies, and Practice, 1763-1789* (Macmillan Press: New York, 1971), p.406.
16   Peter H. Wilson, 'Violence and the Rejection of Authority in Eighteenth-Century German: The Case of the Swabian Mutinies in 1757', *German History*, vol.12, no.1 (February 1994), p.2.
17   Wilson, 'Violence and the Rejection of Authority', p.2.

or tolerant of mutinies – participation in any collective action risked capital punishment. Similarly, choosing not to act against a mutiny garnered the same punishment. Collective action such as mutiny was thus fairly rare in eighteenth-century armies. The same cannot be said for the Continental Army. Mutiny represents an important area of negotiation between officers and the rank-and-file, as well as between soldiers and the Continental Congress, and state authorities.[18] The punishment for mutiny, if any was given, was much more flexible than punishment for other crimes due to a mutual understanding of the importance of the individual soldier, and the validity of their grievances. Even if officers disagreed with enlisted soldiers' method of protest, few disagreed that protest was merited. Due to the consistent manpower shortages within the Continental Army, officers needed to dole out punishments carefully. Soldiers needed to both be punished but see the justice in the punishment – enough to entice them back to service in the army. As such, flexibility and uncharacteristic expressions of forgiveness were common in mutiny court martials, in a way they were not for other crimes. Punishment for mutiny in the Continental Army rarely resulted in death sentences and occurred with relative frequency during the Revolutionary War. Two reasons explain this difference.

First, there was an acknowledgement on behalf of the Continental Army that the grievances of those participating in the mutiny were legitimate. Officers may not have agreed with mutiny as a course of action, but could not deny the lack of supplies, sustenance and pay the soldiers endured. If military service was a contractual agreement then the Continental Army rarely held up their end of the contract in full. Baron Ludwig Von Closen wrote his assessment of the situation, following the Pennsylvania line mutiny: 'The lack of pay, the bad food and dearth of clothing, together with the fact that Congress does not permit them to leave military service, even when their terms expired one or two years ago, are the reason for their being driven to this extremity. In Europe, they would do the same for less.'[19] Mutiny may have been an extreme reaction, but it was one warranted under the extreme circumstances.

Second, it was impractical to punish large groups of soldiers. The Continental Army always lacked manpower, and enough men mutinied in multiple instances that it would have been a severe blow to the army if they punished or executed all involved. In addition, the nature of enlisted men's service in the Continental Army was different to that of most European army soldiers. The men were almost all volunteers – citizens fighting for a cause – and were taught repeatedly by officers to consider themselves as such. Sentencing large groups of soldiers to death who brought forth grievances does not inspire confidence in the cause or the justice system. As a result of the light punishment mutineers received, mutiny was a relatively safe form of protest for individual soldiers, while still ensuring a degree of success for the collective. Although ringleaders of the mutinies were at great risk

---

18   William P. Tatum III, 'The Soldiers Murmured Much on Account of this Usage: Military Justice and Negotiated Authority in the Eighteenth-Century British Army', in Kevin Linch & Matthew McCormack (eds) *Britain's Soldiers: Rethinking War and Society, 1715-1815* (Liverpool: Liverpool University Press: 2021), p.111.

19   Evelyn M. Acomb (ed. & trans.), *The Revolutionary Journal of Baron Ludwig von Closen, 1780–1783* (Chapel Hill: University of North Carolina Press, 1958), 12 January 1781, p.54.

of punishment, it was rare that all participants suffered.[20] The lack of robust punishment undoubtedly ensured the continuing practice of mutiny across the Continental Army.[21]

Although the Continental Army suffered a number of mutinies during the war, and the British Army in North America suffered virtually none, this did not impede the army's victory in 1783.[22] Why, when soldiers were seemingly at their wits end, did they still refuse to leave military service? If, as many historians have argued, their willingness to stay in the army was largely economic, and soldiers were the dregs of society with no other option, why then did they stay despite the lack of pay? Mutinies occurred in European armies, but they occurred less frequently and typically with a preceding or subsequent mass desertion. This culmination of events rarely happened in the Continental Army. The function and character of mutiny in the Continental Army must therefore be analysed as separate to the action in other contemporary armies. Both the mutineers, and the armies that presided over the situations, managed the situations vastly differently in the Continental Army and European armies.

Mutiny in the Continental Army evolved throughout the eight years of the Revolutionary War in a way not comparable to its European counterparts. The newness of the military institution, and soldiers' understandings of their position in society and the military, meant that mutiny was used from the army's inception to highlight soldiers' dissatisfaction. Soldiers, aware of their rights, and wary of a standing army anyway, used mutiny as a form of protest and as a way to highlight their willingness to serve in the army, while simultaneously demonstrating their inability to do so. As a result, the characteristics of mutinies evolved greatly throughout the war. Earlier in the war, mutinies were results of power struggles. They started in 1775, but hardly ever occurred in 1776 or 1777. Mutinies later in the war were typically the result of military authorities' failure to fulfil their contractual obligations to the soldiers. Mutinies increased in frequency from 1778 to 1779, culminating in the largest mutiny of the war in 1781. As military authority and structures were defined throughout the war, mutinies became a last resort for soldiers to protest and address their grievances.

Certain patterns existed in all mutinies during the Revolutionary War. Mutiny was an action carried out by a group of soldiers. Without the group, these acts against the army would be stopped quickly and punished harshly. Coherence safeguarded soldiers' protest. Mutiny was always motivated by a grievance against the army, in one way or another. As the war developed, the nature of these grievances shifted, grew, and amalgamated, but a grievance was always present. In each mutiny there was an emphasis attached to the soldier's

---

20   Neimeyer, *America Goes to War*, p.141.
21   William Pennington, a soldier from New Jersey, angered at the mutiny, argued as such in his diary: 'The mild treatment of the Pennsylvanians met, by the state appointing a committee to treat with them and redress the grievances they supposed themselves to labor under, and was the principal incitement to the Jersey line to take the steps they have been led into by some turbulent fellows.' 'Our Camp Chest, 1780–1781,' Copy of Diary of William S. Pennington of New Jersey, original diary on deposit in the Historical Society of New Jersey, pp.326–327.
22   Only 15 soldiers in the British Army were tried for mutiny during the Revolutionary War. Each of these instances were individual acts of mutiny (disrespecting an officer, or the crown, etc.), rather than collective crimes like the instances of mutiny in the Continental Army. Arthur N. Gilbert, 'British Military Justice during the American Revolution,' *The Eighteenth Century*, vol.20, no.1 (Winter 1979), p.30.

persona. Soldiers accentuated their suffering for the cause – their strongest rhetorical device and the only bargaining chip available to them. These men understood that they needed officers to view them as incredibly loyal but demoralised soldiers with no other choice because of the army's inability to provide for them. Soldiers needed the army to understand that they were forced to mutiny in order to rectify their situation, laying the blame for the mutiny with the army, rather than the soldiers partaking. If a pattern of suffering for the cause could be proven, then perhaps their concerns would be listened to, or, at the bare minimum, their punishments lessened.

Similarly, the timing of mutinies tended to follow specific patterns. On the whole, mutinies most frequently occurred around New Year. That was typically when enlistment terms were up, and they faced additional hardships because of the elements and had been cooped in winter camps for multiple months. The increased time in camp, less consistent but more monotonous duties and clear lack of supplies undoubtedly contributed to the organisation and frequency of these mutinies. Additionally, when soldiers are encamped for months, there is no enemy to fight. With the absence of a clear 'other' in the Crown Forces, the other became Congress and officers. New Year mutinies became so commonplace within the Continental Army that General Anthony Wayne remarked of the month that he 'sincerely wished the ides of January was come and past.'[23] The winter of 1780–1781 in the Morristown encampments was particularly harsh on the soldiers, which contributed to the string of mutinies in which Continental Army soldiers participated.

Soldiers understood their military service as a contract they volunteered to sign. The notion of this contract was crucial in soldiers' conceptions of their role in the broader society as citizens, and therefore what rights they were entitled to. Both parties, in this case the soldier and the army he fought for, were responsible for upholding their side of the bargain. For soldiers, their contracted terms were simple: they would serve in the army for a specified period of time and in return they would receive pay, food, and clothing. When the terms of the contract were not met, problems arose. The army was expected to provide just as soldiers are expected to serve. Failure in this happening resulted in soldiers attempting to leverage the only thing they had: their service. Problematically, however, in the Continental Army, soldiers who participated in mutinies *wanted* to serve. Indeed, as Ilya Berkovich argues, mutiny was not a way for soldiers to reject their military identity. In fact, many soldiers who mutinied did so with an added emphasis on their soldierhood.[24]

The existence and success of mutinies also relied on a sense of shared group identity, making it more likely that experienced soldiers participated rather than newer recruits. The longer a soldier served in the Continental Army, the more hardened they became to the sufferings of military life and the more attached they were to the cause, their service, and their fellow soldiers. Mutiny was the reserve of the experienced soldier – soldiers with limited service experience deserted, rather than protest, in the face of grievance. For instance, army returns for the winter of 1780–1781 at Morristown recorded that no more than 11 percent of the men were on the sick rolls at any time. This would suggest that the men encamped

---

23   Anthony Wayne to Colonel Johnstone, 16 December 1780, quoted in Charles J. Stillé, *Major General Anthony Wayne and the Pennsylvania Line* (Philadelphia, J.B. Lippincott, 1893), pp.240–241.

24   Berkovich, *Motivation in War*, p.117. Mutineers in Europe (Swabian mutinies) proudly marched in formation and wore their regimental colours as a way to highlight their dedication.

in Morristown were more experienced soldiers than their Valley Forge counterparts three years earlier, of which one-third of all soldiers were on the sick roll at all times. Their experience in the army earned them immunity from the diseases that frequented camps.[25] The Continental Army clearly understood that mutinies thrived on bonds between experienced soldiers, as longstanding regiments squashed the larger mutinies. When the Pennsylvania and New Jersey lines mutinied in 1781, New England regiments were called in to stop the protest.[26]

Critical in understanding the action of mutiny is understanding attitudes surrounding the practice. Unlike desertion, starvation or marching – things that happened daily to Continental Army soldiers – mutiny was a discussion almost absent in their diaries. Narratives published after the war, like Joseph Plumb Martin's, included details of the mutinies that Martin participated in and heard about during the Revolutionary War. But diaries written during the conflict leave discussion of mutinies out of their accounts, except on a few occasions when the author helped put down a mutiny.[27] This is not particularly surprising. Mutiny was a crime punishable whether soldiers participated in one, or merely discussed the prospect. A successful mutiny was reliant on a collective action against officers they took by surprise. Regardless, the language used by officers to describe mutiny is telling, and sheds light on our understanding of why they punished it the way they did, as well as how it affected relationships between officers and soldiers more generally.

Officers felt that general dissatisfaction in camp could lead to a mutiny if unchecked and referred to this possibility as a 'spirit of mutiny.' The phrase covered many different behaviours, although it was not used to discuss mutiny when it broke out, only when officers were suspicious it might.[28] The description was used to articulate the rumblings of dissatisfaction within the army they feared would escalate into something more. Officers' description of mutiny as a 'spirit of' highlights their acceptance that the action was gradual. Similarly, officers frequently referred to mutiny as an infection that could and would spread throughout the ranks and the whole army. Yet again, this underscores officers' understanding of the

---

25   James Kirby Martin & Mark Edward Lender, *A Respectable Army: The Military Origins of the Republic, 1763-1789* (Oxford: Wiley Blackwell, 2015), p.168.

26   Neimeyer, *America Goes to War*, p.152.

27   'The mutineers returned to their duty and received a general pardon. This unhappy circumstance will reflect the eternal dishonour on the character of their line, and sully their former actions.' 'Our Camp Chest, 1780–1781,' Copy of Diary of William S. Pennington of New Jersey, original diary on deposit in the Historical Society of New Jersey, p.326.

28   Washington first used the phrase in 1777 concerning pay: 'Nothing can so effectually lay the Foundation of Discontent, and of Course encourage a Spirit of Mutiny and Desertion among the Soldiers, as withholding their Pay from them.' George Washington to John Hancock, 10 May 1777, Philander D. Chase (ed.), *The Papers of George Washington, Revolutionary War Series, vol.9, 28 March 1777–10 June 1777* (Charlottesville: University Press of Virginia, 1999), pp.375–376. On 26 May 1779 Washington wrote again, this time to James Duane, about 'a spirit of mutiny': 'The principal one was that a spirit of mutiny had appeared among the men which I thought it absolutely necessary to suppress rather than encourage.' The spirit itself in both instances is not an indication of mutiny, but rather murmurings about the possibility. The phrase 'spirit of mutiny' was used to describe the feeling of unhappiness within camp, which could result in a mutiny if not contained. George Washington to James Duane, 26 May 1779, Edward G. Lengel (ed.), *The Papers of George Washington, Revolutionary War Series, vol.20, 8 April–31 May 1779* (Charlottesville: University of Virginia Press, 2010), p.633.

grievances and their acknowledgement that the soldiers' situation was cause for such discontent.[29] They understood that there needed to be an evolution of thought and experience over a period of time, which culminated in the expression of dissatisfaction.

Officers in the Continental Army were not oblivious to the hardships soldiers endured during wartime. They also had a vivid understanding of the bonds soldiers formed during their service. Indeed, as discussed in chapters two and three, officers went out of their way to encourage those bonds. Soldiers with deep regimental connections were less likely to desert than those who had recently joined the army. A sense of belonging and brotherhood was essential to the success of individual regiments and the army as a whole. These same bonds were what made mutiny an attractive option to soldiers. The desire to stay in the army and fight alongside their fellow soldiers necessitated another way for soldiers to express their dissatisfaction. As leaving was not a good option, and their circumstances were not changing, they turned to the threat of mutiny.

Officers were deeply concerned that a mutiny in one regiment would cause a domino effect and result in mutinies across others. Inherent to this was an acknowledgement among officers that the complaints of any one unit were almost always universal. Following the Pennsylvania line mutiny, George Washington wrote to George Clinton detailing it, iterating his concern that this may not be a single incidence:

> What will be the event of this affair I do not know, or whether the spirit of defection will be confined to that line. The Officers have been apprehensive of something of a like nature among the troops at these posts, who have the same causes of complaint.[30]

This was a justifiable fear in this particular case, and in many others, as that is exactly what happened. Every mutiny that happened fed off previous ones, building on grievances and changing tactics to be more effective.

Mutinies in 1775 and 1776 were power struggles rather than expressions of grievance. Although the same grievances existed in those years of the war as would come to a head later on, the soldiers' complaints were not the cause of the early mutinies. Instead, these power struggles were undoubtedly manifestations of the confusion wrought from the shift from militia to a standing army, and all that it implied, in June 1775. Early mutinies of the war were of a similar ilk to those of colonial soldiers during the French and Indian Wars. These mutinies started with an expression of grievance – normally about supplies – punctuated by threats for officers and soldiers alike to march home if demands were not met.[31] These actions were somewhere between mutiny and mass desertion. Two mass desertions

29 'An alarming spirit of mutiny and desertion has shown itself upon several occasions, and there is no saying how extensively the infection might spread.' George Washington to William Livingston, 22 April 1779, in Lengel (ed.), 'The Papers of George Washington, vol.20, pp.166–167.
30 From George Washington to Anthony Wayne, 3 January 1781, Founders Online, National Archives, <https://founders.archives.gov/documents/Washington/99-01-02-04428>, accessed September 2023.
31 Fred Anderson, A People's Army: Massachusetts Soldiers and Society in the Seven Years War (Chapel Hill: Published for the Institute of Early American History and Culture, Williamsburg, VA, by the University of North Carolina Press, 1984).

occurred very early in 1775 – one from the Connecticut line in December, and another in October during the Quebec Campaign.[32] Occurrences such as this happened exclusively in 1775, not afterwards, and relied on the manipulation of a nascent institution's regulations. Misunderstanding of power between enlisted soldiers and officers and how the army would function as an institution, resulted in command problems and a number of mutinies.

One of the first mutinies of the war, in September 1775, demonstrated this grey area of authority well. Lieutenant David Ziegler of William Thompson's Pennsylvania Rifle Battalion punished a sergeant for neglecting his duty and confined him. John Leaman, a member of the sergeant's company furious about the arrest, led a group of soldiers determined to set the sergeant free. Ziegler successfully captured Leaman and placed him in jail too.[33] Shortly afterwards, while enjoying his dinner alone with Colonel Thompson, Ziegler and the other officers heard a ruckus outside, only to discover that the other mutineers had broken out Leaman and the original incarcerated sergeant. Undoubtedly frustrated by the persistence of the soldiers, Ziegler and Thompson recaptured Leaman and confined him in Cambridge, a mile away from the encampment. This was successful for about 30 minutes, until members of other companies joined the mutineers and marched to Cambridge to free Leaman. With no other option, Ziegler alerted General Washington, who ordered some 500 soldiers to go and protect the jail. The mutineers, realising their situation was unwinnable, turned back and were eventually captured.[34] In the aftermath of the mutiny, Washington was at a loss about what to do. The men were guilty of mutiny, and the court martial decided that swiftly, but the threat of another mutiny still loomed. The soldiers were sentenced to pay 20 shillings and the leaders of the mutiny were imprisoned for six days – overall, a light sentence given the severity of the crime.[35] Although the authority structure of the Continental Army was clear, this rebellion demonstrated the limits of that authority. The nascent officer corps could not truly exercise the full extent of their authority without severe consequences or the threat of another mutiny.

A similar, and perhaps the most famous, example of mutiny in 1775 happened later that year at Fort Ticonderoga. Benedict Arnold attempted to forbid Ethan Allen's men from plundering after the fort was captured. When Arnold was met with threats, he informed Allen that he would take command of his soldiers, which resulted in the soldiers collectively refusing to obey Arnold and threatening to go home. To appease the men, Arnold allowed Allen to remain their direct commander, and they were allowed to continue plundering

---

32   In December 1775, 80 men deserted from camp in Cambridge due to their 'great uneasiness at the Service and determination to leave it.' George Washington to Jonathan Trumbull Sr, 2 December 1775, Philander D. Chase (ed.), *The Papers of George Washington, Revolutionary War Series, vol.1, 16 June 1775–15 September 1775* (Charlottesville: University Press of Virginia, 1985), pp.471-473. In October 1775, Lieutenant Colonel Roger Enos and his company deserted the Quebec expedition. He was later subject to court martial and acquitted. It was ruled 'the prisoner was by absolute necessity obliged to return with his division'. General Orders, 4 December 1775,' Chase (ed.), *The Papers of George Washington, vol.1*, p.482.

33   'Journal of Phinehas Bemis,' 10 September 1775, File of Phinehas Bemis, W 14278 (National Archives Microfilm Publication M804, roll 210, frames 664–675), p.14. Revolutionary War Pension and Bounty-Land Warrant Application Files, Records of the Veterans Administration, Record Group 15.

34   Nagy, *Rebellion in the Ranks*, p.4.

35   Chase (ed.), *The Papers of George Washington, vol.1*, pp.454–455.

houses in the surrounding area.[36] This incident began a dangerous precedent within the Continental Army. The coherence of Allen's Green Mountain Boys in their refusal to obey Arnold created a situation in which they remained unchallenged. Their collective insubordination resulted in exactly what they had intended it to – they faced no recrimination, and their demands were met. Although at this early stage of the conflict it is not surprising that Allen's men refused to recognise Arnold's, and by extension the Continental Army's, authority over them, it represents a foundational moment in group insubordination and protest. As the war developed, soldiers came to understand that cohesion was the key to their success. If they could create a group willing to challenge the issue at hand, it was likely that they would succeed in their endeavour. If the leaders of mutinies were clearly identifiable and were punished, rarely did all the participants face punishment.

Both of these mutinies highlight an important element to group cohesion, and a force that officers in the Continental Army spent much of the war simultaneously fighting against and encouraging: regionality. The strength of Ethan Allen's Green Mountain Boys lies at least partly in their title – they were 'Green Mountain Boys.' As a unit, they were conceived in Vermont and had an identity predicated on being a united force from the same area. Their coherence stemmed from their shared identity and regional connections, which predated the war. The same can be said of the revolt in September 1775. The Pennsylvania Rifle Battalion was known for their musketry skills and their insubordination.[37] As a unit they understood that they possessed a skill that the army needed, and, as a result, demanded special treatment. Unlike other less specialised battalions, the unit was exempt from fatigue duties and often asserted their own rules, rather than obeying the army.[38] When a member of the battalion was threatened, much of the battalion sided with him, rather than accepting the strictures of military discipline. The Green Mountain Boys and the Pennsylvania Rifle Battalion prioritised their own units over the entire army. The Continental Army officers understood that they were essentially powerless when confronted with such regional loyalty. The soldiers needed to be punished, but, to keep them on side and vaguely cooperative, the army was unable to stretch their military authority far. Both units were known for being highly skilled 'mountain men' – loners with a rebellious streak that set them apart from other soldiers in skill and required obedience.[39] What made these units able to rebel in the way they did was not their skill but their coherence.

Inherently these mutinies say less about morale than later mutinies did. Maintaining morale in the army was, to some degree, about mitigating expectations. These early mutinies represent the confusion inherent in the creation of an army and the defining of the powers within it as well as the shift from militia to regulars. As an institution, the Continental Army lacked the robust structures or authority to quell mutinies with the ease of later years. The officers lacked the reputation and rapport with the men to appeal on a more emotional level, and regionalism still manifested itself in home regiments rather than larger units. The mutinies of 1775 and 1776 were not units threatening to leave service in the army – in fact,

---

36 Benedict Arnold, quoted in John William Kruger, 'Troop Life at the Champlain Valley Forest during the American Revolution.' PhD Dissertation, State University of New York at Albany, 1981, p.29.
37 Nagy, *Rebellion in the Ranks*, pp.3–4.
38 Nagy, *Rebellion in the Ranks*, pp.3–4.
39 Neimeyer, *America Goes to War*, p.146.

the mutinies rarely had anything to do with whether or not service would continue. Instead, the mutinies reflected the process of defining what that service would look like and who it would be under. These soldiers attempted to leverage their service, and the larger need for it, in an attempt to define what exactly their service would look like. By 1779 soldiers were unable to do the same. The structures of the Continental Army had developed enough that expectations of soldiers and structures within the army, although nascent, were at least defined from the outset.

Mutinies in 1777 and onwards were of a markedly different nature to those of 1775. Although power dynamics were being challenged, mutineers did so with specific grievances. These grievances built up and occurred with increasing frequency and severity from 1777 to 1779. Mutiny happened less in 1777 and 1778 than in other years, but still happened. The Continental Army majorly restructured in 1777, which allowed it to better supply the soldiers and deal with grievances before mutinies escalated. Similarly, 1777 was the start of new enlistment terms. As soldiers more frequently deserted within their first nine months of service and mutinies relied on soldiers being loyal to one another, years of high enlistment rates saw lower numbers of mutinies than others. However, the mutinies that occurred in 1777 and 1778 were not often the result of authority disputes as in the previous two years, but rather a consequence of supply and pay issues.

In 1777, Connecticut militiamen mutinied over unequal pay between them and the Continental Army troops of the same state. After Governor Jonathan Trumbull reduced their rations, making militia rations less than their army counterparts, the militiamen mutinied. To end the dispute, Connecticut restored militia rations to normal and the mutiny ended quickly. Similar clashes over inequality between Continental Army regiments also occurred – certain colonies paid soldiers higher bounties than others, and disputes frequently arose surrounding the inequity. Such issues were consistent throughout the Revolutionary War. Washington wrote to John Hancock in 1776, wary of such practices. If states could levy their own bounties, he wrote that he was 'certain when the Troops come to act together, that Jealousy, impatience & mutiny would necessarily arise. a different pay cannot exist in the same Army.'[40] Despite the army's attempts to form a cohesive *Continental* Army, free from regional jealousies in favour of national cohesion, regional distinctions acted as an underlying cause of many issues.

Lack of provisions was also often the cause of mutinies between 1777 and 1779. Within days of arriving at Valley Forge, soldiers in the army mutinied over improper supplies and rations. Famously, the winter at Valley Forge was a trying experience for the army encamped there, but the immediacy with which soldiers experienced hardship upon arrival is often misunderstood. The mutiny, although relatively small, occurred on 21 December, but was quickly put down by 'spirited officers'.[41] The next day, just five days after Washington marched troops into Valley Forge, he wrote to Congress in desperate need of supplies, as he observed soldiers unable to even stand in their weakened state.[42] Brigadier General James Varnum pointed out to Washington that many of his men had not had bread in three days,

40   Philander D. Chase (ed.), *The Papers of George Washington, Revolutionary War Series, vol.7, 21 October 1776–5 January 1777* (Charlottesville: University Press of Virginia, 1997), pp.142–143.
41   George Washington in Nagy, *Rebellion in the Ranks*, p.31
42   George Washington in Nagy, *Rebellion in the Ranks*, p.31.

nor meat in two.[43] The desperation at Valley Forge only increased in severity. With every passing month, officers grew more concerned that the situation would destroy the army. Nathanael Greene described the situation as perpetually being 'on the eve of starving and the army of mutinying' in January 1778.[44] By the middle of February, Greene's prediction came true. After months in camp with few provisions, and even less to do, the 12th Massachusetts regiment approached General John Patterson and threatened to quit if their grievances were not met. Finally, the general agreed to allow the men to leave camp in search of food and the soldiers in turn agreed to end their protest.[45]

These two instances at Valley Forge were so small compared to the mutiny the officers predicted that Washington completely discounted them in his letter to George Clinton on 16 February 1778. In the letter, he praised the soldiers for their fortitude: 'Naked and starving as they are, we cannot enough admire the incomparable patience and fidelity of the soldiery, that they have not been, ere this, excited by their sufferings, to a general mutiny and dispersion.'[46] Washington understood the supply situation at Valley Forge to be so severe that he expected the whole camp to rebel, rather than just smaller groups. The instances of that winter in Valley Forge were the first of many mutinies that arose to address grievances in the following years. A string of mutinies occurred in 1779 highlighting the lack of provisions and pay. The Connecticut line mutinied in 1779 in an attempt to 'raise some provisions, if not, at least to raise a little dust.'[47] Similarly the North Carolina line 'demanded their pay… and would not march till they had justice done them.'[48] In each of these instances, the mutinies were stopped with relative ease.

---

43   Brigadier General James Mitchell Varnum to George Washington, 22 December 1777, Frank E. Grizzard, Jr. and David R. Hoth (eds), *The Papers of George Washington, Revolutionary War Series*, vol.12, 26 October 1777–25 December 1777 (Charlottesville: University Press of Virginia, 2002), pp.675–676.

44   Nathanael Greene to Alexander McDougall, 25 January 1778, Richard K. Showman (ed.), *The Papers of General Nathanael Greene* (Chapel Hill: The University of North Carolina Press, 1980), vol.2, pp.259–261.

45   Frances Dana to Elbridge Gerry, 16 February 1778, Paul H. Smith (ed.), *Letters of Delegates to Congress* (Washington D.C.: Library of Congress, 1982), vol.9, pp.109–111.

46   From George Washington to George Clinton, 16 February 1778, Edward G. Lengel (ed.), *The Papers of George Washington, Revolutionary War Series, vol.13, 26 December 1777–28 February 1778* (Charlottesville: University of Virginia Press, 2003), pp.552–554.

47   Martin, *Ordinary Courage*, pp. 96–99. Joseph Plumb Martin discussed this mutiny at length in his memoir. It left a lasting impression on him. This may be because of the cyclical nature of this particular mutiny. The men spent much of the winter of 1779–1780 in the Morristown encampment 'absolutely, literally starved' (p.96). He described soldiers eating their shoes or birch bark off trees if they could find it – one officer was driven to shoot and eat his dog for provisions. Soldiers raised their grievances and threatened to leave en masse. Officers convinced them to stay and instead to petition the Connecticut General Assembly. Soldiers returned to duty only to mutiny again shortly thereafter for the exact same grievances: 'The men were now exasperated beyond endurance; they could not stand it any longer' (p.98). Officers appealed to the soldiers' patriotism and sense of duty, imploring them to remain with promises of provisions. Soldiers again agreed, received provisions, and within weeks, were starving again.

48   Taken from the testimony of Ann Glover, wife of Samuel Glover, who led the North Carolina line mutiny. The army put down the mutiny quickly, and Samuel Glover was executed for his role in it. Shortly thereafter, his widow petitioned the state for an income, highlighting that her husband's and his conspirators' actions, although morally wrong, were out of love for their family, whom they could not support because the army did not pay them as promised. Petition to the General Assembly from

A similar event happened in Brigadier General James Varnum's brigade in March 1779. Describing the incident to General Washington, Major General John Sullivan wrote:

> … ninety Men of the Brigade, belonging to different Regiments collected, with a view, of relating their Grievances to the officers; imagining I suppose, that their Numbers wou'd give them a consequence. But tho' mistaken in their mode of Address, they had not the appearance of Violence, and were without Force, readily dispers'd.[49]

Although there are examples to the contrary, most mutinies in the Continental Army played out similarly. A large group of soldiers, with a list of complaints, brought them to officers and disbanded quickly after the grievances had been aired.

A letter from Major General Horatio Gates to Major General William Heath, dated 30 April 1779, highlighted this in his plea for more supplies. Gates asked Heath to send 'at least, three hundred Barrels of Flour, to pacify the Troops' immediately and more as soon as possible.[50] The reason for this was that two mutinies within the space of a week had occurred and he was concerned that more would break out. His concern, however, was that he would not be able to bring himself to put the mutiny down. Gates wrote: 'the real Cause of the Mutinies is such, that I dare not, no, with Equity I could not exert the coercive Part of my Authority.'[51] Here it is clear that, although Gates disagreed with how soldiers expressed their discontent, he found their grievances fully justified. Critically, these instances of mutiny between 1775 and 1780 were, for the most part, non-violent. The large group of unhappy armed soldiers marching in union undoubtedly and purposefully created a threatening image, but there were rarely shots fired in the process, let alone casualties. By 1781, this would no longer be the case.

As the war developed so too did the organisation and numbers behind the mutinies. Those that occurred in 1780 were larger than ever before. Mutinies in the Continental Army built off one another steadily for the first six years of the war until everything culminated at the end of 1780: major defection, high desertion rates and the largest mutiny of the war. It is not entirely surprising that 1780 marked a shift in the Continental Army. Currency depreciation was at its worst throughout 1780, the vast majority of soldiers' enlistments expired in the first few months of the year and the winter of 1779–1780 was the worst North America had seen in half a century.[52] The winter encampment at Morristown, New Jersey, marked the

---

Ann Glover, widow of Samuel Glover, 10 January 1780, Walter Clark (ed.), *State Records of North Carolina* (Goldsboro, NC: Nash Brothers, 1898), vol.15, pp.187–188. A further discussion of widows' petitions, and Ann Glover's specifically, can be seen in Royster, *A Revolutionary People at War*, pp.296–297. The revolts of the Pennsylvania and Connecticut line are further detailed in Neimeyer, *America Goes to War*, p.148.

49   Major General John Sullivan to George Washington, 3 March 1779, Philander D. Chase and William M. Ferraro (ed.), *The Papers of George Washington, Revolutionary War Series, vol.19, 15 January–7 April 1779* (Charlottesville: University of Virginia Press, 2009), pp.349–350.

50   Major General William Heath to George Washington, 8 May 1779, *The Papers of George Washington, vol.20*, pp.378–379.

51   *The Papers of George Washington, Revolutionary War Series, vol.20*, pp.378–379.

52   Nagy, *Rebellion in the Ranks*, p.70.

hardest winter encampment of the war – even more so than Valley Forge. The bad weather also meant that roads became impassable and supply lines lagged in delivering the pittance of supplies sent to the starving Continental Army.[53] All of this, unsurprisingly, resulted in three mutinies in the first few months of 1780. On 1 January, the Massachusetts line at West Point mutinied over their enlistment terms. They wanted their three-year term to end immediately at the new year, instead of being extended. The Connecticut line mutinied at Morristown on 25 May over the army's inability to feed or pay the soldiers. Finally, the New York line mutinied at Fort Schuyler in June over pay and lack of supplies.[54]

The three mutinies have one essential thing in common – that they were stopped relatively quickly. The Connecticut line is perhaps the best example of the flaws with using mutiny as protest. Reports of the mutiny all noted that the officers were able to calm it by reminding the soldiers what they were contending for. Joseph Plumb Martin's account of the mutiny following the war described the officers immediately after seeing it as endeavouring 'to soothe the Yankee temper they had excited' and noted that the soldiers only backed down after 'an abundance of fair promises.'[55] Of course, this was the inherent weakness in most mutinies after 1777. The soldiers who participated in mutinies did so because they wanted to remain a part of the army. Soldiers used mutiny as a tool for reform but always failed to completely withdraw their service. As did the officers on their promises. Martin noted that the soldiers 'fared a little better for a few days after this memento to the officers, but it soon became an old story … we endeavoured to bear it with our usual fortitude, until it again became intolerable.'[56] Although a terrifying prospect to the small Continental Army, soldiers' threats to leave the army were only viable as long as soldiers carried through and, within the Continental Army, few did. Instead, after ensuring that their complaints were heard, they continued with their duties until such a time where they needed to raise their grievances again. Mutiny in the Continental Army functioned in this perpetual cycle throughout the war.

Indeed, officers writing to George Washington following the Connecticut line's mutiny all emphasised the soldiers' suffering. Colonel Return Meigs wrote, 'this Brigade is now ten days deficient in Meat, notwithstanding my efforts to have them supply'd – there cannot possibly be a case where mutiny can be admitted: But that this Brigade has been worse served With provisions than any other in the Army.'[57] The lack of meat rations for over a week was not the mutineers' only complaint. In his letter to Joseph Reed following the incident, Washington expounded further: 'The troops very pointedly mentioned besides their distresses for provision' that they had not been paid for five months, and that Continental currency was depreciated to the point of virtually no value. Despite Colonel Meigs' reminders of their service, good conduct and the cause they were contending, Washington continued, the soldiers responded that 'their sufferings were too great – that they wanted present relief – and some present substantial recompense for their service.'[58] In this mutiny, as in so many others,

---

53   Nagy, *Rebellion in the Ranks*, p.74.
54   William M. Ferraro (ed.), *The Papers of George Washington, Revolutionary War Series*, vol.26, *13 May–4 July 1780* (Charlottesville: University of Virginia Press, 2018), pp.250–251.
55   Martin, *Ordinary Courage*, p.99.
56   Martin, *Ordinary Courage*, p.100.
57   Ferraro (ed.), *The Papers of George Washington, Revolutionary War Series*, vol.26, pp.194–196.
58   Ferraro (ed.), *The Papers of George Washington, Revolutionary War Series*, vol.26, pp.220–225.

soldiers emphasised that the army had let them down but would continue in military service when some needs were met. Their ability to endure the war's hardships was nearing its end.

In this vein, understanding mutinies as expressions of morale is useful. The practice of mutiny in the later years of the war exposed the nuances of morale. These large mutinies highlighted dissatisfaction, undoubtedly. Mutiny was essentially soldiers' insistence that although they were *willing* members of the army, if circumstances did not change, they would no longer be *able* members of the army. They reached their limits of endurance, not because of the war itself, or because of their unwillingness to fight it, but because the structures of the army were not providing for them.

Most of the Continental Army's mutinies during the Revolutionary War highlighted similar problems. The mutinies of 1781 were the culmination of those factors, precipitated by Major General Benedict Arnold's defection and the harsh winter the army faced, which in turn resulted in high desertion rates. The year 1781 was the only one when high desertion rates and large-scale mutiny existed simultaneously. In the Continental Army, desertion and mutiny typically functioned independently and inversely of one another. The mutinies in 1781 were distinct because they sustained themselves with violence and took multiple days to squash. Previous mutineers may have marched in formation and carried weapons, but they were rarely used. Officers were shot and killed within minutes of the Pennsylvania line mutiny in January 1781. The mutinies of 1781 truly were a manifestation of all the built-up tensions, anxieties and dissatisfaction growing in the army up until that point.[59]

The Pennsylvania line mutiny of 1781 was the most severe of the Revolutionary War. Three officers and a handful of mutineers were killed in the struggle. It was the only mutiny of the war that the army itself could not stop. Joseph Reed, President of Pennsylvania, ultimately ended it. The mutiny was the culmination of everything the Army and its officers had come to fear over the previous six years. Enlisted men in the Continental Army used mutiny as a form of protest throughout the war. As a practice among soldiers, mutinies developed and evolved alongside the army itself. As an expression of morale, mutiny functioned simultaneously as a manifestation of dissatisfaction and confirmation of dedication and loyalty.

A mutiny of this magnitude raised concerns within the officer corps of the Continental Army that no other had. The seriousness of the situation was not lost on anyone. The officers' immediate concern was losing the Pennsylvania line to a large-scale desertion, or worse, to the British. News of a mutiny this large would travel quickly. Washington was uncertain whether the army would be faced with a mass defection in addition to a mutiny. He wrote to Major General Anthony Wayne immediately after finding out about the revolt, commending him on his attempts to stop it but warning him not to attempt to with force again. Washington feared 'that an attempt to reduce them by force will either drive them to the Enemy, or dissipate them in such a manner that they will never be recovered.'[60] Although driving such a force to the enemy would be catastrophic for the Continental Army, a mass

---

59   The Pennsylvania Line mutiny of 1781 did not happen without warning that soldiers' discontent was brewing. Congress received petitions from the Pennsylvania Line on Christmas Day in 1780 for 'half pay, and of the other Emoluments.' Petition to Anthony Wayne, 25 December 1780 in Herrera, 'Self-Governance and the American Citizen as Soldier, 1775-1861,' p.49.

60   George Washington to Anthony Wayne, 3 January 1781, *Founders Online,* National Archives, <https://founders.archives.gov/documents/Washington/99-01-02-04428>, accessed September 2023.

desertion would inflict as sharp a blow. The Continental Army under Washington from December 1780 to January 1781 had at most 9,000 soldiers – losing 1,500 would have reduced their number by a sixth.[61]

The British saw this mutiny as an opportunity. At 4:00 a.m. on 7 January Major General Wayne was awoken from his sleep by two sergeants who had mutinied six days previously. With them, they had two British soldiers and a letter from the enemy offering them positions within the British Army. Wayne received the message loud and clear. He wrote to Washington eagerly the next morning that 'The Soldiery in General Affect to spurn at the Idea of turning *Arnolds* (as they express it)' and that they should not fear the mutineers defecting.[62] Crucial to the success of mutinies in the Continental Army was the persistent affirmation from those participating that they were loyal soldiers.

A secondary concern was that this would incite other troops nearby. Writing to John Hancock on 5 January, Washington admitted that he was yet unsure how extensive the mutiny would become: 'At present the Troops at the important Posts in this vicinity remain quiet, not being acquainted with this unhappy and Alarming Affair, but how long they will remain so cannot be ascertained, as they labour under some of the pressing hardships with the Troops who have revolted.'[63] Much of the Continental Army was camped within the mid-Atlantic colonies and it would not be long before they found out about the revolt. Washington emphasised to Hancock that these soldiers were without clothes in winter, had not been paid for over a year, and rarely had adequate provisions. With the same grievances as the mutineers, Washington had little confidence that this rebellion would not spark more throughout the army. His fears were legitimate. Rebellion bred rebellion. The aftermath of the Pennsylvania line mutiny was almost as trying for the Army as the mutiny itself. News of the mutiny in its aftermath spread throughout the ranks, and frequent minor incidences occurred across the colonies. Nothing on the same scale was arranged, but the events of the first week of January clearly unsettled the army.

Evaluating mutiny in the Continental Army reveals a consistent pattern of development and escalation in mutinies during the war. From 1775 until the end of the war, officers understood that the army was under a constant threat of mutiny. As the war progressed, so too did the character of the mutinies. In 1775, mutinies represented power struggles inherent in the transition from militia units to a professional army. These early mutinies demonstrated to soldiers that collective protest was an effective tool for change, that also safeguarded the participants from punishment. After 1775, mutinies grew in size, frequency and outlook. They served as protests against the army when specific grievances (lack of pay, clothing, shelter, supplies) were not responded to. Mutinies between 1777 and 1780 provided short-term compromises between the soldiers and the army, however, grievances were often repeatedly raised after the initial promises were not kept. Eventually, these mutinies culminated in a mass desertion and the Pennsylvania Line Mutiny of 1781. The

---

61   See, Charles H. Lesser (ed.), *The Sinews of Independence: Monthly Strength Reports of the Continental Army* (Chicago: University of Chicago Press, 1976).

62   Anthony Wayne to George Washington, 8 January 1781, *Founders Online,* National Archives, <https://founders.archives.gov/documents/Washington/99-01-02-04474>, accessed September 2023.

63   Walter Stewart to George Washington, 4 January 1781, *Founders Online,* National Archives, <https://founders.archives.gov/documents/Washington/99-01-02-04436>, accessed September 2023.

grievances raised that year were essentially a summary of those raised in the preceding years. The Continental Army was unable to quell the mutiny and the state government had to step in. The increase of the number of mutinies after 1777 is closely tied to the creation of regimental bonds between soldiers – the longer soldiers served, the more committed they became to their units as well as to broader revolutionary ideals. Patterns of mutiny clearly demonstrate soldiers' reliance on one another, as well as their understanding of the value of their service to the Army.

Mutiny and its frequency during the Revolutionary War within the Continental Army highlights the agency soldiers had and used to express their dissatisfaction from within the system. The absence of provisions drove soldiers to a breaking point, and mutinies acted as a final way to raise grievances. The subjects of these grievances represent factors important to morale. These soldiers were not merely drill bots who marched on command. The army was a socio-economic sphere with complex relational structures unique to the military. The persistence of mutinies within the Continental Army simultaneously highlights a failure on behalf of the Continental Army and Congress to meet their end of the enlistment contract and provide for their soldiers, but also demonstrates a clear pattern of loyalty amongst enlisted men. The mere existence of these continual mutinies demonstrates that soldiers clearly understood their value to the army, and their position as citizens fighting for a cause. As the war progressed, so too did soldiers' consciousness of the value in their service, and the severity of mutinies. In mutinying, soldiers leveraged their service to obtain what was owed to them. Although an act of protest, mutiny in the Continental Army demonstrates soldiers increased utilisation of the conflict's revolutionary ideals for their own benefit.

Bibliography

Archival Sources
National Archives & Records Administration, Washington, D.C.
National Archives microfilm publications; M0332, Papers of the Continental Congress 1774-1789, reel 170, vol.9

Primary Sources
Anon., 'Diary of the Revolt – Pennsylvania in the war of the revolution battalions and line 1775–1783,' in John Blair Linn and William H. Egle (eds), *Pennsylvania archives*, (Harrisburg: Clarence M. Busch, 1896), 2d ser. vol.11, pp.659–706

Bemis, Phinehas. 'Journal of Phinehas Bemis.' File of Phinehas Bemis, W 14278. (National Archives Microfilm Publication M804, roll 210, frames 664–675). Revolutionary War Pension and Bounty-Land Warrant Application Files, Records of the Veterans Administration, Record Group 15. National Archives and Records Administration – Northeast Region (Waltham, MA)

Closen, Ludwig von, Evelyn M. Acomb (trans. & ed.), *The Revolutionary Journal of Baron Ludwig von Closen, 1780–1783* (Chapel Hill: University of North Carolina Press, 1958)

Glover, Ann, 'Petition to the General Assembly from Ann Glover, widow of Samuel Glover,' 10 January 1780, Walter Clark (ed.), *State Records of North Carolina* (Goldsboro, NC: Nash Brothers, 1898), vol.15, pp.187–188

Martin, Joseph Plumb (ed. James Kirby Martin), *Ordinary Courage: The Revolutionary War Adventures of Joseph Plumb Martin* (Chichester: Wiley Blackwell Publishing, 2013)

Pennington, William S., 'Our Camp Chest, 1780–1781,' Copy of Diary of William S. Pennington of New Jersey, Society of the Cincinnati

Reeves, Enos, 'Letterbook Extracts January 2–17, 1781', 2 January 1781, in John Rhodehamel (ed.), *The American Revolution: Writings from the War of Independence, 1775–1783* (New York: Library of Congress, 2001)

Showman, Richard K. (ed.), *The Papers of General Nathanael Greene* (Chapel Hill: The University of North Carolina Press, 2000)

Simes, Thomas, *The Military Medley Containing the Most Necessary Rules and Directions for Attaining a Competent Knowledge of the Art: To Which is Added an Explanation of Military Terms, Alphabetically Digested* (London: n.p., 1768)

Smith, Paul H. (ed.), *Letters of Delegates to Congress, 1774–1789* (Washington D.C.: Library of Congress, 1976–2000)

Washington, George, *The Papers of George Washington, Founders Online,* National Archives, <https://founders.archives.gov/>

Washington, George, Various (eds), *The Papers of George Washington, Revolutionary War Series* (Charlottesville: University of Virginia Press, various years)

Washington, George, Worthington Chauncey Ford, (ed.), *The Writings of George Washington* (New York and London: G. P. Putnam's Sons, 1889–1893)

Secondary Sources

Anderson, Fred, *A People's Army: Massachusetts Soldiers and Society in the Seven Years War* (Chapel Hill: Published for the Omohundro Institute of Early American History and Culture, by the University of North Carolina Press, 1984)

Berkovich, Ilya, *Motivation in War: The Experience of Common Soldiers in Old-Regime Europe* (Cambridge: Cambridge University Press, 2017)

Gilbert, Arthur N., 'British Military Justice during the American Revolution,' *The Eighteenth Century,* vol.20, no.1 (Winter 1979), pp. 24–38

Herrera, Ricardo, 'Self-Governance and the American Citizen as Soldier, 1775-1861,' *The Journal of Military History,* vol.63, no.1 (January 2001), pp.21–52

Higginbotham, Don, *The War for American Independence: Military Attitudes, Policies, and Practice, 1763-1789* (Macmillan Press: New York, 1971)

Hobsbawm, E.J. 'The Machine Breakers', *Past & Present,* vol.1, no.1 (February 1952), pp.57–70

Kruger, John William, 'Troop Life at the Champlain Valley Forest during the American Revolution,' PhD Thesis, State University of New York at Albany, 1981

Lesser, Charles H. (ed.), *The Sinews of Independence: Monthly Strength Reports of the Continental Army* (Chicago: University of Chicago Press, 1976)

Martin, James Kirby and Mark Edward Lender, *A Respectable Army: The Military Origins of the Republic, 1763–1789* (Oxford: Wiley Blackwell, 2015).

Nagy, John A., *Rebellion in the Ranks: Mutinies of the American Revolution* (Yardley: Westholme Publishing, 2016)

Neagles, James C., *Summer Soldiers: A Survey & Index of Revolutionary War Court-Martial* (Salt Lake City: Ancestry Incorporated, 1986)

Neimeyer, Charles Patrick, *America Goes to War: A Social History of the Continental Army* (New York: New York University Press, 1996)

Royster, Charles, *A Revolutionary People at War: The Continental Army and American Character, 1775–1783* (Chapel Hill: University of North Carolina Press, 1979)

Stillé, Charles J., *Major General Anthony Wayne and the Pennsylvania Line,* (Philadelphia, J.B. Lippincott, 1893)

Tatum, William P. III, 'The Soldiers Murmured Much on Account of this Usage: Military Justice and Negotiated Authority in the Eighteenth-Century British Army', in Kevin Linch & Matthew McCormack (eds), *Britain's Soldiers: Rethinking War and Society, 1715-1815* (Liverpool: Liverpool University Press: 2021), pp.95–113.

Way, Peter, 'Rebellion of the Regulars: Working Soldiers and the Mutiny of 1763–1764,' *William and Mary Quarterly,* vol.57, no.4 (October 2000), pp.761–792

Wilson, Peter H., 'Violence and the Rejection of Authority in Eighteenth-Century Germany: The Case of the Swabian Mutinies in 1757,' *German History,* vol.12, no.1 (February 1994), pp.1–26

4

To Do the Duty of Soldiers in Every Respect: The Loyalist Militia of New York, 1776–1783

Todd W. Braisted

On a statue pedestal in Concord, Massachusetts, Ralph Waldo Emerson's words state 'Here once the embattled farmers stood.' They of course refer to the militiamen that rallied to the challenge of British encroachment, as they saw it, of their rights as free British subjects. The events of 19 April 1775 and the words Emerson so eloquently wrote, encapsulated the feelings of many Americans in that tumultuous spring of 1775. That militia companies so quickly turned out that April morning should have been no surprise to the British regulars who faced off against them outside of Boston. Militia companies, troops and regiments were the backbone of the colonial military establishment practiced by most American colonies. The citizen-soldier, the farmer, mechanic, labourer one day, temporary soldier the next. Men fighting not so much for the idea of empire but for their home and kin, their native province, county, or town.

The British Army that faced off against George Washington in the late summer 1776 consisted of roughly 24,000 British and German soldiers, along with the embryonic beginnings of an American Provincial Corps. Why would this vast (and growing) force need militiamen to assist in their efforts of crushing the rebellion and restoring British rule? What role could part-time soldiers play alongside a professional army such as that assembled by Britain?

Some idea might be formed from Timothy Ruggles' instructions to Captain Francis Green in Boston the previous autumn. Green commanded a company of the Loyal American Association, under Ruggles' command, which supplanted the Boston Militia as a Loyalist equivalent once hostilities broke out. Far from engaging in a life and death struggle alongside the army, Green and his men would 'prevent all disorders within the district by either Signals, Fires, Thieves, Robers, house breakers or Rioters.'[1] The Association, along with the volunteer companies of Royal North British Volunteers and Loyal Irish Volunteers, would provide internal security for Boston, serving until the evacuation of that city and no further.

---

[1]   The National Archives (TNA): AO 13/45: p.476, Ruggles to Green, Boston, 15 November 1775.

It would be nearly the same in Newport, Rhode Island, where in 1777 the British commander, Major General Robert Pigot formed a volunteer unit, the Loyal Newport Associators 'for the Purpose of preserving the internal Peace and Security of the Town.'[2]

The task of establishing, or perhaps more correctly, reconstituting New York's militia for the British would fall to the colony's royal governor, William Tryon. Tryon's military background would serve him well during the conflict, having entered the army with the purchase of an ensigncy in the British Foot Guards during the Seven Years War. Before taking over the New York government in 1771, Tryon had raised and led a force in North Carolina where he then governed against a revolt by the so-called Regulators, defeating them at the Battle of Alamance on 16 May 1771.

Royal authority in New York declined rapidly in the first half of 1775, including the evacuation of the small garrison of British troops in June. Governor Tryon attempted to maintain some authority, appointing David Mathews mayor of the city, a post he held until his arrest in June 1776 for alleged involvement in a plot to assassinate George Washington. Tryon himself was forced to govern from on board the ship *Duchess of Gordon* after seeking shipborne refuge in October 1775. While local committees and newly-raised armed companies ruled the city, many inhabitants still harboured loyalist sentiments, most quietly, some indiscreetly. One of the latter was a merchant named Joseph Moon, who overheard a rebel captain 'Curse his Majesty and his Ministers,' upon which Moon 'called for a blessing upon them.' Moon's words provoked a beating from the infuriated officer, leaving him 'almost dead'. Moon later signed an address of loyalty to the British and served in the New York City Militia.[3] Such speech would of course provoke any number of similar responses after the Declaration of Independence was read in the city on 9 July 1776, when a crowd tore down a statue of King George III in Bowling Green. Subsequent events soon completely changed the political complexion of the New York metropolitan area.

A British fleet appeared off Sandy Hook the end of June 1776 and within days effected an unopposed landing on Staten Island, formally called Richmond County. A key reason that General William Howe had moved the scene of war from Boston to New York was the number of loyalists, commonly referred to as 'friends to government,' in that city and the surrounding area. This was apparent immediately on the arrival of the first British vessels that summer. Washington, commanding the defences of New York, knew the general sentiments of the islanders and wisely chose not to make a defence there, at most driving some of the cattle across the water to New Jersey.

On 2 July 1776, the first British troops landed unopposed on Staten Island, and were generally greeted warmly by the inhabitants. One who tried to escape to his family in New Jersey was seized at the ferry with whatever property he could carry. The next day he related to the commander of the New Jersey Militia that the British let him go, returned his goods to him and told him to return with his family to the island 'to live in peace assuring him that they came not to injure but to protect the inhabitants.'[4]

2   *The Newport Gazette*, 23 October 1777. Orders given by Robert Pigot, Newport, 15 October 1777.
3   TNA: AO 13/56: pp.260–261, Petition of Joseph Moon to the House of Commons, no date.
4   Library of Congress (LOC): GW Papers, Series 4, General Correspondence, 1697–1799, MSS 44693, Reel 037: Livingston to Gen. Hugh Mercer, Elizabeth Town, 3 July 1776.

With the troops was Governor Tryon, who immediately summoned the militia to appear at Richmond Town, where on 6 July 1776 nearly 400 were mustered.[5] The extract strength of the Richmond County Militia has never been ascertained. A February 1774 muster of the regiment showed 20 officers and 447 other ranks, divided into three infantry companies and one troop of light horse.[6] By 9 July 1776, 493 Staten Islanders had taken the oath of allegiance to King George, by which it may be reasoned the strength of the militia was roughly the same as it had been two years previously.[7] The Richmond County regiment of 1774 was commanded by Colonel Christopher Billopp, who would retain his command under the British for the rest of the war.[8]

The defeat of Washington's army at Brooklyn on 27 August 1776 led to their evacuation of all Long Island. While Kings County was the first of the island's three counties restored to British rule, the ongoing campaign put immediate formation of their militia on hold. The British landing at Kip's Bay, Manhattan on 15 September 1776 instantly ended rebel control of New York City for the next seven years. A scene of anarchy no doubt took place, with slow-footed Continentals and others seeking a passage across the Hudson to safety or making their peace with the arriving British. Some New Yorkers took matters into their own hands as far as security was concerned. One was Patrick Walsh, who described the action that night:

> ... on the 15th September 1776, the Rebel Troops evacuated New York, the British Colours being Hoisted upon Fort George, as I was then High Constable of the City I was Appointed by a Lieutenant of the Royal Navy to take the Command of the Fort ... Cornelius Ryan Joined me with 27 Loyalists Chiefly Deserters from the Rebels, and who had been concealed by him for some time ... and all that night he Patroled the Streets.[9]

Rebels were not the only ones facing danger that night. Loyalist New York City Alderman and Justice of the Peace William Waddell had his home just north of the city broken into by British and Hessian troops, losing £123 in property, including six dozen bottles of Madeira wine plus a further two hogsheads and quarter cask of the same beverage 'stove in the Heads & carried off in pails.'[10]

For the next five to eight weeks, Governor Tryon and others brought the chaos to order, raising one battalion of city militia consisting of 10 companies from the seven city wards. The battalion was commanded by George Brewerton, commissioned colonel commandant on 23

---

5   TNA: CO 5/1107: p.372, Tryon to Lord George Germain, 8 July 1776.
6   Staffordshire Record Office (SRO): Earl of Dartmouth Papers, Microfilm Edition, Reel 10, D(w)1778/II/824: Return of the Militia of Richmond County, 8 Febraury 1774. A fourth company of foot was added before the end of that month.
7   New York State Library (NYSL): Elliot Papers, K 13349, Box 4, f.11: Staten Island Oath of Allegiance list, 9 July 1776.
8   TNA: AO 13/117: p.110, Billopp's commission as colonel was signed by Tryon and dated 18 November 1772.
9   TNA: AO 13/26: p.436, Certificate of Captain Patrick Walsh, Westminster, 2 October 1788.
10   TNA: AO 13/56: p.491, Estimate of effects and property lost by William Waddell by the British, 16 September 1776.

October 1776. Brewerton was an odd choice, as he had been commissioned the previous month as colonel commandant of the 2nd Battalion, DeLancey's Brigade, a Provincial regiment which he presumably was busy trying to raise at that time.[11]

The militia battalion's actual strength beyond its 39 officers is unknown. The city could muster about 3,000 men of fighting age, including a handful of free blacks. Firemen and Quakers were legally exempt from militia duty by the British, accounting for some 400 additional men.[12] If the city militia battalion of 10 companies followed traditional British regimental strength, it would have consisted of between 500 and 600 officers and men. It does not appear to have served long, as several of its officers were busily engaged in the Provincial Forces, such as Garret S. DeWint in the King's Orange Rangers and Waldron Blaau in the 2nd Battalion, New Jersey Volunteers, among others.

To be sure, the British much preferred raising provincials as opposed to militia. The Provincial Establishment in effect created an army of American regulars for duty anywhere in America, embodied for the duration of the war, provisioned, armed, uniformed, paid and disciplined the same as the British regular army. Tryon himself commanded the Provincial Forces at New York for the 1777 campaign, expending as much energy organizing them as the militia.[13]

Long Island & Westchester

William Tryon was not in New York City when it was captured, nor when a mysterious fire took hold of the city on 20 September 1776 and burned a good portion of it; he was at the estate of William Axtell on Long Island. He informed Lord George Germain on 26 November that as the New York Militia Law was still in effect, he would use it to commission officers.[14] The Militia Act passed just prior to hostilities in 1775 stipulated every male between 16 and 50 years of age be enlisted in their county regiment or an independent company under penalty of a monthly fine for non-compliance.[15] Under this law, Tryon had the legal authority to organize and embody all the militia in areas under British control in New York. The more area restored to the Crown in New York, the more militia that could serve, and conversely, the fewer that might fight against them.

11   W. Coventry, H. Wadell, 'New York Militia of 1776', *The New York Genealogical and Biographical Record*, vol.2, no.3 (July 1871), pp.156–157. 'Return of officers of the Regiment and Independent Companies of the New York Militia.'

12   TNA: CO 5/1108: pp.71–101, Alphabetical list of persons in New York City who took oath of allegiance to the British, 13 January 1777–26 February 1777.

13   University of Michigan, Clements Library (CL): King's American Regiment Orderly Book. General Orders 20 April 1777.

14   Peter Force, *American Archives, Fifth Series* (Washington, DC: Clarke & Force, 1853), vol.III, p.855. Tryon to Germain, 26 November 1776.

15   New York (state) *Laws of the colony of New York, passed in the years 1774 and 1775: Fourteenth and fifteenth George III. Republished under direction of Frederick Cook, Secretary of State, pursuant to chapter one hundred and seventy-one, laws of eighteen hundred and eighty-eight* (Albany: J.B. Lyon, 1888), p.100.

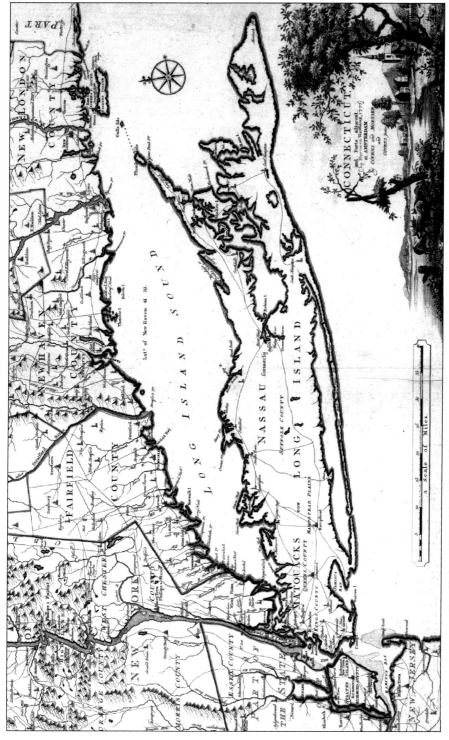

New York and Long Island. Detail from map 'Connecticut and Parts adjacent,' 1777 (Library of Congress)

The first order of business was to politically cleanse the island of any remnants of rebel authority and administration. This was particularly true for Suffolk, most distant from New York City and which county had raised companies for the Continental Army. While many of the leading Whigs had fled to Connecticut, enough congressional adherents silently remained behind to cause the British concern throughout the war. The submissions came about in rapid succession and were duly published in the newspaper, all being similar in text. Each township dissolved the local committee formed during the revolutionary period and 'renounce and disavow the Orders and Resolutions of all Committees and Congresses whatsoever, as being undutiful to our lawful Sovereign, repugnant to the Principles of the British Constitution, and ruinous in the extreme to the Happiness and Prosperity of this County.'[16] Suffolk had the most physical territory to cover and it would be impossible for the British to even consider large garrisons there. They would need an active militia to help keep order.

Former militia officers under the State of New York, such as Colonels Phineas Fanning and Thomas Conklin, would not be acceptable to command the reformed county regiment. While Suffolk's population more than justified multiple regiments, Tryon decided that one regiment would do for the entire county. No return of the newly modelled corps exists, but it appears the British were content to have the men arranged in captains' companies under three field officers: Colonel Richard Floyd, Lieutenant Colonel Benjamin Floyd and Major Frederick Hudson. Richard Floyd owned an extensive manor property in Brookhaven and had previous militia experience, having been commissioned major around 1759 and then lieutenant colonel in 1773; Tryon commissioned him colonel on 28 December 1776.[17] A 1778 oath of allegiance list of the townships in the county gives some idea of the regiment's relative strength: Brookhaven, 536 men; Southampton, 544; Easthampton, 274; Huntington, 561; Smithtown, 111; Islip, 88; Southold 563. Not all of these 2,677 men were eligible for militia service, some not falling within the age range specified in the militia law.[18] Tryon met with nearly 800 militia at Brookhaven on 12 December 1776, probably the only time for the remainder of the war so many men of the Suffolk regiment were together in one muster.

Prior to reaching Suffolk, Governor Tryon visited Hempstead, where he mustered 820 men of the Queens County Militia on 10 December. Both here and in Brookhaven, the governor took care to win over hearts and minds. 'I took much pains in explaining to the People (having formed them into Circles) the iniquitous Arts &c that had been practised on their Credulity to Seduce and Mislead them, and I had the Satisfaction to observe among them a general return of Confidence in Government,' Tryon had the satisfaction to report to Lord George Germain on that Christmas Eve.[19] A pre-war muster of the Queens regiment

---

16   *The New-York Gazette and the Weekly Mercury*, 11 November 1776. Declaration of the Township of Huntington, 21 October 1776.

17   TNA: AO 13/12: p.455, Memorial of Richard Floyd by his attorney to the Commissioners for American Claims, London, 9 March 1784; TNA: AO 13/12: p.454, Commission of Richard Floyd by William Tryon, 28 December 1776.

18   TNA: CO 5/1109: pp.2-49, List of persons in Suffolk County who took the oath of allegiance before Gov. Tryon, 1778.

19   TNA: CO 5/1108: pp.19–20, Tryon to Germain, New York, 24 December 1776.

Oath of Allegiance of Hendrick Wyckoff, Kings County, October 1776. (Private collection)

under Colonel Jacob Blackwell showed 14 companies with 1,361 officers and men.[20] By 1775, Blackwell had been replaced by Colonel Gabriel G. Ludlow, who was instrumental in refusing to have the county to cooperate in any opposition to the British. Some 1,238 Queens residents signed a published address to Tryon on 21 October 1776, showing the strong loyalist tendencies of the county.[21] When Sir William Erskine led a British force to Jamaica, Queens, it was Ludlow who greeted him, at the head of 700 county men.[22]

There was but one problem with retaining Ludlow as commander of the militia: like George Brewerton in New York City, Ludlow was also a colonel in the Provincial Forces, having received a commission as colonel of the 3rd Battalion, DeLancey's Brigade. Oliver DeLancey had been a major general in the New York Militia under the crown but soon after Howe's success at Brooklyn, the commander-in-chief gave him a warrant to raise a brigade of three Provincial battalions.[23] There were some initial thoughts, among DeLancey and others, of drafting men from the militia into the Provincial battalions if enough volunteers could not be found. DeLancey had gone so far as to warn Colonel Phineas Fanning of Suffolk County that only a sufficient number of volunteers would prevent 'the Disagreeable business of Detaching them' from the militia.[24] Despite not recruiting enough men, at least initially, none were drafted. Volunteers from the island numbered well into the hundreds,

---

20   SRO: Earl of Dartmouth Papers, Microfilm Edition, Reel 14, D(w)1778/II/1639: 'A Return of Col. Blackwell's Regiment of Militia in Queens County.'

21   *The New-York Gazette and the Weekly Mercury*, 2 December 1776. Address of David Colden to Tryon, Queens County, 21 October 1776.

22   TNA: AO 12/25: pp.139-140, Evidence on the Claim of Gabriel G. Ludlow, Saint John, 13 February 1787.

23   CL: CP 123:22a: Oliver DeLancey, Sr. to Oliver DeLancey, Jr. New York, 15 September 1780.

24   NYSL: Mss No. 6059, Oliver DeLancey: DeLancey to Fanning, Jamaica, 5 September 1776.

perhaps over a thousand, which reduced the strength of the militia to some degree. As an example, a return of Captain Seaman's Queens company showed four out of 75 in the company enlisting in Provincial units in 1778.[25]

As Ludlow soon departed to take full command of his Provincial battalion, a newcomer to the county, Archibald Hamilton, was appointed to take his place in the militia. Hamilton had only settled in Flushing (on an estate he dubbed 'Innerwick') in 1774. He had served as an officer in the British Army since 1747 until marrying the daughter of Lieutenant Governor Cadwallader Colden, a Long Islander, in 1766.[26] Hamilton's military experience helped mould the Queens regiment into an efficient part-time military organization even though he was not familiar with most of the officers and men under his command.

Tryon had started his Long Island tour in Kings County on 30 November 1776 and after giving the same speech he would give the rest of the island, he found 'a hearty disposition among them in favour of Government.'[27] The county's battalion before and after hostilities commenced looked very similar. The February 1774 muster showed Colonel Johannes Lott's Kings County Regiment with a strength of seven infantry companies and one troop of light horse, divided between Gravesend, Flatlands, Brooklyn, Bushwick, New Utrecht and Flatbush, with a strength of 422 officers and men.[28] By comparison, in the muster of November 1777, their strength increased to 435 officers and men, now under the command of Colonel William Axtell.[29] Axtell, for whatever reason, questioned the loyalty of some of his men. In August 1777 he requested Major Jeremiah Vanderbilt to muster the regiment, instructing the captains commanding companies to 'make a Secret mark Against the Names of those Persons' they conceived not friendly to the Crown.[30] Of the enlisted men, the only ones in question, some 80 out of 409, were 'doubtful,' the most suspect, by far, being in Captain Patrus Lott's Bushwick Township company, with 37 out of 67 having dubious characters.[31]

Westchester was unique among the counties Tryon visited in that it was not dominated by the British, other than the areas bordering Kingsbridge on Manhattan. Prior to the revolution, the county was able to field three battalions of militia and a troop of light horse, mustering some 2,181 officers and men under the command of Colonel James Van Cortland.[32] Tryon published an order for the militia of Westchester to muster at White Plains on 4 November 1776, scarcely a week after the major battle fought there between Howe and Washington.[33] Despite the proximity of significant Continental forces, and barely 48 hours' notice to muster, as many as 1,500 men came out to take the oath of allegiance.[34] The colonel

---

25   Brooklyn Historical Society (BHS): MSS File 162, Correspondence of Major John Kissam: Return of Capt. Samuel Seaman's Company, 9 June 1778.

26   TNA: AO 13/114: pp.282–283, Memorial of Hamilton to the Commissioners for American Claims.

27   TNA: CO 5/1107: p.429, Tryon to Germain, New York, 2 December 1776.

28   SRO: Earl of Dartmouth Papers, Microfilm Edition, Reel 14, D(w)1778/II/803, 812-86 & 82-823: Muster of Kings County Militia, February 1774.

29   CL: CP 267:C: Return of the Kings County Militia, 7 November 1777.

30   NYSL: Elliot Papers, K13349, Box 4, f.3: Axtell to Vanderbilt, Flatbush, 24 August 1777.

31   NYSL: Elliot Papers, K13349, Box 4, f.3: Muster Roll of Capt. Patrus Lott's Company, 27 August 1777.

32   SRO: Earl of Dartmouth Papers, Microfilm Edition, Reel 14, D(w)1778/II/804: Return of the strength of the regiment of Westchester, 31 January 1774.

33   TNA: AO 13/15: p.89, Tryon to the officers of the Westchester Militia, 2 November 1776.

34   *The New-York Gazette and the Weekly Mercury*, 11 November 1776.

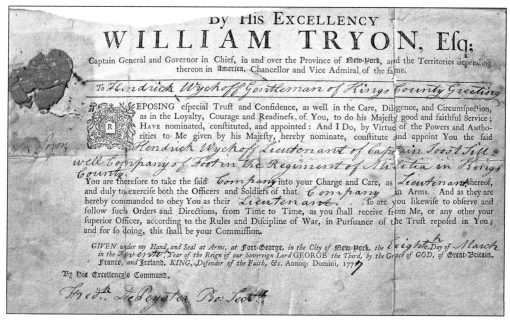

Commission of Lieutenant Hendrick Wyckoff, Kings County Militia, 18 March 1777. (Private collection)

of the Westchester County Militia throughout the war was James DeLancey, the 29 year-old nephew of Brigadier General Oliver DeLancey, even though operationally others took command for two years while he was a prisoner of war.[35] Given that the men who eventually served in this corps came from both Westchester and elsewhere, such as Connecticut, it was typically known as DeLancey's Refugees, using the term applied primarily to Loyalists who had been forced from their homes and into British lines. Despite the large turnout of men for Tryon, as far as militia was concerned the numbers would prove deceptive. Recruiting the Provincial regiments being raised at that time, throughout Westchester, Dutchess, Orange and Ulster counties, drew many hundreds from those who turned out for the militia in November 1776. Others resided behind what would become the rebel lines, often referred to as the 'neutral ground' north of British lines, rendering their militia service unlikely.

New York City and the Leveé en Masse

The initial composition and design for the New York City regiment seemed to have fallen by the wayside within months of its inception. By March 1777, William Waddell requested to raise a battalion of three companies to be raised out of the militia, to consist of none 'but

---

35   For a good account of James DeLancey's life and family, see George DeLancey Hanger's 'The Life of Loyalist Colonel James DeLancey' published in the *Nova Scotia Historical Review*, vol.3, no.2, 1983, pp.39–56.

good citizens.'[36] It appears that no men were taken from the regiment itself, but instead the three independent companies raised in October 1776 joined together; Christopher Benson's New York Rangers, Normand Tolmie's Independent Highland Volunteers, and the German Independents commanded by Captain Frederick William Hecht. Little is known about the German company other than it seems to have disappeared after 1777. Normand Tolmie was a native of the Island of Skye off Scotland but since 1756 had been a ship chandler in New York City. After the war he wrote that 'He raised an independent Company of Highland Militia immediately after the British took Possession of New York which were supported entirely without Expence to Government.'[37] Not entirely. Governor Tryon's expense account records purchases of, among other things, leather pouches and 'a stand of colours' for the company.[38] On 10 October 1776, Christopher Benson was officially commissioned captain of the New York Rangers. The original articles of association by their 115 officers and men, pledging themselves to 'do the Duty of Soldiers in every respect during the present contest,' were probably similar to those for the other companies.[39]

In October 1777, New York City was nearly stripped of troops to undertake an expedition up the Hudson River under Sir Henry Clinton in an attempt to aid General John Burgoyne's ill-fated troops at Saratoga. Proposals came in to form volunteer companies to supplement Benson's and Tolmie's units. Nine independent companies were formed, including one commanded by Mayor David Mathews called The Mayor's Independent Company of Volunteers.[40] The companies filled up quickly, easing the strain on troops doing garrison duty. 'I entered a volunteer at New York,' wrote one recruit to a friend in England, 'in a company called the Massachusetts Volunteers, for the defence of that city. Our company consists of about 75, all hearty jolly fellows (except myself); we are regimented at our own expence, though Gen. Clinton finds us arms, and each man 18 rounds of cartridges.'[41] The desire for professionalism was exemplified by Captain Allen McDonald, a North Carolina refugee commanding a company, extolling his men to drill better: 'What a shocking Sight it must be to see a handsome young Gentleman genteelly dressed in his Uniform, with an excellent Firelock on his Shoulder, without the Knowledge of using it properly.' All the efforts greatly pleased General James Robertson, who as commandant undertook the endeavour in Clinton's and Tryon's absence up the river. Writing to Abijah Willard, who organized the Massachusetts Volunteers, he had no doubts these companies 'will greatly tend to extirpate Anarchy and overawe Rebellion.'[42]

What made the British garrison normally somewhat secure was that Manhattan, Long Island and Staten Island were all islands. If the Royal Navy could sail through the waterways, Washington's forces did not dare attack, particularly Manhattan, for fear of being cut off. But the winter of 1779–1780 in New York City was the coldest and most severe in human

36   TNA: T 1/651: p.376, Waddell to Howe, New York, 29 March 1777.
37   TNA: AO 13/54: pp.577–578, Tolmie to the Commissioners for American Claims, London, 11 March 1784.
38   TNA: AO 1/1300: p.473, Tryon declared accounts.
39   New York Historical Society (N-YHS): Benson Papers. Articles for the New York Rangers, circa October 1776.
40   *The Royal Gazette* (New York), 6 December 1777.
41   'Regimented,' that is, uniformed. *The London Chronicle*, 12 May 1778.
42   CL: CP 25:12: Robertson to Willard, 16 October 1777.

memory. Cold set in to such a degree that by the middle of January all the waterways were completely frozen. There were no more islands. Add to this, Sir Henry Clinton sailed off in December 1779 with 7,500 men, perhaps half the garrison, to lay siege to Charleston, South Carolina. With Manhattan in effect landlocked, the city's commandant, Brigadier General James Pattison of the Royal Artillery, quickly organized a militia of all able-bodied men, volunteers or not (with exemptions for firemen and Quakers), into 40 companies. Those serving in the volunteer companies from 1776 and 1777 continued their service with them. Within one week, 2,662 officers and men were serving in 40 new companies of New York City Militia.[43]

New York needed every available man. The number of posts, redoubts, forts, magazines, stores, etc. that needed defending totalled 38, everything from the King's Shipyard to Trinity Church Yard and the stockaded Hay Magazine. The British and German troops available amounted to about 4,300; all the volunteer and militia companies added 5,796 more, of which about 4,600 were equipped with firearms.[44]

In addition to the militia and volunteer companies, there were new sources of manpower, primarily the civil branches of the army and ordnance along with seamen from Royal Navy and other vessels that were ice-locked and not going anywhere. These men formed new corps:

> Loyal Ordnance Volunteers, 4 Companies
> Engineers Volunteers, 1 Company
> Quartermaster General's Volunteers, 1 Company
> Loyal Commissariat Volunteers, 2 Companies
> Barrack Master General's Volunteers, 1 Company
> King's Dock Yard Volunteers, 3 Companies
> The Royal Navy Battalion
> Seaman armed with pikes from Navy Transports
> Seamen armed with pikes from Navy Victuallers
> Seamen armed with pikes from small craft
> New York Pilots armed with pikes[45]

In November 1779 the New York Marine Society, formed by Royal Charter nine years earlier, raised a company of artillerymen under Captain Vincent Pearce Ashfield.[46] There was likewise a sabre-armed troop of 60 cavalry formed from the Horse Department of the Royal Artillery's Civil Branch. The drawback with having so many men taken from the civil branches was that, during a time of siege, many would be need for their normal functions of providing food, ammunition, transportation, wood, etc. The Loyal Commissariat

---

43   *The New-York Gazette and the Weekly Mercury*, 14 February, 1780.
44   CL: CP 83:31: Disposition of the Garrison & Embodied Citizens of New York in case of alarm, 28 January 1780.
45   CL: CP 85:57: Return of the Armed Forces in New York, 19 February 1780.
46   Royal Artillery Institute (RAI): Pattison Papers, 1777–1781: Record of Commissions, Warrants and Appointments Granted by Major General Pattison Commandant of New York Commencing 6 July 1779, pp.12–13. Commission of Vincent Pearce Ashfield, 26 January 1780.

Volunteers garnered some fame for providing an escort of 60 men under Lieutenant Samuel Jarvis for about 100 sleighs loaded with provisions, which remarkably crossed the ice from Manhattan to Paulus Hook, New Jersey, and from thence over the frozen kills to Staten Island.[47]

By the beginning of summer 1780, the 40 companies of city militia were organized into four battalions of 10 companies each, the 1st Battalion commanded by Lieutenant Colonel William Walton, the 2nd by Alexander Wallace, the 3rd by Isaac Low and the 4th by Philip Kearney of New Jersey.[48] On the same day the militia battalions were formed, it was thought 'Expedient to form the seven Volunteer Companies of this City into one Battalion, in Order to render their Establishment still more respectable and useful, and to appoint a Lieutenant Colonel Commandant, and a Major to the same.'[49] Seven of the volunteer companies raised in November 1777 were therefore joined together to form the Loyal Volunteers of the City of New York, commanded by the mayor, Lieutenant Colonel David Mathews, and Major Stephen Skinner. Skinner was from New Jersey, the brother of Brigadier General Cortland Skinner, commander of the New Jersey Volunteers. The Massachusetts Volunteers remained an independent unit for the rest of the war.

Not everyone was pleased. Captain Abel Hardenbrook, Junior, objected to the promotion of Henry Dawson to major of the 2nd Battalion, claiming seniority. He was granted permission to remove his company from the battalion and serve the remainder of the war officially known as 'The Old Volunteer' company.[50]

Having several thousand men under arms with little or no military training was of limited value until others were found to discipline them. Luckily for the British, several veterans stepped forward to assist. One was Thomas Mason, a former sergeant of the 27th Foot and 27-year veteran of the British Army. At the close of the previous war he had settled in New York City and bought two houses worth £600 which he somehow managed to earn during his time of service (both of which he lost in the great fire of 1776). During the turmoil of 1776 he was arrested and confined on suspicion of being a Loyalist until eventually released. Around the age of 60 and too infirm for active service, 'he voluntarily acted as drill Serjeant and assisted in forming the New York City Militia, in which Corps he served during the whole time they were embodied without receiving the least pay or Emolument.'[51]

The Loyal Volunteers of the City of New York benefitted from the experience of another old British soldier, Æneas Mackay. Mackay served 22 years in the army, the last two as adjutant of the 52nd Foot before retiring in 1777. Settling in New York City, he joined one of the volunteer companies raised later that year and eventually became adjutant. General Robertson recommended him at the end of the war, acknowledging that 'he turnd the

---

47   TNA: AO 13/114: pp.536–539, Memorial of Samuel Jarvis to the Commissioners for American Claims, London, 3 November 1785.

48   RAI: Pattison Papers, p.41: 'Abstract of Field and Staff Officers of the City Volunteer & Militia Battalions 12 Augt. 1780.'

49   RAI: Pattison Papers, p 29: Commission of Lieutenant Colonel David Mathews, 26 July 1780.

50   Anon. (ed.), 'Official Letters of Major General James Pattison, Commandant of New York,' *Collections of the New-York Historical Society for the Year 1875* (New York: Printed for the Society, 1876), p.423.

51   TNA: AO 13/56: pp.162–163, Memorial of Thomas Mason to the Lords of the Treasury.

knowledge he had while an adjutant in the army acquired, to the advantage of the Kings Service by teaching a volunteer regiment of respectable Inhabitants the use of their arms, and brought them to be very well disciplined and to make a fine appearance.'[52]

Perhaps the best-known professional to serve in these corps was Sergeant Roger Lamb, whose memoirs have been published several times. A regular soldier who was captured under both Burgoyne and Cornwallis, Lamb escaped to New York City in the spring of 1782, where he was appointed 'adjutant to the Merchants Corps of volunteers, who were then on permanent duty in the town.'[53]

Two officers with name recognition in the militia were John Ramage and James Potter. Ramage was an artist who painted numerous miniature portraits. At the age of 27 he was living in Boston when in 1775 he became a second lieutenant in the Loyal Irish Volunteers.[54] When Boston was evacuated, he went with the army to Halifax and at some point made his way to New York City where he became a second lieutenant in the militia on 2 February 1780. It would be hard to overstate the value of James Potter to the British Army, particularly the Provincial Forces. A sword cutler, he established his shop on Maiden Lane in Manhattan. Between January 1779 and December 1781, Potter's shop manufactured no less than 1,600 cavalry broad swords. They equipped such Provincial cavalry as the British Legion and the Queen's Rangers among others. Potter was commissioned a second lieutenant in the 4th Battalion, New York City Militia on 26 July 1781.[55]

By July 1781, the Loyal Volunteer Battalion was well-organized and disciplined, with two companies of light infantry, five battalion companies and perhaps even a band of music. Wishing to reward their service, James Robertson, who replaced Tryon as governor in 1780, presented them with a pair of colours, which an onlooker described as 'one the Union, and the other the City Arms on a Crimson Field.'[56] Captain Frederick Mackenzie of the adjutant general's department commented on the ceremony and field day:

> One of the Battalions of this City Militia is Commanded by Mr. David Mathews, the Mayor, and is Composed of the Merchants and traders of New York. General Robertson, the Governor, having made them a present of a pair of Colours, they were out a few days ago to be reviewed by him, and some of the principal Officers, in describing what they could do, told him, they could, March, Wheel, form Columns, Retire, Advance, & *Charge*; 'Yes, Gentlemen' said the General, 'I am convinced you can *Charge* better than any Corps in His Majesty's service.'[57]

52   TNA: AO 13/56: pp.96–97, Certificate of James Robertson, London, 27 June 1783.
53   Don N. Hagist (ed.), *Roger Lamb's American Revolution* (Yardley, PA: Westholme, 2022), p.146.
54   Anon. (ed.), 'Kemble Orderly Book,' *Collections of the New-York Historical Society for the Year 1883* (New York: Printed for the Society, 1884), pp.270–271.
55   National Archives of Scotland (NAS): Henderson of Fordell Collection, Robertson Papers, GD 172/2608, pp.7–8: Commissions issued to the 4th Battalion of New York Militia.
56   *The Public Advertiser* (London), 31 January 1782. 'Letter from an Officer arrived in the last Fleet from New York.'
57   Frederick Mackenzie, *The Diary of Frederick Mackenzie* (Cambridge, MA: Harvard University Press, 1930), p.582.

Arms and Uniforms

The Militia Law stipulated that each militia infantryman 'shall be provided with a good well fixed Musket or Fuzee, a good Sword, Belt and Cartridge Box, Six Cartridges of Gun Powder and Six sizeable Bullets.'[58] The pre-war requirements for militia weapons clearly put the burden on the individual, rather than the Colony of New York. An armed population in theory could turn out men already armed and equipped without the need of government stores (or cost). It never envisioned a civil war, a conflict where one part of the population would rise up and control the other, opposing part, which is exactly what happened at the commencement of the war in America. Queens County residents were by far the most vocal in opposition to the rebellion and hence received rigorous treatment from their rebellious neighbours. This manifested itself in February 1776 when the county was swept through by a thousand New Jersey troops under William Alexander, Lord Stirling. The experience of Queens County Loyalist Douwe Van Dine was typical; he related, 'he never took any part with the Rebels, in consequence he was disarmed.'[59] If the British were going to rely on local militia to supplement their security, they would have to help re-arm them.

Queens County's regiment, by far the largest, would need to be rearmed somehow by the British. Tryon related the situation to General Howe, who delivered 795 muskets to be distributed to 'the most faithfull Subjects.'[60] Colonel Ludlow punctually distributed the muskets (470 of which did not come equipped with bayonets) along with 7,850 cartridges and 870 flints to the 15 companies of the regiment.[61] The number was insufficient to cover all the militia, and the arms were not of the best quality. A return of Captain Daniel Youngs' Oyster Bay Company showed 71 men, 17 of whom had 'bad arms' while two others 'received old arms.' The others had received a musket, bayonet, 10 cartridges and a flint, which were to be considered as a loan of government property.[62] Some further old muskets, with wooden ramrods, were obtained in June 1778 from the Provincial 1st and 3rd Battalions of DeLancey's Brigade, which received newer ones with steel rammers.[63] In early 1780, Colonel James DeLancey's Westchester regiment was in woeful shape in point of arms. The regiment, unquestionably the most active, had barely half of their infantry armed with muskets and only about 40 percent of the cavalry armed with swords, with not a pistol or carbine among them.[64]

When the winter of 1779–1780 set in and the new companies and corps were raised, the British ordnance stores issued out 2,819 muskets of different sorts to 16 of the companies and corps. Surprisingly, over half the weapons were the new short land pattern, only 233 of

58   New York (state), *Laws of the Colony of New York*, pp.102–103.
59   TNA: AO 12/25: p.69, Testimony of Douwe Van Dine to the Commissioners for American Claims, Saint John, 26 January 1787.
60   TNA: CO 5/1108: p.45, Tryon to Germain, New York, 20 January 1777.
61   NYSL: Elliot Papers, K13349, Box 4, f.10.
62   East Hampton Free Library (EHFL): Pennypacker Long Island Collection, Document Book #1, f.35: Return of arms delivered to Capt. Daniel Youngs Company, Oyster Bay, 22 January 1777.
63   Anon. (ed.), *Orderly Book of the Three Battalions of Loyalists Commanded by Brigadier-General Oliver DeLancey 1776-1778* (New York: New-York Historical Society, 1917), p.99. Orders, Headquarters Long Island, 17 June 1778.
64   CL: CP 87:31: State of the Westchester County Militia, 1 March 1780.

the total being the older long land type.[65] As late as May and July 1783, Brigadier General Samuel Birch, commandant of New York City, was paying for the cleaning of 'City Arms,' weapons belonging to Tolmie's Highlanders and Oliver Templeton's Company of the Volunteer Battalion. Whether these muskets were part of those issued out by the Ordnance Department or owned by the city itself is not clear.[66]

The challenge of completely arming the militia would vex each side during the war, and it was never fully resolved.

As far as clothing was concerned, the bulk of the militia served in what they wore in their everyday lives, looking no different than their rebel counterparts. There were some exceptions. The initial three volunteer companies were expected to provide their own uniforms, but only that of the New York Rangers was ever specified, the officers and men agreeing to furnish them-

Sword Belt Plate, Kings County Militia. (Private collection)

selves with 'a short red Coat with blue Lappells Cuffs and Cape with white lining [and] a round Buck Hat [with] a black Feather it being the Uniform of the Company.'[67] When the next wave of volunteer companies was raised in the autumn of 1777, they too opted to provide themselves with uniforms 'at their own expence.'[68] While there is no record of what the uniforms of all the volunteer companies consisted of while they were independent, there is a description from an officer after they were consolidated into the Loyal Volunteers of the City of New York: 'Their Cloathing is Scarlet, faced with the same, with white Lining; the only Distinction between the Officers and private Gentlemen Volunteers is, the former wearing a Sword and Epaulete.'[69]

65   CL: Frederick Mackenzie Papers: Return of Arms issued out of His Majesty's Stores, 1 January to 10 March 1780.
66   N-YHS: Samuel Birch New York City Account Book, p.21: Repairs of Militia Arms.
67   N-YHS: Benson Papers: Articles for the New York Rangers, circa October 1776.
68   CL: CP 25:49: James Robertson to Sir Henry Clinton, 28 October 1777.
69   *The Public Advertiser* (London), 31 January 1782. 'Letter from an Officer arrived in the last Fleet from

Officers of at least two county militias provided themselves with uniforms at some point during the war. Abraham Van Tassel served four years as a private in the Westchester regiment 'without receiving either Clothing or pay' but the same was not entirely true of his commanding officer.[70] Two known portraits of Colonel James DeLancey show him in a red uniform coat faced with blue and a silver epaulette or epaulettes. This appears to be very similar to what Colonel Archibald Hamilton ordered the officers of his Queens County regiment to provide for themselves, 'a uniform or regimentals ... to be scarlet, faced with blue, with white lining, white waistcoat and breeches, and silver buttons, with a silver epaulet, a well cocked hat with silver button and loops and silver hat-band.'[71] Failure to wear the uniform upon duty would result in a fine. A short coatee, attributed to a member of the Weekes family exists today in the Oyster Bay Historical Society, and is likewise red faced with blue, trimmed in narrow silver lace. This is perhaps the uniform of an officer or sergeant of one of the regiment's three cavalry troops in which this family was represented.

Temporary Corps: The Westchester Chasseurs and The Nassau Blues

Twice during the course of the war units were embodied from among the militia for fixed, brief periods of service. The first time was in August 1777 and was a cavalry unit known as the Westchester Chasseurs. Led by the commander of that county's militia, Colonel James DeLancey, the unit's 60 or so officers and men received arms, accoutrements, caps and boots from the British, while the members provided their own uniforms and horses.[72] Governor Tryon extolled the troop's virtues as much for apprehending British deserters as for their service against the rebels. 'This Troop is truly the Elite of the County, and their Captain Mr. James DeLancy, who is also Colonel of the Militia of Westchester County. I have much confidence in them, for their spirited behaviour.'[73]

The troop was involved in only one known action, occurring on 5 October 1777. The unit marched from Kingsbridge to White Plains, returning with barrels of flour, black cattle, sheep, pigs and oxen, for the loss of five horses and 'Mr. Purdy, a very respectable Inhabitant of West Chester County.'[74] There were two of this large Loyalist family in the troop, a Joseph and Jotham, and it appears to have been the latter who was killed at the age of 26. The campaign ending shortly thereafter, the troop was disbanded on 3 November. On 28 November, less than a month after his Chasseurs were disbanded, James DeLancey was captured by a party of rebels while at the house of Robert Hunt 'at West Farms, between Morrissania and Westchester Town.'[75] His capture was heralded in the lower Hudson Valley and coastal Connecticut:

New York.'
70   TNA: AO 13/26: pp.506–507, Estimate of losses of Abraham Van Tassel, no date.
71   BHS: MSS File 162: Correspondence of Major John Kissam: Regimental Order of Col. Archibald Hamilton, 7 February 1780.
72   NYSL: Elliot Papers, K13349, Box 4, f.16: 'Conditions for raising a Militia Troop of West Chester Chasseurs,' Kingsbridge, 12 August 1777.
73   TNA: CO 5/1108: pp.159–160, Tryon to Germain, Kingsbridge, 3 October 1777.
74   *The Royal American Gazette* (New York), 9 October 1777.
75   *The New-York Gazette and the Weekly Mercury*, 1 December 1777.

JAMES DELANCEY, late sheriff of West-Chester, and Col. of the Enemy's Militia, was taken last week by one of our scouts; the Colonel was found under a bed, and for better defence had himself surrounded with a bulwark of baskets. He was dragged from his humble redoubt, put under a proper guard and sent to a place, better secured.[76]

He would remain a prisoner for the next 26 months.

The second temporary corps raised from the militia came about in 1779 and was named the Nassau Blues. Judge Thomas Jones of Long Island, no fan of much of the conduct of the war, related their raising in his own unique style:

William Axtell, Esq., of Kings County, upon Long Island, and a member of his Majesty's Council, was commissioned by the Commander-in-Chief as Colonel of a regiment to consist of 500 men, to be raised by him on the King's account, the officers to have the same rank, and pay, as the other provincial corps, with this condition however, they were to be disbanded on the first day of the ensuing December. Axtell's recruits amounted to about thirty. These formed his regiment. It was in pay from the 1st of May, 1779, to the 1st of December following, seven months. It was encamped in his court yard. It guarded his house, his poultry, his hogs, his sheep, and his cows. No other service did the regiment do, except, that two attended him whenever he took a ride. Yet, he received full pay, clothing, arms, and provisions, for 500 men the whole time.[77]

A late nineteenth century New York newspaper went so far as to state that rebels referred to the corps as 'The Nasty Blues,' and that the prisoners they took were held in a secret dungeon under Axtell's spacious dwelling.[78] The actual corps was authorized to consist of 642 men, with 289 provided by Suffolk, 290 from Queens and 63 from Kings, with the counties responsible for their uniforms and the British providing everything else.[79] They mustered only about 60 officers and men, drawing rations and clothing only for that number, despite what Judge Jones had feared. Of the men raised, only a dozen appear to have been from Long Island; the rest were either discharged British and Provincial soldiers, refugees or deserters from the rebels.[80] The corps existed through the end of December 1779 and was then disbanded. Eight of the men volunteered to serve under Captain Lieutenant Frederick DePeyster in a temporary ranger corps commanded by Patrick Ferguson in South Carolina. The few survivors of this, including DePeyster, later became a part of the Provincial New York Volunteers.

---

76   *The New-York Packet, and the American Advertiser* (Fishkill), 4 December 1777.
77   Thomas Jones. *History of New York During the Revolutionary War* (New York: The New-York Historical Society, 1879), pp.304–305.
78   *The New York Herald*, 15 September 1883. Neither statement is supported by any evidence.
79   CL: CP 90:18: Plan for raising the Nassau Blues, New York, 14 June 1779.
80   Library and Archives Canada (LAC): RG 8, "C" Series, Vol. 1894: Muster Roll of the Nassau Blues, Flatbush, 1 July 1779.

In Defence of Home and Hearth

With the exception of New York City, all the militia saw some action during the war, primarily defending their own counties. It would be impossible to relate all the actions, particularly in Westchester, whose regiment between the period October 1779 to May 1782 alone was responsible for capturing no less than 27 officers and 432 other ranks, making it one of the most active units in all the army.[81] Not all militia behaved the same way, or was available when needed, a trait common to those on both sides. When Major General Lord Stirling led 2,700 Continental troops onto Staten Island on 15 January 1780, Lieutenant Colonel John Graves Simcoe and the Queen's Rangers occupied the redoubts at Richmond Town and sought to add the island's militia to the garrison while he led the Rangers to attack Stirling's force. But it was not to be, as he later wrote:

> On these ideas, he desired Col. Billop, (who commanded the militia of Staten Island,) to get them to assemble to garrison Richmond; but neither entreaties, the full explanation of the advantage such a conduct would be of, nor the personal example of Col Billop, had any effect: not a man could be prevailed upon to enter the garrison. They assembled to drink at various public houses, and to hear the news, or were busy in providing for the temporary security of their cattle and effects; and these were not disaffected persons, but men who were obnoxious to the rebel governors, many of them refugees from the Jersies, some who had every reason to expect death, if the enemy succeeded, and all the total destruction of their property.[82]

Simcoe and Billopp had just been incarcerated together in a New Jersey dungeon. It was Billopp's second imprisonment. Simcoe knew there was no questioning his courage.

In July 1781, a combined French-rebel expedition sailed from Newport, Rhode Island, to attack the loyalist fort at Lloyd's Neck, just north of Huntington. The post had recently been taken over by the refugees of the Associated Loyalists, commanded by Lieutenant Colonel Joshua Upham. The four companies of Suffolk Militia in Huntington should have provided a sufficient source of support, but Upham soon learned otherwise: 'I called on the Huntington militia, but saw nothing of them, nor was I disappointed.' Queens County however, upheld their reputation, as 'Capt. Young's troop, and Capt. Vanwyck's company of foot, came last evening to our assistance; they posted themselves on West Neck, and behaved exceeding well.'[83] Lloyd's Neck held off the attack successfully without the benefit of Huntington's assistance.

Colonel James DeLancey resumed command of the Westchester regiment after being released from captivity in February 1780. In his absence, the regiment had fallen into disorder, particularly since the British held so little of the territory of Westchester. The corps

---

81   TNA: AO 13/113, Part I: pp.285–290, 'List of American Prisoners taken by Colonel Delancey's Refugees,' 6 June 1783.

82   John Graves Simcoe, *Simcoe's Military Journal: A History of the Operations of a Partisan Corps, called The Queen's Rangers commanded by Lieut. Col. J.G. Simcoe During the War of the American Revolution* (New York: Bartlett & Welford, 1844), pp.123–124.

83   *The New-York Gazette and the Weekly Mercury*, 16 July 1781.

was commanded in 1778 by Major Mansfield Baremore, a former sergeant in the Provincial Guides & Pioneers, and in 1779 by Lieutenant Colonel Isaac Hatfield, a former subaltern in the Queen's Rangers.[84] Under DeLancey again, the Westchester regiment grew into a formidable force of cavalry, light infantry and rangers, often the focus of attempts against them by militia, state troops, and Continentals. Such was the activity of the corps when compared to the other counties, Westchester lost two captains mortally wounded in just a three-month period in 1780, while no other loyalist county is known to have had any officers killed during the entire conflict.[85] A detachment of cavalry under a subaltern, Elijah Vincent, even went so far as to ambush a detachment of French cavalry from Lauzun's Legion, killing an officer, 'a gentleman of very elegant figure and dress.'[86] Recounting of all the actions of the regiment would fill a volume.

While all three counties on Long Island saw some action, that of Queens surpassed the other two combined. Typical actions were against plundering parties from the Connecticut shore, but there were exceptions. On 4 July 1780, the four-year anniversary of the Declaration of Independence, HMS *Galatea* chased a rebel privateer sloop of 52 men, the *Revenue*, ashore near Hog Island, near Hempstead, Queens.[87] Immediately a party of 13 men of the Queens County regiment under Ensign Elijah Wood engaged the stricken crew, capturing 10 men after six hours of skirmishing. A reinforcement of 26 more militia secured the remainder of the crew.[88]

None of these small encounters, and there were many, altered the course of the war or affected the outcome of any campaign. They were insignificant to most except the men who took part in them. These small actions, however, were the norm of the war, not the rarity. This was life within British-held New York, little different in many ways from the countryside surrounding it.

Offensive Actions

Given the relative strength of the British, German and Provincial Forces in and around New York City, the militia and volunteer companies were not needed for offensive operations. There were three known minor excursions. One is gleaned from the financial accounts of William Waddell who noted that in March 1777, at the request of Governor Tryon, he paid two pounds to 'a man to watch & for discovering John Hopper Junior a noted Rebel, who made it a practice to Seduce the Auxillery Troops to desert.'[89] The next entry stated 'Paid Expences of the Party of Rangers under my command to Fetch to Town the said Hopper, Brevoort & Devoe, the party out all night, March 6th 1777.' Executing the raid cost Waddell

---

84   TNA: AO 12/23: pp.78–79, Evidence on the claim of Isaac Hatfield, Jr, Digby, 22 October 1786.
85   *The Royal American Gazette*, 9 February 1780 and *The Royal Gazette* (New York), 3 June 1780. The captains were Hazard Wilcox and Solomon Fowler. Wilcox had commanded a company of pioneers in the 1777 Burgoyne Campaign while Fowler had raised a troop of 30 cavalry before his death.
86   *The New-York Gazette and the Weekly Mercury*, 23 July 1781.
87   *The Royal Gazette* (New York), 8 July 1780.
88   *The Royal Gazette* (New York), 15 July 1780.
89   'Auxillery', that is, German.

two pounds, eight shillings.[90] The Rangers were no doubt Christopher Benson's New York Rangers; the only other corps with that word in their name at the time was the Queen's Rangers under Robert Rogers, over whom Waddell had no authority. While it is not stated where this raid took place, the names mentioned were all common to Bergen County, New Jersey, across the river from Manhattan.

The next offensive raid did not occur until 27 June 1781, when a party of 36 officers and men of the Provincial 1st Battalion, New Jersey Volunteers were joined by 34 men described as 'Refugees and Militia' from Staten Island under the command of Captains 'Robins and Durham,' raided Tremley's Point in Essex County, New Jersey (present-day Linden). One of officers was Captain Nathaniel Robins, who commanded a company of 40 men described as 'partisans.' There is no record of any officer named Durham, although a half-pay New Jersey Volunteer officer named Asher Dunham may be the person mentioned. The whole party was under the command of Lieutenant William Hutchison of the New Jersey Volunteers. While it is unknown how many of Colonel Billopp's Staten Islanders took part in the raid, none were killed or wounded in the successful action, which was primarily to collect cattle. About 40 rebel Essex County Militia under Captain Isaac Morse pursued the raiders, 'harassing the Rear as usual. Lieutenant Hutchinson formed an Ambuscade unperceived by the Rebels, which had its desired Effect, 15 Rebels past hollowing, Damn the Refugees, cut them down; up the Troops arose from the Place where they were secreted, the Rebels observing this stood aghast, threw down their Arms, others stood with Arms in their Hands.'[91] Captain Morse and 19 of his men were captured, some of whom were wounded, and escorted to Richmond on Staten Island.

Given the activity of the Queens County Militia, it is interesting that they never took part in any of the whale boat raids against Connecticut, primarily conducted by Refugee corps such as the Associated Loyalists at Lloyd's Neck. On 29 October 1781, Lieutenant Colonel Joshua Upham, commanding at Lloyd's Neck, led about two dozen Associators and Queens County Militia under Captain Thomas Jackson over to Connecticut to destroy an enemy brig driven up on the shore. Traveling on board the Royal Navy Sloop *Beaumont*, the detachment returned without incident in about 48 hours.[92]

Although covering an extensive coastline, there is only evidence of a single armed vessel being employed at the expense of any of the counties, a gun boat manned by Staten Island. The craft was paid for by the commissioners of the county and had a crew of eight, commanded by a Captain James Stewart, possibly a half-pay officer from the 5th Battalion, New Jersey Volunteers.[93] Other vessels were used; one of the most effective privately-maintained gun boats was operated off the northern part of Staten Island by Elizabethtown, New

90   TNA: AO 13/10: pp.254–256, Account of sundry expenses, William Waddell, from 15 September 1776.

91   *The New-York Gazette and the Weekly Mercury*, 2 July 1781; National Archives and Records Administration (NARA): Collection M-804, Pension and Bounty Land Application Files, No. W478: Jacob Brookfield, New Jersey.

92   TNA: ADM 36/9643: Ship Muster Book of HMS *Beaumont*, October–November 1781.

93   J.J. Clute. *Annals of Staten Island from its Discovery to the Present Time* (New York: Charles Vogt Press, 1877), p.156; TNA: AO 13/111: p.479, Memorial of James Stewart to the Commissioners for American Claims, London, 24 February 1784.

Jersey Loyalist Cornelius Hatfield and commanded by Staten Islander Job Smith.[94] Indeed, Hatfield's boat was instrumental in retaking the Sloop *Neptune* which on 15 October 1779 had been boarded and the crew captured by a small detachment of New Jersey State Troops.[95]

Life as a Militiaman

Militia duty done by each side had many similarities. particularly in point of guard mounting. With innumerable landing places on all the islands that comprised the British territory, the duty could be both fatiguing and tedious. The June 1781 order of *Generalmajor* von Riedesel shows the extent that needed to be covered in the area of his command on Long Island:

> … each Company of Militia will furnish every tenth Man daily, of Horse and Infantry to be Mounted if possible or more if the exigency of the Service requires it; and these Partys will make Patroles with Horse and Foot, and post Guards where it may be thought necessary all along the North and South Shore and across the whole Island: From Denyces along the South Shore to Hampstead and Judge Jones's Fort Neck, and across the Island by Jericho as far as Cold-Spring and from Cold-Spring Westward along the North Shore to Hallets Cove and Kills, and from Guannes to Denyces.[96]

On Staten Island, when much of the army was at Elizabethtown Point after the Battle of Connecticut Farms in 1780, militia duty was especially hard in order to compensate for the absence of troops, 'The Militia to the amount of 170 men Patrole along the Coasts in their own Districts and form detachments to Cover their Habitations and Support their Patroles from a place called Prawles to Billops point, and from thence to the Great Kills, Half way from Billops point to the Flag Staff.'[97]

Throughout British lines, fortifications dotted the landscape. While the army was expected to help build such works, the militia were typically called upon to lend assistance. One fort was built completely by the militia in New York City near the East River and was named the Citizens Redoubt in their honour.[98] In November 1780, Colonel Archibald Hamilton announced to his corps that they would be taking over the Clinton Redoubt at Whitestone: 'So Publick a testimony of His Excellency Sir Henry Clinton's confidence in our Loyalty, must stimulate every Breast that wishes well to his King and the British Constitution, and surely will induce us to do our Duty with double ardour.'[99] Weekly rotations of militia maintained the post for the remainder of the war.

---

94   TNA: AO 13/25: pp.442–443, Memorial of Job Smith to the Commissioners for American Claims, Shelburne, 5 April 1786.
95   *The Pennsylvania Packet or the General Advertiser* (Philadelphia), 28 October 1779, 'Extract of a letter from an officer in the State regiment at Elizabeth Town, dated October 15'; *Supplement to The Royal Gazette* (New York), 20 October 1779.
96   TNA: AO 13/99: pp.183–184, Orders by Major General Riedesel, Brooklyn, 22 June 1781.
97   CL: Frederick Mackenzie Papers: Report of Lt Col John Gunning, Staten Island, 12 June 1780.
98   *The Royal Gazette* (New York), 3 June 1780.
99   TNA: AO 13/99: pp.176-177, Queens County Militia Regiment Orders, 2 November 1780.

Other works did not get the same zeal and attention. Forts at Staten Island, Brooklyn and Huntington all suffered for want of labour, to the point that Sir Henry Clinton ordered one unfinished redoubt at Richmond Town demolished for lack of militia assistance in either building or defending it. When one was constructed at the Flag Staff, near the Narrows on the east side of the island, the militia were paid and provisioned the same as the civil branches of the army were for their labour. Brigadier General John Campbell, commanding on the island in 1777, hoped the lure of food and money 'added to their Zeal for the Publick Good,' would have the men 'turn out cheerfully & willingly.'[100] Men from the four companies of Suffolk County Militia at Huntington worked on fortifications there in 1777 and at Lloyd's Neck two years later. The works at Brooklyn were supposed to be carried on by the militia of all three Long Island counties, but Suffolk proved backward in providing men. Upon being prodded to supply their quota, Colonel Richard Floyd replied,

> I am willing to exert myself in any thing for the assistance of Government in my power, but the situation of this County at present is such that is impracticable for me to comply with the request, without Laying myself so Exposed that I must quit my residence here, as I have not been able to lodge in my house this three weeks past and plundered within that space.[101]

Floyd had already been captured at home once and rightly feared being taken again. The works went on, in fits and starts, through the remainder of that summer.

Living in the midst of an army, even one you may ostensibly support, was not a fully secure experience for many. Troops from both armies, despite orders and the threat of severe punishment, occasionally took to licentious behaviour, particularly robbery and plundering. Loyalists in the counties controlled by the British might grudgingly expect such behaviour from British or German troops, men with no connection to America. It was harder to accept when it came from fellow Loyalists. The Amberman Family of Queens County found this out on two terrifying occasions over scarcely two months in 1780.

Derrick Amberman was not a member of the militia, having long since passed the age of mandatory service. On 3 March 1780, two officers on half-pay, Captain Richard Robert Crowe of the Black Pioneers and Major Richard W. Stockton of the 6th Battalion, New Jersey Volunteers appeared at Amberman's home and enquired if any officers were quartered there. Upon being told no, the officers informed him that soon that would change. Words were exchanged and soon Amberman was beaten and stabbed to death in front of his wife and daughter. Both officers were arrested and tried by general court martial. According to Amberman's widow, Sarah, she asked Stockton why he had killed her husband, to which he supposedly answered, 'I have killed him because he is a damned Rebel Son of a Bitch.' Ironically, Colonel Archibald Hamilton testified on behalf of Captain Crowe, the two having served together as officers in the 48th Foot in Albany during the French and Indian War. Crowe was acquitted while Stockton was found guilty and sentenced to death.[102]

---

100 TNA: AO 13/117: pp.69–70, Campbell to Colonel Christopher Billopp, 11 November 1777.
101 CL: CP 60:45: Floyd to Jones, 12 June 1779.
102 TNA: WO 71/92: Court Martial Proceedings of Richard Robert Crowe and Richard W. Stockton, 4 April to 5 May 1780.

Paul Amberman of Jamaica, Queens County was a militiaman under Colonel Hamilton. This Amberman had been arrested prior to the arrival of the British in 1776 and tried 'by a County Committee' for being a Loyalist and refusing service in the rebel militia. Escaping from confinement, he gladly greeted the British upon their arrival in September 1776. After this happy event, he 'immediately took up arms in defence of His Majesty's Government.'[103] What fate awaited him could not have been expected when in the overnight hours of 6 May 1780, a group of men pounded on his door for entry. It proved to be 10 men of the King's American Regiment, their faces blackened, intent on robbing him and his family. To add insult to injury, the King's American Regiment was raised in the winter of 1776–1777 in the New York City area, aided by financial donations provided by the inhabitants, those of Kings and Richmond alone contributing over £800 to recruit the corps.[104] Amberman was threatened with death, whereupon he surrendered £180 in cash, along with silverware and other effects.[105]

After further robberies in Jamaica the next night, on the 8th the gang arrived at the home of William Creed, Junior, where their luck ran out. Creed's house happened to be the quarters of Sergeant Donald McCraw of the 42nd Highlanders, who had a special fondness for the Creed family due to their kindness towards him. Upon hearing the gang break open the house, McCraw confronted them, running one, John Yeomans, through the body with his sword, and wounding another, Stephen Ogden, in the head. By morning, all the gang were rounded up and eventually tried by court martial, with four being sentenced to death, three sentenced to either 500 or 1,000 lashes with a cat of nine tails, and two acquitted. Yeomans never stood trial because he died shortly after the incident.[106]

Despite the harsh sentences, neither Stockton nor any of the King's American Regiment were executed. The militia would have to rely on their own vigilance to prevent further depredations from friend and foe alike. Even as late as Christmas 1782, Captain Daniel Rapalje of Queens County was seeking the robbers of sleigh-born travellers, 'said to be soldiers.'[107]

End of British Rule

The end of the war brought an end to royal administration of the militia. There were no grand reviews or tearful disbandings. There was no known official proclamation besides an order in New York for the volunteer and city companies there to turn in whatever arms had been issued by the British during the preceding three and a half years.[108] The Loyalists who

---

103 TNA: AO 13/24 p.4, Memorial of Paul Amberman to the Commissioners for American Claims, undated.

104 *The New-York Gazette and the Weekly Mercury,* 27 January 1777; TNA: AO 13/100: p.13, William Tryon certificate, 9 February 1784.

105 TNA: AO 13/24: p.5, 'Estimate of Losses sustained by Paul Amberman…'.

106 TNA: WO 71/92: pp.227–238, Court Martial Proceedings of Sergeant Henry Norris, Peter Christian, Luman Pringle, Jonathan Ogden, Adam Ringsdorf, Enos Fluellon, Stephen Ogden, John Merrit, and Frederick Fisher, King's American Regiment, 20–22 July 1780.

107 *The Royal Gazette* (New York), 8 January 1783.

108 *The Royal Gazette* (New York), 11 June 1783. Orders by Major of Brigade Edward Williams, 10 June

had done as much as seven years of duty now looked to take care of their own lives, either as part of the British empire elsewhere or as citizens of the newly-recognized United States of America. For some, there were immediate needs. Peter Braistead, a militiaman under Christopher Billopp on Staten Island, had been severely wounded while on guard duty on the night of 16 August 1779, no doubt in one the many cross-water incursions from New Jersey. The result was the loss of one arm and severe injuries to the other, leaving him 'incapable of doing any kind of Work, and himself and family reduced to great distress.' Pleading to Sir Guy Carleton, the final British commander-in-chief in America, for assistance, he was granted £20 in New York Currency on 20 March 1783 'as a present relief.'[109] Samuel Wade was a fellow Staten Islander, a blacksmith who eventually served as a second lieutenant in the New York City Militia. The end of the war left him with a nearly blind wife and he himself intensely suffering from a leg wound received while a sergeant in the 48th Foot in the previous war. He spent at least a year after the war destitute in hospital, supporting his wife, a daughter with scarlet fever, and a teenage son, begging the government for support.[110]

Any number of accounts and sums were due to those who provided firewood, horses, wagons, cattle, crops, labour, etc. As was typical in cases where the British evacuated a post they long held, a board of officers reviewed claims and made payment where due. The board sat for weeks in 1783, reviewing hundreds of claims, many of them from Staten Island and Queens. Typical was a bill over two years old for 18 Queens County militiamen, six of whom were officers, for providing a little over 55 cords of firewood for Anspach officers quartered at Oyster Bay, a charge originally submitted for payment in April 1781.[111]

The end of the war saw the departure of many officers and men from the militia and volunteer companies. Many became commissioned officers in the newly formed militia companies heading for Port Roseway, Annapolis Royal and the Saint John River in Britain's Canadian provinces. These were not military companies per se, but administrative units to better organize and provide for the thousands of refugees heading for Nova Scotia and elsewhere. Some of the many departing merchants tried to sell their homes, shops and effects before the city was ceded to the United States, but there were few takers, buyers fearing the properties were already forfeited to the State of New York under the confiscation acts. Those that did sell got but a fraction of what they had paid, or of its current worth. Captain Normand Tolmie's wife, acting on his behalf while he was filing a claim in England, was able to get £100 for a wharf on the East River 'very much under its value.'[112]

In contrast to the other county regiments drifting into history without fanfare or regularity, the Westchester corps had the most significant number of officers, men and families depart together, to establish new homes in the area of Cumberland, Nova Scotia, very close to Fort Cumberland and what would soon be the new Province of New Brunswick. The corps had been reduced to six companies and embarked for the Maritimes on 5 June 1783.

1783.
109 TNA: PRO 30/55/6809: Petition of Peter Braisted to Carleton, Staten Island, 25 January 1783.
110 TNA: AO 13/56: p.504, Wade to unknown, no date.
111 TNA: AO 13/97: p.603, Invoice for firewood provided Anspach officers in winter quarters, Oyster Bay, 3 July 1783.
112 TNA: AO 13/54: pp.592–593, Examination of Norman Tomie by the Commissioners for American Claims, 25 October 1786.

It was but a shadow of its former self, when less than two years earlier it could muster its peak of 490 officers and men. But on that June day, 175 men, 86 women, 219 children and 13 servants left for a distant land where they hoped to continue the bonds that brought them together in the Hudson Valley before that April Day in 1775 when the world changed for all of them.[113]

Bibliography

Primary Sources
The National Archives (TNA)
> ADM 36 Admiralty, Royal Navy Ships' Musters (Series I)
> AO 1 Auditors of the Imprest and Commissioners of Audit, Declared Accounts
> AO 12 American Loyalists Claims, Series I
> AO 13 American Loyalists Claims, Series II
> CO5 Board of Trade and Secretaries of State: America and West Indies
> PRO 30/55 Howe, correspondence and papers as C-in-C in the American colonies
> T1 Treasury Board Papers and In-Letters
> WO 60 Commissariat Department, Accounts
> WO 71 Courts Martial Proceedings
The National Archives of Scotland (NAS)
> Robertson Papers
Royal Artillery Institute (RAI)
> James Pattison Papers
Staffordshire Record Office (SRO)
> Earl of Dartmouth Papers
Library and Archives Canada (LAC)
> RG 8, "C" Series
Brooklyn Historical Society (BHS)
> Correspondence of Major John Kissam
East Hampton Free Library (EHFL)
> Pennypacker Long Island Collection
Library of Congress (LOC)
> George Washington Papers
National Archives and Records Administration (NARA)
> M-804, Pension and Bounty Land Application Files
New-York Historical Society (N-YHS)
> Christopher Benson Papers
> Samuel Birch New York City Account Book
New York State Library (NYSL)
> Andrew Elliot Papers
> Misc. Mss Oliver DeLancey
University of Michigan, William L. Clements Library (CL)
> Frederick Mackenzie Papers
> Orderly Book of the King's American Regiment
> Sir Henry Clinton Papers

---

113 TNA: WO 60/27: 'Return of Loyalists and Troops sailed for the undermentioned Places, N. York 10th October 1783.'

Printed Primary Sources

Anon. (ed.), 'Kemble Orderly Book,' *Collections of the New-York Historical Society for the Year 1883* (New York: Printed for the Society, 1884)

Anon. (ed.), 'Official Letters of Major General James Pattison, Commandant of New York,' *Collections of the New-York Historical Society for the Year 1875* (New York: Printed for the Society, 1876)

Anon. (ed.), *Orderly Book of the Three Battalions of Loyalists Commanded by Brigadier-General Oliver DeLancey 1776-1778* (New York: New-York Historical Society, 1917)

Force, Peter, *American Archives, Fifth Series, Volume III* (Washington, DC: Clarke & Force, 1853)

Hagist, Don N., *Roger Lamb's American Revolution* (Yardley, PA: Westholme, 2022)

Jones, Thomas, *History of New York During the Revolutionary War* (New York: The New-York Historical Society, 1879)

New York (state), *Laws of the colony of New York, passed in the years 1774 and 1775: Fourteenth and fifteenth George III. Republished under direction of Frederick Cook, Secretary of State, pursuant to chapter one hundred and seventy-one, laws of eighteen hundred and eighty-eight* (Albany: J.B. Lyon, 1888)

Mackenzie, Frederick, *The Diary of Frederick Mackenzie* (Cambridge, MA: Harvard University Press, 1930)

Simcoe, John Graves, *Simcoe's Military Journal: A History of the Operations of a Partisan Corps, called The Queen's Rangers commanded by Lieut. Col. J.G. Simcoe During the War of the American Revolution* (New York: Bartlett & Welford, 1844)

Newspapers

The London Chronicle
The Newport Gazette
The New-York Gazette and the Weekly Mercury
The New York Herald
The New-York Packet and the American Advertiser (Fishkill)
The Pennsylvania Packet or the General Advertiser (Philadelphia)
The Public Advertiser (London)
The Royal American Gazette (New York)
The Royal Gazette (New York)

Published Secondary Sources

Clute. J.J., *Annals of Staten Island from its Discovery to the Present Time* (New York: Charles Vogt Press, 1877)

Coventry, W., Wadell, H., 'New York Militia of 1776,' *The New York Genealogical and Biographical Record*, vol.2, no.3 (July 1871), pp.156–157

Hanger, George DeLancey, 'The Life of Loyalist Colonel James DeLancey,' *Nova Scotia Historical Review*, vol.3, no.2, (1983), pp.39–56

5

We Destroyed Men, Women and Children: The Tactical and Strategic Impact of Massacres on the Frontier During the American Revolution

Robbie MacNiven

In mid-December 1778 Colonel John Cantine, commander of the 3rd Ulster County Regiment, a unit of New York militia, received a chilling letter at his headquarters in Marbletown. Written by a group of senior Iroquoian leaders, mostly from the Seneca tribe, it stated that 'your Rables [Rebels] came to Oughquago [Onaquaga] when we Indians were gone from our place, and you Burned our Houses, which makes us and our Brothers the Seneca Indians angrey, so that we Destroyed men, women, and Children at Chervalle [Cherry Valley].' It went on to threaten Cantine and Marbletown with the same unless the militia ceased raids into Native territory; 'we, therefore, Desire that you will Let our brothers live in peace, least you be worst delt with, then your Nighbours the Cheryvalle People was. You may think its a Hard winter will hinder us from Coming to you. I have Big Shouse [snowshoes] and can come in a few days to your place.'[1]

The Seneca were referring to the attack on the settlement of Cherry Valley, a prominent colonial outpost close to the New York frontier that was sacked on 11 November 1778 by a combined force of British, Loyalist American and Native American troops. The letter referenced the burning of the Iroquois villages of Unadilla and Onaquaga in October 1778 as one of the reasons behind the attack. These villages had themselves be burned partly in retaliation following the Battle of Wyoming, where revolutionaries claimed a massacre had taken place. The destruction of Cherry Valley would help to trigger a series of invasions by rebel forces in 1779 which devastated Iroquois holdings.

Four years after the Cherry Valley massacre, Colonel William Crawford led a force of frontier militia on a raid against Native settlements along the Sandusky River. The expedition was defeated by Crown Forces and Native allies on the Sandusky Plains, and Crawford

---

1   Joseph Ceskwrora, William George, John, William Johnston, 'A Threatening Letter from Four Indian Chiefs, Decemb'r 13th 1778', quoted in Anon. (ed.), *Public Papers of George Clinton, First Governor of New York. 1777 –1795 1801 –1804* (Albany: James B. Lyon, 1900), vol.IV, p.364.

was captured. According to the narrative of Moravian preacher John Gottlieb Ernestus Heckewelder, the Natives upbraided Crawford for 'the murder of the Christian Indians on the Muskingum,' a reference to a massacre committed by rebel militia at the Moravian Lenape village of Gnadenhutten, near the Muskingum River, on 8 March 1782, three months before Crawford's capture.[2] Crawford had not been present at Gnadenhutten, but the Natives tortured and murdered him as an act of revenge.

Taken together, the massacres at Cherry Valley and Gnadenhutten, as well as surrounding events such as the battles of Wyoming and Sandusky, offer stark examples of how fighting on the frontiers during the American Revolution degenerated into a cycle of extreme violence. While the spectres of massacre and atrocity had stalked Native-colonial relations almost since first contact, the American Revolutionary War saw a marked escalation in acts of aggression on both sides. Atrocities bred a desire for retaliation, which lead to both tactical and strategic consequences which often continued the cycle. For example, the disrespect of frontier militia shown towards the Continental Army officers ostensibly commanding them – outsiders who were often believed to not truly appreciate the damage wreaked on local communities by enemy raids – contributed considerably to disaster at the Battle of Wyoming, and to the massacre at Gnadenhutten and Crawford's subsequent failed expedition. Conversely, the influence of British and Loyalist officers over their Native auxiliaries had a marked impact during combat and after. The Crawford expedition quite likely avoided annihilation because the commander in the field had been injured early during the battle, while the Cherry Valley massacre occurred in no small part because the Natives had lost all respect for their erstwhile leader.

Wyoming and Cherry Valley

The settlement of Cherry Valley was first established in the Mohawk Valley by English and Scottish colonists in 1739. By the outbreak of the Revolutionary War in 1775 it was one of New York's most prominent frontier settlements, and was soon under the control of local rebel forces.

The defeat of a Crown army under Lieutenant General John Burgoyne at Saratoga in October 1777 resulted in British policy in the northernmost colonies reverting to small-scale raiding of rebel-held forts and settlements sympathetic to the revolution. These operations were typically conducted by 'hybrid' war bands of Native Americans, Loyalist Provincials, Loyalist militiamen and volunteers and, occasionally, small forces of British regulars. The foremost northern commanders of these units in the field were John Butler and his son Walter Butler, and Mohawk chief Joseph Brant.

On 3 July 1778 one such war party led by John Butler seized two small rebel forts, Jenkins and Wintermute, in Wyoming Valley, Pennsylvania. They then turned their attentions towards neighbouring Forty Fort, a more substantial defensive work whose garrison included a small number of Continental soldiers. Butler demanded the fort's surrender. The

---

2   John Heckewelder, *A Narrative of the Mission of the United Brethren Among the Delaware and Mohegan Indians* (Philadelphia: McCarty & Davis, 1820), p.338.

Continental officer in command of the garrison refused, knowing the raiders were unlikely to be able to conduct a long-term siege. He intended to simply wait them out, but the militiamen under his command had other ideas.

Believing they outnumbered Butler's force, and anxious to defend their homes from the raiders, members of the militia accused their commander of cowardice, suggested he was a secret Loyalist, and declared that they would march from the fort's safety to face the foe. Indiscipline feeding into ill-considered operational choices was hardly a new thing for militia forces. At the Battle of Oriskany on 6 August 1777, it was senior figures in the militia who urged their commander to continue his march despite his misgivings, resulting in an ambush. As we shall see, the militia displayed similar irregularity at Gnadenhutten and Sandusky. The inability of Continental officers on the frontier to control the actions of local militia severely hampered Congressional efforts at the tactical and up to the operational level. In July 1778, threatened by Butler's forces, the militia marched from the relative safety of Forty Fort.

Butler's scouts, while out collecting cattle, noted the movements of the enemy. In order to encourage them in their mistake, Butler ordered that Wintermute 'be set on fire, which deceived the enemy into an opinion that we had retreated.'[3] Such ruses were not unusual during frontier warfare. In particular, it was common to attempt to mislead enemies about the exact location of forces, and exaggerate strength while weak, or weakness while strong. Torching the forts seems to have played its part as, after a brief pause, the rebels continued onwards. This, according to Butler, 'pleased the Indians highly, who observed they should be on equal footing with them in the woods.'[4]

Butler did indeed place his men 'in a fine open wood' with orders to 'lay upon the ground, waiting their approach.'[5] His centre and left consisted of his Provincial Corps rangers, while his Native allies were concealed on the right. The rebels approached and fired a premature volley 'within two hundred yards.'[6] The rangers, according to Butler's later report, 'continued upon the ground, without returning their fire, until they had fired three volleys.'[7] The inexperienced militia continued to fire, reload, advance and fire, their shots having almost no effect on their prone enemy. With the rebels now within one hundred yards, the Natives struck from the right, and the rangers likewise opened fire.

The commander of the Congressional force writes that 'our men stood the fire well for three or four shots … but, unfortunately for us, through some mistake, the word *retreat* was understood from some officer on the left, which took so quick that it was not in the power of the officers to form them again.'[8] Panic gripped the militia, further accentuated as the whooping Natives rushed in for the kill. Outflanked, the rebel line collapsed within half an hour of making first contact, with the Natives pursuing vigorously. Casualties were particularly high among the rebel officers, who seem to have been killed during the brief firefight

3   John Butler, Lacuwanack, 8 July 1778, quoted in George Peck (ed.), *Wyoming; its History, Stirring Incidents, and Romantic Adventures* (New York: Harper and Brothers, 1858), p.53.
4   Peck, *Wyoming*, p.52.
5   Peck, *Wyoming*, p.53.
6   Peck, *Wyoming*, p.53.
7   Peck, *Wyoming*, p.53.
8   Zebulon Butler, 10 July 1778, in Peck, *Wyoming*, p.50.

or while trying to rally their men as they broke. The Continental commander at Forty Fort related the deaths of a colonel, a lieutenant colonel, a major and seven captains. Butler also claimed that 13 lieutenants and 11 ensigns were among the slain, along with 268 private soldiers and militiamen.[9]

In his after-action report, Butler stated that his expedition had taken 227 scalps and only five prisoners during the engagement. He wrote that 'the Indians were so exasperated with their loss last year near Fort Stanwix that it was with the greatest difficulty I could save the lives of those few.'[10] The mention of Fort Stanwix was an allusion to the bloody battle of Oriskany, for which some Natives seemingly still sought vengeance.

Following the crushing defeat, Forty Fort's few remaining defenders surrendered. Two salient points indicate the primary objectives of commanders leading offensive operations on the frontier. Firstly, Butler's report talked about how he 'killed and drove off about one thousand head of horned cattle, and sheep and swine in great numbers.'[11] He followed up by stating that his next intention was to 'harass the adjacent country, and prevent them from getting in their harvest. The settlement of Scohary or Minisinks will be my next object, both of which abound in corn and cattle, the destruction of which cannot fail of greatly distressing the rebels.'[12] The second point of note is that he claimed that 'in the destruction of this settlement not a single person has been hurt of the inhabitants but such as were in arms; to these, indeed, the Indians gave no quarter.'[13] Indeed, one of the local settlers admitted that 'happily these fierce people, satisfied with the death of those who had opposed them in arms, treated the defenseless ones, the woman and children, with a degree of humanity almost hitherto unparalleled.'[14] Even the commander of the vanquished Congressional forces at Wyoming admitted 'that the Indians have killed no persons since, but have burned most of the buildings, and are collecting all the horses they can.'[15] In the immediate aftermath, Butler's force mounted follow-up attacks on the pro-rebel settlements of German Flats, Shawnee Flats and Lackawanna, all of which were conducted without violence towards civilians.

Butler was therefore successfully fulfilling the two core objectives of British raiding on the frontier, namely seizing resources whilst depriving the enemy of them, and inspiring terror and panic in the local populace without going so far as to conduct a massacre of innocents, one that would have negative propaganda implications for Crown Forces. But, despite his care in this regard, events were already in motion that would see the restraint following Wyoming undone.

Butler seemed to view the killing of fleeing and surrendering enemy combatants at Wyoming as unfortunate, but also believed that his subsequent treatment of civilians in the aftermath fell within the bounds of humane restraint. That, however, was not the

---

9   Peck, *Wyoming*, p.54.
10   Peck, *Wyoming*, p.53.
11   Peck, *Wyoming*, p.54.
12   Peck, *Wyoming*, p.55.
13   Peck, *Wyoming*, p.54.
14   John Hector St. John Crevecoeur, *Letters from an American Farmer and Other Essays* (Harvard: Harvard University Press, 2013), p.279.
15   Peck, *Wyoming*, p.51.

view among either rebel forces, or many of the local inhabitants who the local Continental commander described as 'strolling in the country destitute of provisions.'[16] Accounts of the killings at Wyoming rapidly multiplied and became exaggerated. It was claimed that Butler had burned non-combatants alive, and one survivor even went so far as to fabricate a story about a Native American woman accompanying the war party who supposedly took it upon herself to tomahawk 15 helpless prisoners, one after the other.[17] Over the coming months and years, historian Max Mintz notes, 'accounts abounded of the wanton slayings, torture of captives, and sufferings of exposed women and children fleeing through the swamps.'[18] Even while he printed the correspondence of those involved on both sides – which agreed that Native forces showed restraint to civilians encountered in the aftermath of the battle – one nineteenth-century author claimed that Butler surely must have ordered his allies to,

> … shoot down the settlers in the field; kill and scalp their wives and children; rob, burn, and scalp on as large a scale as possible. All this was done by the same agency as that by which the people were prevented from 'getting in their harvest;' and if Colonel John Butler did the one, the same Colonel John Butler did the other.[19]

Motivated by the initial claims of massacre and the raiding of Butler and Brand, a series of retaliatory efforts were conducted by Continental and militia forces in the latter half of 1778. Continental Colonel Thomas Hartley commanded a strike into Iroquois territory in September that burned Native villages and purportedly massacred civilians, including a Native leader known as Queen Ester who was killed 'for her part in the Wyoming massacre.'[20] A few weeks later Continental and militia forces led by Lieutenant Colonel William Butler (not to be confused with John Butler and Walter Butler, the Loyalist officers) torched the Iroquois towns of Unadilla and Onaquaga, which had been abandoned before the advancing revolutionaries. What worsened these acts in the eyes of the Natives was the fact that a number of men involved in the raids had been captured at Forty Fort and had given their parole, promising not to take up arms against the tribes or the Crown again. A number of these men also resided in Cherry Valley, which had become a hub for rebel forces operating along the north-western frontier. As the cycle of retaliatory killings continued to escalate as 1778 drew to a close, Cherry Valley was singled out as a target.

John Butler's son, Walter Butler, and Mohawk chief Joseph Brant led a fresh raiding force into Cherry Valley in early November. Their number consisted of two companies of Butler's Rangers, a little over 300 Natives – most of them Senecas but also including Mohawks, Cayugas, Onondagas, Delawares and Tuscaroras – and around 50 British regulars from the 8th Foot. Command and control issues bedevilled the expedition from the

---

16   Peck, *Wyoming*, p.51.
17   Harry M. Ward, *The War for Independence and the Transformation of American Society* (London: University College London Press, 1999), p.199.
18   Max M. Mintz, *Seeds of Empire: The American Revolutionary Conquest of the Iroquois* (New York: New York University Press, 1999), p.97.
19   Peck, *Wyoming*, p.55.
20   Lloyd A. Brown and Howard H. Peckham (eds), *Revolutionary War Journals of Henry Dearborn, 1775–1783* (Cirencester: Heritage Books, 2007), p.171.

beginning. Walter Butler did not show the finesse displayed by his father during such operations. Seemingly jealous of Joseph Brant's ability to attract Loyalist volunteers to his war party rather than to his own rangers, he fell out with the Native chief over an argument concerning rations. In doing so, Butler ensured that the Natives, who comprised half the expedition's strength, were far less likely to answer to him as overall commander than they were to Brant.

Despite this less-than-ideal start, fortune favoured the Crown troops. Cherry Valley was protected by a small palisade fort, buts its commander, Continental Colonel Ichabod Alden, refused to take rumours of the enemy's approach seriously. He failed to put the fort into a defensive state and continued to live outside it with many of his officers in the home of the family of John Wells. After the rebel pickets were taken without managing to raise the alarm, Cherry Valley's garrison was caught completely by surprise. Alden and most of his officers were among the first to die as the Wells house was overrun by vengeful Seneca. To their number was added the Wells family themselves, the Natives heedless of the fact that they counted Joseph Brant as a personal friend.

Despite the surprise, the Continentals within the fort were able to secure it before the enemy could reach them. They could only watch as the Natives, especially the Seneca, began to indiscriminately murder Cherry Valley's civilian populace, including not only those with rebel sympathies and neutrals, but also Loyalist families caught up in the attack. Throughout, Walter Butler seems to have done little to try and impose discipline on his allies, and the Loyalist provincial soldiers and remaining volunteers were deployed around the fort to keep the garrison contained. Unlike Butler, Brant did his best to curb the aggression of those under his command. Aided by his own Mohawk warriors, he was able to personally intervene to save a number of Loyalist civilians.[21]

Amidst the killing and the looting, the settlement was torched. Knowing that news of the attack would quickly spread and that a relief force would be sent, Butler and Brant decided to withdraw rather than attempt to lay siege to the fort. Continental Army Captain Benjamin Warren, who saw out the massacre in the fort, left a vivid retelling of the sight that awaited him when he stepped out the next day, following the withdrawal of the raiding party:

> Such a shocking sight my eyes never beheld before of savage and brutal barbarity; to see the husband mourning over his dead wife with four dead children lying by her side, mangled, scalpt, and some their heads, some their legs and arms cut off, some torn the flesh off their bones by their dogs – 12 of one family all killed and four of them burnt in his house.[22]

Nor were all the victims maimed and murdered during the attack itself. The Natives, again mostly the Seneca, took around 70 settlers with them as prisoners. Brant worked hard to secure the release of 40, who were allowed to return to the ruins of their homes, but not all

21   Barbara Graymont, *The Iroquois in the American Revolution* (Syracuse, NY: Syracuse University Press, 1972), pp.188–189.
22   Benjamin Warren, quoted in Francis Whiting Halsey, *The Old New York Frontier: Its Wars with Indians and Tories, Its Missionary Schools, Pioneers and Land Titles, 1614–1800* (Westminster, MD: Heritage Books, 1901), p.242.

were released. One old woman who could not keep up with the pace of the war party was killed.[23]

The massacre caused outrage among those sympathetic towards Congress. Ironically, while Brant had been accused of atrocities at Wyoming despite not having person-ally been present, the rage of commentators was drawn to Walter Butler, who was seen as having allowed, or even presided over, the massacre at Cherry Valley. There were accounts of 'between 30 & 40 Women & Children butchered in the most unheard of manner,' while Brant argued with Butler, claiming that 'he would never have a hand in Massacring the Defenceless Inhabitants.'[24] One commentator finished by stating that 'had the British leaders or the British King been actuated by Sentiments of this sort the American War would not have been Stained with such unparalleled cruelty, nor the name of Briton so justly execrated throughout these States.'[25] One pro-Congress news-paper, the *New Jersey Gazette*, reported in the weeks following the raid that 'the enemy killed, scalped, and most barbarously murdered, thirty-two inhabitants, chiefly women and children, also Colonel Alden ... They committed the most inhuman barbarities on most of the dead ... the lieutenant-colonel, all the officers and continental soldiers, were stripped and drove naked before them.'[26] Meanwhile, Continental Army General James Clinton wrote to Walter Butler admonishing him for the perceived part he had played in the killings and highlighting the fact that mercy had been shown to his own family while in rebel captivity:

> The enormous murders committed at Wyoming and Cherry Valley would clearly have justified a retaliation; and that your mother did not fall a sacrifice to the resentment of the survivors of those families who were so barbarously massacre, is owing to the humane principles which the conduct of their enemies evinces a belief that they are utterly strangers to.[27]

Indeed, highlighting the apparent baseness and brutality of their opponents was becoming common practice among Congressional commanders, politicians and publications, and Walter Butler's seeming betrayal of not only his principals but of his very race in standing by while civilians were murdered by Natives nominally under his command provided a golden propaganda opportunity.

For his own part, Walter Butler could not avoid the fact that a massacre had truly taken place at Cherry Valley, though he did seek to lessen his own involvement and land the blame squarely on the Natives. They were out of control, he claimed, driven beyond reason by the

23   Graymont, *The Iroquois*, p.189.
24   Isabel Thompson Kelsay, *Joseph Brant, 1743-1807; Man of Two Worlds* (Syracuse, NY: Syracuse University Press, 1984), p.233.
25   Kelsay, *Joseph Brant*, p.233.
26   *The New Jersey Gazette*, 25 November 1778, quoted in Frank Moore, *Diary of the American Revolution: From Newspapers and Original Documents* (New York: Charles Scribner, 1858), vol.2, p.105.
27   General Clinton to Captain Butler, Albany, 1 January 1779, quoted in William Leete Stone, *Life of Joseph Brant Thayendanegea Including the Border Wars of the American Revolution* (New York: Alexander V. Blake, 1838), vol.1, p.383.

false accusations levelled at them following the engagement at Wyoming. In a letter to his superior at Fort Niagara, he set out that:

> Not withstanding my utmost precautions to save the women and children, I could not prevent some of them falling victim to the fury of the savages … The death of the women and children on this occasion may, I believe, be truly ascribed to the rebels having falsely accused the Indians of cruelty at Wyomen. This has much exasperated them, and they are still more incensed at finding that the colonel and those who had then laid down their arms, soon after marched into their country intending to destroy their villages.[28]

Walter Butler's protestations did nothing to ameliorate the attitudes of settlers towards him. In fact, 'Cherry Valley quarter' was supposedly shouted by an Oneida Native allied to the revolutionary cause, when he killed and scalped Walter Butler in 1781. The bloodshed of Wyoming and Cherry Valley would continue to spawn further violence for years to come.

In the immediate aftermath of the massacre, the forces of Congress sought to retaliate. With little in the way of British offensive operations in the east in early 1779, George Washington authorized a large-scale invasion into Iroquois territory, giving the expedition's objectives as:

> The total destruction and devastation of their settlements, and the capture of as many prisoners of every age and sex as possible. It will be essential to ruin their crops now in the ground and prevent their planting more … that the country may not be merely overrun, but destroyed. But you will not by any means listen to any overture of peace before the total ruinment of their settlements is effected.[29]

The expedition, commanded by Major General John Sullivan, struck almost unopposed into the Iroquois heartlands, burning over 40 Native settlements along with large quantities of food and supplies. The campaign caused the massed displacement of Native peoples, many of whom fled to the British garrison at Fort Niagara, seeking protection. Starvation and exposure took its toll, and Iroquois operations were sharply restricted for the next few years as they struggled to recover from the blow. The expedition was framed by supporters of the revolution as what historian Barbara Alice Mann describes as 'righteous retaliation for Wyoming and Cherry Valley.'[30] While it achieved its broad aims of turning the tide against the Crown at least on that portion of the frontier, not all such expeditions would meet with success or progress unopposed. Nor did massacres produce retaliation only on the side of the rebels.

---

28   Walter Butler to Colonel Bolton, camp at Unadilla, 17 November 1778, quoted in Anon. (ed.), *Transactions of the Canadian Institute* (Toronto: Murray Printing Company, 1898), vol.5, p.259.

29   George Washington, Middlebrook, 31 May 1779, quoted in Edward G. Lengel (ed.), *The Papers of George Washington* (Charlottesville: University of Virginia Press, 2010), vol.20, pp.716–719.

30   Barbara Alice Mann, *George Washington's War on Native America* (Westport, CT: Praeger Publishers, 2005), p.20.

Gnadenhutten and Sandusky

The Revolutionary War proved devastating not only for Natives American tribes that became embroiled on one side or the other, but also for those who sought to remain neutral. Among the latter were the Moravian Lenape of Delaware. Converted by missionaries of the Czech Protestant Moravian denomination, these 'Christian Indians' held an avowedly pacifistic stance, even as the wider Lenape tribe became split between support for the Crown or Congress. While non-violent appeasement of both sides might have been viewed as the best policy for avoiding the horrors and tumult of war, in reality it simply made the Moravian Natives easy targets.

Both the Congressional headquarters at Fort Pitt, near the western Pennsylvanian frontier demarcated by the Ohio River, and the British operating out of their stronghold at Fort Detroit on the far side of Lake Erie, viewed the Moravians with suspicion. While the Moravians refused to take up arms, they did not stop raiding parties that were passing through the area from taking food and shelter, which caused the revolutionaries to suspect that they were secretly in league with the Crown. The British meanwhile found they could not persuade the Moravians to actively join them, and correctly suspected them of feeding some intelligence about Crown movements back to Fort Pitt.

Matters came to a head in late 1781, when Natives allied to the British arrived at the Moravian settlements and ordered the populace to relocate to the Sandusky River, closer to Fort Detroit. The missionaries themselves were questioned by the commander of the Crown's efforts on that part of the frontier, Major Arent Schuyler De Peyster, while the flock were housed in a destitute settlement they called Captive Town. This arrangement was quickly found to be insufficient, as the Moravians had not been allowed to bring stores of food with them for the winter, and the British were unable to adequately supply them. Not wishing to force the Moravians into starvation, De Peyster permitted a number to return to their villages throughout the winter to harvest crops and collect grain that had been stored up. This they did for a time, but the situation became rapidly more fraught.

The early months of 1782 saw an increase in raiding conducted by Crown-allied Natives in the region. The partially-abandoned Moravian settlements provided useful layovers for the war parties heading out on, or returning from, their expeditions. Moravian missionary John Gottlieb Ernestus Heckewelder related how one such party, passing by the Moravian village of Gnadenhutten following a raid, stated that they had 'taken a woman and child prisoner, whom they killed and impaled on this side of the Ohio river, and supposing, that the white people in consequence of what *they* had done, might make up a party and pursue them; they advised them [the Moravians] to be on their guard, and make off with themselves as soon as possible.'[31]

Retaliation was indeed forthcoming. A force of 160 rebel militiamen assembled at Mingo Bottom under the command of militia colonel David Williamson. Without orders from Fort Pitt, they set out to remove the Moravian presence once and for all on 4 March 1782. Ironically, the acting Continental commander at Fort Pitt, Colonel John Gibson, learned of

---

31   Heckewelder, *A Narrative*, p.312.

the militia's decision to strike unilaterally at the Moravians and attempted to warn them, but his message arrived too late.

Williamson chose to divide his force in two, with part bound for Gnadenhutten directly while the rest moved to cut off anyone fleeing the area. The militia arrived at the Tuscarawas River but could find no spare canoes to cross with. One of the militiamen swam over and discovered a sugar trough, with which he returned. A group of the militia then stripped down and, depositing their clothing as well as, presumably, their arms and ammunition in the trough, swam with it across the river. On the other bank they discovered a Moravian named Joseph Schebosh, who was out looking for a stray horse. The son of a white missionary and a Native woman, Schebosh begged for his life but was murdered by the militia.[32]

The rebels carried on to Gnadenhutten, where they found those Moravians who were present in the village out working their fields. The militia feigned friendship, convincing them to surrender what weapons they had and telling them they were moving them to Fort Pitt for their own protection, where they would do what the British could not and provide them with food. The Moravians appeared to believe the militia and complied with their demands.

It was not long before the tenor of the interactions between the two groups changed markedly. The militia made a number of accusations against the Moravians, such as:

> That the horses found with them, had been taken from white people, they being branded with letters, with which the Indians were unacquainted; that the axes found with them, had the names of white people stamped upon them. Pewter basins and spoons were stolen property; the Indians making use of wooden bowls and spoons. Tea-kettles, pots, cups and saucers, was also declared stolen property. In short, every thing they possessed, was said to have been taken from the white people whilst at war with them.[33]

Using the stolen objects as a pretext, the militia separated the men from the women and children and confined them to two buildings. They then voted on whether or not to kill the Natives, with all but 18 of the militia casting in favour of a massed execution. After giving them the night to pray and prepare themselves, the militia set about their gruesome work.

One militiaman procured a cooper's mallet, which he used to strike each victim on the head in turn. When he grew tired, he handed the mallet to another man to continue. Knives and tomahawks were also employed. One second-hand retelling related how a militiaman named Nathan Rollins, whose brother, father and uncle had all been killed in Native raids, 'tomahawked nineteen of the poor Moravians, & after it was over he sat down & cried, & said it was no satisfaction for the loss of his father & uncle after all. – so related Holmes Jr who was there – who was out on both Moravian campaigns, & Crawford's.'[34]

After murdering the Natives, the militia torched the buildings, then withdrew. They intended to strike at other nearby settlements, but word of their presence had spread and the remaining Moravians in the area had fled. A total of 96 Natives were killed, 29 of them

---

32   Anon., *The History of Tuscarawas County, Ohio* (Chicago: Warner, Beers & Co., 1884), p.296.
33   Heckewelder, *A Narrative*, p.317.
34   J.T. Holmes, *The American Family of Rev. Obadiah Holmes* (Columbus, OH: Stoneman, 1915), p.199.

women and 39 children. Only two children survived, one by playing dead before slipping away, the other by hiding in a cellar and then escaping before the building burned down.

News of the massacre was met with mixed reactions by whites on the frontier, but among many Native tribes the killings caused outrage every bit as potent as the outcry among the revolutionaries following Wyoming and Cherry Valley. Robert G. Parkinson writes that 'Ohio Indians were furious at what had happened.'[35] The massacre also had the effect of causing a partial revival of nativistic religious traditions, including the ritualised torture of enemy captives.[36] If the Moravian Lenape had adhered strictly to the tenets of Christian pacifism, and had still been slaughtered by their supposed coreligionists, then why would any other Native be expected to follow the white man's faith?

The Natives of the Ohio region – primarily the Wyandots, Shawanese, Delawares and Mingos, would not have to wait long for a chance at vengeance. In May a militia expedition was organized with the intention of striking at the Native communities along the Sandusky River and thus clearing the frontier, much as the Sullivan Expedition had done further north in 1779. It had initially been hoped that Fort Detroit itself might be threatened, but neither Congress nor the Continental Army could offer the support necessary to make such an objective viable, and so the operation had to be conducted entirely on the initiative of the frontier militia.

The murder, on 12 May 1782, of Baptist minister John Corbley's family by Natives helped to motivate volunteers to turn out for the expedition.[37] Instructions were given 'to destroy with fire and sword (if practicable) the Indian town and settlement at Sandusky, by which we hope to give ease and safety to the inhabitants of this country.'[38] A force of 480 militiamen assembled at Mingo Bottom, the same muster point used by the militia force that had committed the Gnadenhutten massacre – indeed, it seems that many of the same men joined the expedition, including the commander of the Gnadenhutten atrocity, David Williamson.

As was standard practice, the militia elected their officers by vote. Williamson lost out to William Crawford, an experienced frontier campaigner who had only recently left the Continental Army. Despite his involvement combating Natives, Crawford's election victory was a narrow one, due in no small part to the fact that 'the general and common opinion of the people of this country is that all Continental officers are too fond of Indians.'[39] Continental Army frontier commander General William Irvine noted on numerous occasions the disregard the local militia showed towards Continental officers and their anger when those officers tried to restrain attacks on Natives, writing that 'they are unwilling to comply with the most necessary orders of the commanding officer of this department, therefore … I shall pay much less regard to a people so much averse to serving themselves,

35   Robert G. Parkinson, *The Common Cause: Creating Race and Nation in the American Revolution* (Chapel Hill, NC: University of North Carolina Press, 2016), pp.537–538.
36   John Grenier, *The First Way of War: American War Making on the Frontier, 1607–1814* (Cambridge: Cambridge University Press, 2005), p.161.
37   C. W. Butterfield, *An Historical Account of the Expedition against Sandusky Under Col. William Crawford in 1782* (Cincinnati: Robert Clarke & Co, 1873), p.61.
38   Butterfield, *An Historical Account*, pp.69–70.
39   William Irvine in Anon. (ed.), *Memoirs of the Historical Society of Pennsylvania* (Philadelphia: J. B. Lippincott & Co., 1858), vol.VI, p.150.

much less their country.'[40] Fearful of the reactions of frontier settlers, he even cautioned his wife not to show any regret for the Gnadenhutten massacre, noting, 'whatever your private opinion of these matters may be, I conjure you by all the ties of affection, and as you value my reputation, that you will keep your mind to yourself, and that you will not express any sentiment for or against these deeds.'[41] As was often the case, militia indifference towards the orders of their supposed leaders would quickly start to negatively affect Crawford's expedition.

The force moved out of Mingo Bottom on 25 May. On 3 June they reached the Sandusky Plains, an area of open prairie dotted with clumps of woodland. They reached the first Native settlement, the Wyandot village known as Upper Sandusky, the next day, but found it abandoned. Concerned that their approach had been discovered, Crawford halted the advance and held a council of war. As he did so, mounted scouts were sent ahead to range across the prairie and try and ascertain if any Natives were nearby.

The council decided that, since it seemed likely word had gone ahead of their approach and the other villages along their route would also be abandoned, it was best to turn back. As this determination was reached, word came from one of the outriders. The scouts had advanced to a slightly elevated clump of trees in the grassy plain and then passed beyond, where they had made contact with a Native war party. These were Delawares who had been moving towards the trees from the opposite direction, likewise intending to occupy them while waiting to link up with a Wyandot party on their way to join them.

Seemingly eager to engage the enemy, the militia abandoned their planned withdrawal and advanced towards the copse. After a short skirmish they successfully occupied the trees. Meanwhile, the Wyandots arrived to reinforce the Delawares, who had been driven back but not routed. They quicky and efficiently circumvented the island of trees and began to attack the militia from the rear while the fighting was renewed from their front.

Crawford's aide, John Rose, later reported that 'at 4 P.M. the action was general, close and hot. Both parties contended obstinately for a piece of Woods.'[42] The commander of the Crown Forces, Captain William Caldwell of Butler's Rangers, was injured by a musket ball which passed through one leg and lodged in the other; he 'left the field in the beginning of the action.'[43] This caused some disruption in command and control of the Crown Forces. A stalemate ensued until sunset. As long as they were amongst the trees, the militia were well-sheltered and able to conduct an all-round perimeter defence without having to worry about their flank being turned. On the opposite side, the Natives could use the tall grass of the prairie not only as cover, but to conceal their movements as they encircled the copse. Although some of the militia climbed into trees to better pick out their foes, it was difficult for them to ascertain the size or concertation of the enemy force.

---

40   Irvine in Anon. (ed.), *Memoirs*, p.149.
41   William Irvine, Fort Pitt, 12 April 1782, quoted in C. W. Butterfield (ed.), *Washington-Irvine Correspondence* (Maddison: David Atwood, 1882), p.344.
42   John Rose, Mingo Bottom, 13 June 1782, quoted in Butterfield (ed.), *Washington-Irvine Correspondence*, p.370.
43   John Turney, Camp Upper Sandusky, 7 June 1782, quoted in Butterfield (ed.) *Washington-Irvine Correspondence*, p.368.

The firefight endured until dusk. Casualties were uncertain, but almost certainly light – Rose put the militia's losses on the first day at five dead and 11 wounded.[44] Crown and Native casualties were reported as one ranger, one white interpreter and four Natives killed, and three rangers (including Caldwell) and eight Natives wounded.[45] During the night both sides lay on their arms and built fires around the perimeter of the trees in order to reduce the possibility of a surprise attack. There was no source of fresh water in the wood and that, combined with the heat of the previous day and the sharp fighting, left many of the militia with a dire thirst.

Firing resumed around 6:00 a.m., though it was desultory. The militia 'were so much incumbered with our Wounded and Sick, that the whole day was spent in their care and in preparing for a general attack the next Night.'[46] But the militia's determination to go on the offensive evaporated when Crown reinforcements began to arrive, first a mounted detachment of Provincials from Butler's Rangers, then a fresh war party of Shawanese. The sight of these arrivals caused despair in the surrounded militia. Rose wrote, since the enemy 'could collect all their forces in a circuit of about 50 Miles, who Kept pouring in hourly from all Quarters to their relief, prudence dictated a retreat.'[47]

That night the militia organised themselves for a breakout. They buried their dead and lit fires over them to disguise the graves. Litters were made for the wounded, the pickets were silently called in, and Crawford divided his command into four sections. Things began to deteriorate almost immediately. One group, under Captain John Hardin, despite orders, moved off too early, alerting the Crown forces to the plan – 'the ennemy observing our intentions begun a hot fire.'[48] This in turn caused panic in the group that was supposed to act as the vanguard, who rushed off in the wrong direction, passing between the encampments of the Shawanese and Delawares. The other three groups maintained more coherence and succeeded in skirting out past the main body of the enemy in the dark. Word of the militia's withdrawal did not reach the rangers until midday, which delayed their pursuit. Caldwell later complained that, had he not been injured, he would have been able to coordinate the militia's total defeat.

At daybreak the main body of the militia collected themselves at Upper Sandusky. It soon became apparent however that Colonel Crawford was missing. He had delayed initially to try and stop a number of the wounded from being left behind, then had become caught up looking for family members on the expedition – his son, son-in-law, and nephew. Separated from the main body, Crawford and a few other stragglers were captured a day later by a band of Lenape.

Command fell to Williamson, who succeeded in holding off the pursuing Crown Forces long enough to make it off the Sandusky Plains and back to safety. In a letter to Washington, General Irvine was scathing of the tactical and strategic mistakes made by the militia:

---

44   Butterfield (ed.), *Washington-Irvine Correspondence*, p.370.
45   Butterfield (ed.), *Washington-Irvine Correspondence*, p.368.
46   Butterfield (ed.), *Washington-Irvine Correspondence*, p.371.
47   Butterfield (ed.), *Washington-Irvine Correspondence*, p.372.
48   Butterfield (ed.), *Washington-Irvine Correspondence*, p.372.

I am of opinion had they reached the place in seven days (in stead of ten,) which might have been done especially as they were chiefly mounted they would have succeeded, they should also have pushed the advantage evidently gained at the commencement of the Action; they failed in another point which they had my advice and indeed positive orders for Viz. to make the last days march as long as possible and attack the place in the night, but they halted in the evening within nine miles, fired their Rifles at seven in the morning before they marched.[49]

Crawford's fate served not only as a warning for those intending to take the fight to Native settlements, but as a stark indicator of the fallout from the Gnadenhutten massacre. Crawford was falsely accused as having participated in the killings and was also recognised – correctly – as having been involved in an earlier raid in 1778 that had included the murder of a number of Native American women and children. Requests by the British to spare Crawford's life were rejected, and he was subjected to ritual torture and execution before a crowd of onlookers at the Lenape settlement of Pipe's Town. Crawford was stripped, beaten, and had blank charges of gunpowder fired into him at point-blank range. His ears were cut off, he was branded, and made to walk on hot coals. He was scalped then covered in hot coals before he eventually died. In his report back to Washington, General Irvine wrote that 'the unfortunate Colonel in particular, was burned and tortured in every manner they could invent.'[50] Most of the other captives were tomahawked and scalped.

Crawford's death caused outrage among American colonists and would continue to be used for propaganda purposes for decades to come. In the short-term, prominent revolutionaries acknowledged that Crawford's death was a direct consequence of the Gnadenhutten massacre, which had ushered in a fresh wave of killings. Irvine noted that the atrocity 'struck the people of this Country with a strange mixture of fear & resentment, their solicitations for making another excursion are increasing dayly, and they are actually beginning to prepare for it.'[51] He also wrote that survivors of the expedition had been 'assured by sundry Indians they formerly knew, that not a single soul should in future escape torture, and gave as a reason for this conduct, the Moravian affair.'[52]

Prominent Virginian politician Edmund Pendleton wrote to Irvine, likewise noting:

The torture of Colo. Crawford by the Indians to the Westward I suppose was in Revenge for the Massacre of the poor Moravians by our people some time agoe; yet resentment for this will take place in our back people, and perhaps continue for years a scene of mutual bloodshed.[53]

---

49   William Irvine, Fort Pitt, 16 June 1782, quoted in Butterfield (ed.), *Washington-Irvine Correspondence*, p.121.
50   Butterfield (ed.), *Washington-Irvine Correspondence*, p.126.
51   Butterfield (ed.), *Washington-Irvine Correspondence*, p.127.
52   Butterfield (ed.), *Washington-Irvine Correspondence*, p.127.
53   Edmund Pendleton, Virga, 12 August 1782, quoted in William T. Hutchinson and William M.E. Rachal (eds.), *The Papers of James Madison* (Chicago: The University of Chicago Press, 1967), vol.5, p.45.

Similarly, in a letter to Irvine, Washington bemoaned the defeat at Sandusky and Crawford's fate, and left grim instructions to those fighting on the frontier:

> I lament the failure of the former Expedition – and am particularly affected with the disastrous fate of Colo. Crawford – no other than the extremest Tortures which could be inflicted by the Savages could, I think, have been expected, by those who were unhappy eno' to fall into their Hands, especially under the present Exasperation of their Minds, for the Treatment given their Moravian friends. For this reason, no person should at this Time, suffer himself to fall alive into the Hands of the Indians.[54]

Conclusion

Throughout the war commanders strove – with varying levels of success – to impose strategies amidst the chaos of the frontier, while at the same time negating those of the enemy. These efforts were complicated by the enhanced violence inherent in frontier warfare, and the cycle of revenge and retaliation undermined efforts to impose coherency on a conflict that, in many ways, outgrew the major theatres of operations further east.

The massacres that occurred on the frontier did little to aid the cause of the aggressors. Cherry Valley proved to be a propaganda gift for Congress and did not stop rebel control of the region. Its most lasting strategic effect was to trigger a response in the form of Sullivan's expedition, striking a blow against the Iroquois which, though not decisive, did all but knock them out of the war for several years. Similarly, Gnadenhutten served only to turn Natives away from assisting the forces of the revolution and hardened the attitudes of those already in arms against them. The death of Crawford – in defiance of the will of the British – indicated Native agency in a war that was wreaking devastation on the tribes and their attempts to maintain their own independence.

Acts of massacre also ensured that exercising strategic or tactical authority became harder for commanders. While John Butler handled relations with his Native auxiliaries excellently, his son Walter failed to do the same, and the massacre at Cherry Valley was the consequence. Meanwhile, a string of Continental officers tried and failed to exercise control over the frontier militia. Often outsiders who were believed not to appreciate the fraught nature of existence on the frontier, their failure to earn respect and exert authority resulted in both tactical and strategic disasters such as Wyoming and Sandusky Plains.

Bibliography

Anon. (ed.), *Memoirs of the Historical Society of Pennsylvania* (Philadelphia: J.B. Lippincott & Co., 1858)
Anon. (ed.), *Public Papers of George Clinton, First Governor of New York, 1777 – 1795 – 1801 – 1804* (Albany: James B. Lyon, 1900)

---

54 George Washington, Head Quarters, 6 August 1782, quoted in Butterfield (ed.), *Washington-Irvine Correspondence*, pp.131–132.

Anon. (ed.), *Transactions of the Canadian Institute* (Toronto: Murray Printing Company, 1898)

Anon., *The History of Tuscarawas County, Ohio* (Chicago: Warner, Beers & Co., 1884)

Brown, Lloyd A. and Howard H. Peckham (eds), *Revolutionary War Journals of Henry Dearborn, 1775 – 1783* (Cirencester: Heritage Books, 2007)

Butterfield, C.W. (ed.), *Washington-Irvine Correspondence* (Maddison: David Atwood, 1882)

Butterfield, C.W., *An Historical Account of the Expedition against Sandusky Under Col. William Crawford in 1782* (Cincinnati: Robert Clarke & Co, 1873)

Crevecoeur, John Hector St. John, *Letters from an American Farmer and Other Essays* (Harvard: Harvard University Press, 2013)

Graymont, Barbara, *The Iroquois in the American Revolution* (Syracuse, NY: Syracuse University Press, 1972)

Grenier, John, *The First Way of War: American War Making on the Frontier, 1607 – 1814* (Cambridge: Cambridge University Press, 2005)

Heckewelder, John, *A Narrative of the Mission of the United Brethren Among the Delaware and Mohegan Indians* (Philadelphia: McCarty & Davis, 1820)

Holmes, J.T., *The American Family of Rev. Obadiah Holmes* (Columbus OH, 1915)

Hutchinson, William T. and William M.E. Rachal (eds.), *The Papers of James Madison* (Chicago: The University of Chicago Press, 1967)

Kelsay, Isabel Thompson, *Joseph Brant, 1743-1807; Man of Two Worlds* (Syracuse, NY: Syracuse University Press, 1984)

Lengel, Edward G. (ed.), *The Papers of George Washington* (Charlottesville: University of Virginia Press, 2010)

Mann, Barbara Alice, *George Washington's War on Native America* (Westport, CT: Praeger Publishers, 2005)

Mintz, Max M., *Seeds of Empire: The American Revolutionary Conquest of the Iroquois* (New York: New York University Press, 1999)

Moore, Frank, *Diary of the American Revolution: From Newspapers and Original Documents* (New York: Charles Scribner, 1858)

Parkinson, Robert G., *The Common Cause: Creating Race and Nation in the American Revolution* (Chapel Hill, NC: University of North Carolina Press, 2016)

Peck, George, *Wyoming; its History, Stirring Incidents, and Romantic Adventures* (New York: Harper and Brothers, 1858)

Stone, William Leete, *Life of Joseph Brant Thayendanegea Including the Border Wars of the American Revolution* (New York: Alexander V. Blake, 1838)

Ward, Harry M., *The War for Independence and the Transformation of American Society* (London: UCL Press, 1999)

Whiting Halsey, Francis, *The Old New York Frontier: Its Wars with Indians and Tories, Its Missionary Schools, Pioneers and Land Titles, 1614 – 1800* (Westminster, MD: Heritage Books, 1901)

6

'The pleasure of their number' 1778: Crisis, Conscription, and Revolutionary Soldiers' Recollections

John U. Rees

Contrary to popular belief, Revolutionary American military forces drafted men throughout that conflict (1775–1783). At the simplest and most elementary level, most state militias divided males, ages 16 to 50, into classes by company, county, or district, then called out (drafted) one or several of a county's classes for service ranging from weeks to months. For ongoing, routine service the militia classes or divisions did duty by rotation. Having served the allotted time, the men returned home, and another class took their place. Similarly, Continental regiments were often augmented with state militia drafts, each county class providing a volunteer, a draft, or a substitute in place of a drafted man. The men thus gained served as Continental soldiers for a stipulated term.[1]

---

1   For information on militia classing in the several colonies and states see: 'An Act in further Addition to an Act entitled An Act for forming and regulating the Militia, and for the Encouragement for military Skill, for the better Defence of this State' (passed 18 December 1776), *The Public Records of the State of Connecticut, from October, 1776, to February 1778, inclusive* (Hartford: Lockwood & Brainard, 1894), pp.93, 95; 'The plan for further regulating the Militia, etc.' (passed 16 August 1775), *Extracts from the Journal of Proceedings of the Provincial Congress of New-Jersey Held at Trenton in the Months of May, June and August, 1775* (Burlington: Collins, 1775), pp.28, 32–33; 'An Act to explain and amend an Act, intitled, An Act for the better regulating the Militia, and the Supplemental Act thereto' (passed 23 September 1777), *Acts of the General Assembly of the State of New-Jersey, At a Session begun at Princeton on the 27th Day of August, 1776, and continued by Adjournments till the 11th of October 1777* (Burlington: Collins, 1777), p. 99; 'An Act to regulate the Militia of the Commonwealth of Pennsylvania' (passed 17 March 1777), *The Statues at Large of Pennsylvania from 1682 to 1801* (Harrisburg, PA: William Stanley Ray, 1903), vol IX, p.79; 'An act for providing against Invasions and Insurrections' (passed 1 May 1777), William Waller Hening (ed.), *The Statutes at Large. Being a Collection of All the Laws of Virginia, from the First Session of the Legislature, in the Year 1619* (Richmond: J. & G. Cochran 1821), vol.IX, pp.291–292; 'An Act to Establish a Militia in this State' (passed 8 April 1777), Walter Clark (ed.), *The Colonial records of North Carolina* (Goldsboro, NC: Nash Bros., 1905), vol.24, pp.1–3.

This chapter examines state efforts resulting from the first Congressionally authorized widespread United States army draft, the effect on troop strength, and old soldiers' recollections of their short-term service, with New Jersey as the lead example.

So, why the need for a draft law? While American forces were first organized as a Continental army in the summer and autumn of 1775, the real impetus for widespread conscription began with the autumn of 1776 plan known as the 88-Battalion Resolve, when Congress increased the number of Continental regiments to be raised. Beginning in January 1777 most states' units were reorganized and reenlisted, others formed anew. Each state had a unit quota, apportioned according to population (see below). All enlistments spanned three years or the war's duration, in what became known as the Continental Army Second Establishment. There were several exceptions, including six North Carolina and nine Virginia regiments, all formed in 1776 with enlistments expiring in 1778 or early 1779. Besides these units there were organizations like the 1st and 2nd Canadian Regiments, and the German Battalion, the latter formed in 1776 of three-year soldiers in companies enlisted in either Maryland or Pennsylvania. When Maryland drafted levies in 1778, the Pennsylvania companies did not receive a share. Also included in the 88-Battalion Resolve were 16 Additional Regiments, only 14 of which were actually formed, with varying success. Though recruited wholly or partially in regions comprising one or several states, these units had no official state affiliation, and when the 1778 draft laws went into effect, they, too, received no levies.[2]

1777 State Quotas[3]

States Authorized for 1778 draft	Infantry Regiments Actually Raised	
	Regular	Additional (not included in state quota)
New Hampshire	3	0
Massachusetts	15	3
Rhode Island	2	½
Connecticut	8	1½
New York	5 (quota was 4)	½
New Jersey	4	2
Pennsylvania	13 (quota was 12)	2½ (incl. half of German Battalion)
Delaware	1	0
Maryland	7 (quota was 8)	(half of German Battalion)
Virginia	15	3
North Carolina	9	1

General George Washington recommended a draft in January 1777, writing to Governor Nicholas Cooke of Rhode Island,

---

2   Robert K. Wright, Jr., *The Continental Army* (Washington: Government Printing Office, 1984), pp.12–44, 91–93.
3   Wright, *The Continental Army*, pp.93.

Sir … You must be sensible the Season is fast approaching, when a new Campaign will open … It is of the last importance to the interest of America, that the New Regiments be speedily levied … I hope the Powers of Government are such, as to Compleat the New Levies by draught, if they cannot be fill'd Seasonably by Voluntary inlistments. Necessity obliges me to Call upon you, as I shall upon every other State, in the most pressing terms, to compleat without delay your proportion of the Eighty Eight Battalions.[4]

Wartime armies are often under-strength, with men *hors de combat* for various reasons. Elements of the Continental Army never had their full complement of men from their inception. Colonel Israel Shreve of the 2nd New Jersey Regiment enumerated his difficulties gathering new men, including 'coming home [in December 1776] through the state of New York, [where] several of our recruits for the war deserted,' then when 'the flying camp [militia] broke up, [and] the men [were] discharged … many … were enlisted by my recruiting officers, [were] sworn, received their bounties and went off.' Shreve continued, 'Another thing at that very time [late 1776, that] encouraged desertion was the enemy having possession of part of our state. Many that were enlisted deserted and enlisted in the enemys [Loyalist] New Levie Regts. The whole of these disadvantages caused great numbers to desert that never did duty in the Regt. after they enlisted.' Colonel Shreve provided this accounting:[5]

Second New Jersey Regiment Enlistment Statistics, 1777

Company	Mustered 1 January 1777	Joined After 1 January 1777	Total	Never Joined or Mustered	Left the Regiment After 1 June 1777	Total Never Joined or Left the Regiment
Hollinshead	64	2	66	21	15	36
Cummings	90	7	97	31	21	52
Dillon	64	3	67	33	7	40
Maxwell	57		57	33	6	39
Laurie	30	1	31	4	6	10
Anderson	57		57	31	1	32
Luse	74	8	82	30	21	51
Yard	44		44	19	5	24
Stout	65		65	25	7	32
Total	545	21	566	227	89	316

---

4   John C. Fitzpatrick (ed.), *The Writings of George Washington from the Original Manuscript Sources 1745–1799* (Washington: Government Printing Office, 1932), George Washington to Nicholas Cooke, 20 January 1777, vol.7, pp.42–43.

5   National Archives, US (NA): Revolutionary War Rolls (Microfilm Publication M246), Record Group 93, microfilm reel 57, section 23, 2nd New Jersey Regiment (Miscellaneous Records), Israel Shreve to Congress, 30 December 1786 (regarding funds for recruiting in 1777).

In May 1777 the regiment contained 247 men. Optimum enlisted strength for a 1777 Continental regiment was 640 privates and corporals (rank and file), 32 sergeants, and 16 drummers and fifers; 688 in total.[6]

The rigorous 1777 campaigns reduced the army yet further. In October Washington wrote to the President of Congress about 'the general defective state of the Regiments which compose our armies … they do not amount to near half their just complement … it is certain every idea of voluntary enlistments seems to be at an end.' Nine days after arriving at Valley Forge the general voiced his concern to Virginia Governor Patrick Henry: 'I really do not know what plans will be most likely to succeed for filling your Battalions or those of the other States. It is an Object of infinite, indeed of the last importance, and must be effected if possible.'[7] In January 1778 the commander in chief reported to a Congressional Conference Committee on 'completing the regiments and altering their establishment,

> Voluntary inlistments seem to be totally out of the question; all the allurements of the most exorbitant bounties and every other inducement … have been tried in vain … We may fairly infer, that the country has been already pretty well drained of that class of Men, whose tempers, attachments and circumstances disposed them to enter permanently, or for a length of time, into the army; and that the residue of such men, who from different motives, have kept out of the army, if collected, would not augment our general strength in any proportion to what we require. If experience has demonstrated, that little more can be done by voluntary inlistments, some other mode must be concerted, and no other presents itself, than that of filling the Regiments by drafts from the Militia. This is a disagreeable alternative, but it is an unavoidable one.[8]

Washington went on to discuss reenlistment incentives and future prospects.

> As drafting for the war, or for a term of years, would probably be disgusting and dangerous, perhaps impracticable, I would propose an annual draft of men, without officers, to serve 'till the first day of January, in each year; That on or before the first day of October preceeding, these drafted Men should be called upon to reinlist for the succeeding year; and as an incitement to doing it, those being much better and less expensive than raw recruits, a bounty of twenty five dollars should be offered … upon ascertaining … the number of men, willing to re-engage, exact returns should be made to Congress of the deficiency in each regiment, and transmitted by them to the respective states, in order that they may have their several quotas immediately furnished, and sent on to Camp … so as to arrive by … the first day of January.

---

6   Wright, *The Continental Army*, p. 47.
7   Washington to John Hancock, 13 October 1777, Fitzpatrick, *Writings of Washington*, vol.9 (1933), pp.366–367 and Washington to Patrick Henry, 27 December 1777, vol.10 (1933), pp.208–209.
8   Washington to Continental Congress Conference Committee, 29 January 1778, Fitzpatrick, *Writings of Washington*, vol.10 (1933), pp.362–402.

This method, though not so good as that of obtaining Men for the war, is perhaps the best our circumstances will allow; and as we shall always have an established corps of experienced officers, may answer tolerably well. It is the only mode, I can think of, for completing our batalions in time, that promises the least prospect of success; the accomplishment of which is an object of the last importance; and it has this advantage, that the minds of the people being once reconciled to the experiment, it would prove a source of continual supplies hereafter.[9]

General Washington also spoke against state bounties and the use of substitutes, measures included in most 1778 levy laws.

In light of Washington's comments, it is interesting to note that the Revolutionary draft system had much in common with 1860's Union Army conscription. Both endeavours enjoyed a large proportion of volunteers or substitutes over drafted men, achieved by enlistment bounties, penalties apportioned to individuals or local governments, and varying degrees of community will. One source notes that the 1863 law was used 'to force volunteering,' a perhaps unintended outcome of the 1778 legislation, too.[10]

The 1778 Recruiting Acts

Thus, was conceived the first and possibly most successful Continental Army draft measure. On 26 February the Continental Congress resolved to require 11 states, South Carolina and Georgia excepted, 'to fill up by drafts from their militia, (or in any other way that shall be effectual,) their respective battalions of continental troops … That all persons drafted, shall serve in the continental battalions of their respective states for the space of nine months.' During spring and summer 1778 many states put into effect recruiting laws with varying degrees of success, some containing provisions for a draft. In this manner hundreds of men were added to army infantry regiments, many in time to take part in the June campaign and the Battle of Monmouth.[11]

The New Jersey Draft in Actuality

The New Jersey 'Act for the speedy and effectual recruiting of the four NewJersey Regiments in the Service of the United States,' passed by the General Assembly on 3 April, was typical of other states' levy legislation. The law's mainstay lay in procuring volunteers, drafts, or substitutes from the state militia to serve in New Jersey's Continental regiments. In order

9   Washington to Continental Congress Conference Committee, 29 January 1778, Fitzpatrick, *Writings of Washington*, vol.10 (1933), pp.362–402.
10   Eugene C. Murdock, *One Million Men: The Civil War Draft in the North* (Madison: The State Historical Society of Wisconsin, 1971), p.6; Edward A. Fitzpatrick, *Conscription and America: A Study of Conscription in a Democracy* (Milwaukee: Richard Publishing Co., 1940), pp.21, 25, 27.
11   Worthington Chauncey Ford (ed.), *Journals of the Continental Congress 1774-1789* (Washington: Government Printing Office, 1908), vol.X, 1778, pp.199–203.

to effect this, militia regiments were divided 'into Classes of eighteen Persons in each.' Any class that did not furnish a volunteer was 'to detach by Lot one Person … who shall, on his being mustered and approved, be entitled to the Bounty of Money and Cloaths … specified.' Only men involved in 'the making of Salt at the Pennsylvania SaltWorks' were exempted, and any person drafted to serve could procure a substitute 'within five Days from the said Allotment.' New Jersey levies served a 'Term of nine Months, unless sooner discharged, the said Term to be computed from the Date of his joining the Army.' Additionally,

> the Pay of every Person enlisted or detached as aforesaid, shall commence from the Day of Enlistment or Allotment … and he shall receive One Third of a Dollar by the Day as Subsistence Money, until he shall be mustered and marched to join his Regiment; and further, may enter into any Company of any one of the four Regiments of this State at his Choice, provided such Company be not complete.[12]

Three states' 1778 draft laws stipulated a clothing allotment. Maryland allotted their levies 'a full suit of cloaths.' New Jersey militiamen who volunteered within 10 days of mustering were to be given a bounty of 'Forty Dollars, together with the following Articles of Cloathing … a Blanket, a Hunting Frock, a Pair of Cloth Breeches, a Hat, a Shirt, a Pair of Stockings and a Pair of Shoes; and on the first Day of October next, if not sooner discharged, a regimental Coat, a Shirt, a Pair of Stockings and a Pair of Shoes.' North Carolina levies were to receive 'from the commanding Officer of the County [of origin] a Pair of Shoes and Stockings, two Shirts, a Hunting Shirt, Waistcoat with Sleeves, a Pair of Breeches and Trousers, a Hat and a Blanket, and Five Yards of Tent Cloth.'[13]

New Jersey regiments greatly needed men, and that state's draft particularly proved its worth. Never before during the war, except a brief period in 1776, were regimental strengths so high. At the end of the 1776 campaign, when the state's three-regiment contingent was briefly united at Ticonderoga, it comprised 1,355 soldiers; being late in the campaigning year the regiments were undoubtedly smaller than they were the preceding spring. In 1777, the number of Jersey regiments was increased from three to four. New Jersey brigade strength from May 1777 to July 1779 was as follows (nine-month levy numbers are included in the June 1778 to February 1779 returns):[14]

---

12 'Act for the speedy and effectual recruiting of the four New-Jersey Regiments in the Service of the United States,' 3 April 1778, Anon., *Acts of the General Assembly of the State of New-Jersey … begun at Trenton on the 28th Day of October 1777* (Burlington, N.J: Collins, 1778), pp.64–71.

13 Library of Congress (LOC): William Sumner Jenkins (ed.), *Records of the States of the United States of America: A Microfilm Compilation* (Washington, 1949), Session Laws, vol. B2, *Laws of Maryland Made and Passed at a Session of Assembly, Begun and held … on the seventeenth of March [1778]*, chapter V, 'An Act to procure troops for the American army,' 'Act for the speedy and effectual recruiting,' pp.64–71; LOC: Jenkins, *Records of the States.*, vol. B2, pp. 35, *Acts of Assembly of the State of North Carolina*, 14 April 1778, 'An Act for raising Men, to complete the continental Battalions belonging to this State.'

14 Continental Army returns, 1776–1783, in Charles H. Lesser, *Sinews of Independence: Monthly Strength Reports of the Continental Army* (Chicago: University of Chicago Press, 1976), pp.46, 50, 53, 54, 58, 68, 72, 80, 84, 88, 92, 96, 100, 104, 108, 112, 124.

Private, Massachusetts Grand American Army, 1775.

 At least 90 New Jersey nine-months levies are known to have worn their own clothing and equipment during their 1778 term of service. This a good example of how they may have looked, though the levies would have carried military cartridge pouches, rather than a hunting bag and powder horn. Illustration by Donna Neary, from Marko Zlatich, *New England Soldiers of the American Revolution* (Santa Barbara, CA: Bellerophon, 1993). (Reprinted courtesy of Bellerophon Books)

New Jersey Continental Line

Month and Year	Brigade Strength	Month and Year	Brigade Strength
May 1777	1,259	September 1778	1,683
October 1777	1,142	October 1778	1,678
November 1777	1,148	November 1778	1,690
December 1777	1,085	December 1778	1,772
January 1778	1,144	January 1779	1,658
May 1778	1,059	February 1779	1,624 – Quota Reduced to Three Regiments
June 1778	1,691	March 1779	1,114
August 1778	1,692	April 1779	1,082
		July 1779	1,075

These figures include men sick, deserted, or on detached duty. According to Brigadier General William Maxwell, his New Jersey brigade strength at the Battle of Monmouth on 28 June 1778 was 900, much less than the 1,691 shown on the June muster rolls. The 4 July return reveals 288 men sick, plus 108 on detached duty. Others may not yet have rejoined their units after serving in detached parties during the nine-day pursuit of the British columns.[15]

The efficacy of New Jersey's 1778 levy is most evident when compared with later years. In March 1779, 487 nine-month men were discharged. Post-1778 returns show a marked decline in New Jersey regiment troop numbers; total strength for each of the last four years was only slightly more than half the number of troops serving in August 1778. Just prior to the June 1783 dissolution New Jersey unit strengths fell to their lowest point.

New Jersey Continental Line[16]

Month & Year	Strength
June 1780	920 Three regiments
June 1781	852 Two regiments
June 1782	885 Two regiments
May 1783	832 One regiment and one battalion

New Jersey troop returns for April through August 1778 show an increase of 633 soldiers, still leaving shortfall of 1,271 men. A more detailed accounting taken directly from muster rolls shows 670 levies serving, an almost 40 percent increase in brigade field strength.

---

15   Anon. (ed.), 'Proceedings of a General Court Martial … for the Trial of Major General Lee. July 4th, 1778 …,' The Lee Papers, vol.III, 1778–1782, *Collections of the New-York Historical Society for the Year 1873* (New York: New-York Historical Society, 1874), John Brooks testimony, pp.143–156; Lesser, *Sinews of Independence*, p.72.

16   Lesser, *Sinews of Independence*, pp.168, 204, 228, 252.

1778: Number of Levies in the New Jersey Regiments[17]

Regiment	Total Number of Enlisted Men	Number of Levies	Levies in Proportion to the Whole
1st New Jersey	501	257	51.3%
2nd New Jersey	476	218	46.0%
3rd New Jersey	369	118	32.0%
4th New Jersey	325	77	23.5%
Total N.J. Levies: 670 (39.7% of the whole)			

Just how effective was the Jersey effort when compared to other states during the same period? As before stated, 11 states were required 'to fill up by drafts from their militia, (or in any other way that shall be effectual,) their respective battalions of continental troops.' Four states resorted to a draft, enjoying much the same success as New Jersey; six others, for various reasons, failed to gather any appreciable number of recruits through a levy or alternate method.[18] First, let us look at levy proportions in other Continental brigades, after which we will examine 1778 recruiting efforts state by state. The following numbers were extracted from a 'Return of Number of Men whose term of service will expire between the 27 October 1778 and the Spring':

Proportion of Nine-Month Levies in Eight Continental Brigades, October 1778[19]

Maryland: 1st. Brigade and 2nd. Brigade
3,558 men in 2 brigades, incl. 426 levies: 12% of whole

New Jersey
N.J. Brigade: 1,690 men, incl. 670 levies; 39.7%

New York: Clinton's Brigade
Clinton's Brigade: 1,130 men, incl. 313 levies; 27.8%

---

17   Sources for the 1778 New Jersey levy numbers and wartime regimental strength may be found in: '"The new Leveys are coming in dayly …": The Nine Month Draft in the Second New Jersey Regiment and Maxwell's New Jersey Brigade,' <https://www.academia.edu/95432677/_The_new_Leveys_are_ coming_in_dayly_The_Nine_Month_Draft_in_the_Second_New_Jersey_Regiment_and_Maxwells_ New_Jersey_Brigade_1778_>, appendix in John U. Rees, '"I Expect to be stationed in Jersey sometime …": An Account of the Services of the Second New Jersey Regiment, December 1777 to June 1778' (1994, unpublished TMs: copy held in the collections of the David Center, American Philosophical Society, Philadelphia, PA); NA: Rev. War Rolls, reels 55-62, 1st, 2nd, 3rd, and 4th New Jersey (Continental) muster rolls, 1778.

18   Ford, *Journals of the Continental Congress 1774–1789*, vol.X, 1778, pp.199–203.

19   NA: The Papers of the Continental Congress 1774–1789 (Microfilm Publications M247), Washington, DC (1958), reel 168, p.431, 'Head Qrs. Fredericksb.g 27:th Octobr. 1778 Return of the Number of Men whose term of Service will expire between this time and the Spring.'

Connecticut: Parson's Brigade[20]
1,877 men, incl. 204 levies; 39.7%

Massachusetts: Nixon's, Patterson's, and Learned's Brigades
(minus Wood's Levy Regt)
4,566 men in 3 brigades, incl. 1172 levies: 26 %

Wood's Regt of Massachusetts 9 Mo. Men: 349
Poor's Regt of Massachusetts 9 Mo. Men: 352[21]

Here we can see that levy proportions ranged from a high of 39.7 percent for the Connecticut and New Jersey brigades, to 12 percent for the Maryland division. Brigadier General James Clinton's New York brigade and the three Massachusetts brigades show healthy proportions of 26 and 27 percent respectively.

States that Relied on Previous Enlistment Laws

Four of the 11 states failed to enact special recruiting legislation, instead relying on the 1776–1777 acts enlisting men for three years or the war. While Pennsylvania, Delaware, Connecticut, and New Hampshire were all similar in this respect they differed in other ways.

Pennsylvania experienced severe recruiting shortfalls in 1778, so much so that during the summer three regiments from the state were disbanded and incorporated into senior units. On 18 April 1778 Major General John Armstrong informed the Pennsylvania State Council President, 'The Drafting of our Militia, in order to fill up the regular Regiments of the State however laudable that measure may be … is liable to the additional obstruction arising from the absence of a part of that Body which is to be drafted; I mean the Militia necessarily in the field.' This obstacle was never overcome, and the 27 October 1778 'Return of the Number of Men whose term of Service will expire between this time and the Spring' correctly noted of the state, 'All her troops inlisted for the War.' In a similar manner the single regiment from Delaware remained under-strength in 1778, gathering only a few new men. All Delaware's soldiers were 'inlisted for 3 Years or the War.' (The 27 October 1778 document hereafter will be referred to as the 'Term of Service' return.)[22]

Many Connecticut regiments were also undersize, and several combined for 1778 field service. Beginning the year with a two-thousand-man shortfall, the state relied on a 1777

---

20   Connecticut's levies were the result of a 1777 law 'detaching' militia soldiers for short-term service in Continental regiments.
21   Wood's and Poor's regiments served as state militia, not Continental troops.
22   Washington to Horatio Gates, 26 May 1778, Fitzpatrick, *Writings of Washington*, vol.11 (1934), p.459; NA: Rev. War Rolls, reel 80, 2nd Pennsylvania Regiment September 1778 returns (nine companies) September 1778; NA: Rev. War Rolls, reels 29–31, Delaware Regiment returns; Samuel Hazard (ed.), *Pennsylvania Archives* (Philadelphia: Joseph Severns & Co., 1853), vol.VI, pp.412–413; NA: PCC, October 1778, 'Term of Service' return.

statute that set recruiting quotas for selected towns, met by 'detaching' (drafting) men from the local militia to serve 10 months as Continental soldiers. Unfortunately, even with the threat of a draft, only 484 men enlisted in 1778, plus 248 detached militia, disappointing numbers compared to 1777, when a total of 4,019 men enlisted. The October 1778 return reflects the levies, noting 212 short-term soldiers in two Connecticut brigades.[23]

New Hampshire is the final state for which no special recruiting legislation can be found, though a study of the 1st Regiment muster rolls brings to light a puzzle. August 1778 returns for eight 1st New Hampshire companies reveal a solitary nine-month man. It is possible returns for the rest of the 1st Regiment's companies or the state's other regiments may contain more short-term men, though in the absence of any known draft legislation their presence is hard to explain. Whatever the case, the October 'Term of Service' return notes 27 New Hampshire soldiers due for discharge before spring 1779.[24]

Alternative Measures Adopted by Rhode Island and Virginia

Two states, Rhode Island and Virginia, passed special recruiting measures in 1778 but relied largely on laws outside the aegis of the February Continental Congress resolution. Rhode Island's Continental recruiting legislation (passed 28 May or shortly thereafter) made no mention of the enlistment term but did impose a levy of 839 men. This levy was apportioned to 24 towns in accordance with a computation that took into account taxes assessed on each and the number of 'fencible' men (i.e., suitable for military service) in their population. Any towns deficient in raising the required number were liable to a £30 penalty for each man less than their allotment. These levies were slated for state regiments, rather than the Continental units. A February 1778 law was enacted to augment the state's Continental contingent. That called for enlistment of 'Negro, Mulatto or Indian' enslaved men in the state's Continental forces; any enslaved men so accepted received their freedom. Unpopular with many residents, in early May the legislature set a 10 June 1778 cut-off date for slave recruiting. Just over 200 men, free and enslaved, veterans and new soldiers, joined the reformed 1st Rhode Island Regiment. From March 1778 to July 1780 that regiment was composed of Black and Indian private soldiers, led by White officers and non-commissioned officers.[25]

---

23   'An Act for raising and compleating the Quota of the Continental Army to be raise in this State,' Anon. (ed.), *The Public Records of the State of Connecticut, From October, 1776, to February, 1778* (Hartford: Lockwood & Brainard Company, 1894), pp.240–242; NA: PCC, October 1778, 'Term of Service' return.

24   NA: Rev. War Rolls (microfilm), reels, 43, 44, September 1778 returns, 1st New Hampshire Regiment; Jonathan Smith, 'How New Hampshire Raised Her Armies for the Revolution,' *The Granite Monthly: New Hampshire State Magazine*, vol. LIV (1922), pp.7–18; NA: PCC, October 1778, 'Term of Service' return.

25   'At the General Assembly … of the State of Rhode-Island … begun on the Second Monday in February,' 1778 (Attleborough, Ma.: S. Southwick, 1778), pp.14–17; 'State of Rhode-Island … in General Assembly, May second session, A.D. 1778,' begun 28 May 1778 (Attleborough, MA: S. Southwick, 1778), pp.3–5; 'State of Rhode-Island … in General Assembly, May first session, A.D. 1778,' begun 6 May 1778 (Attleborough, MA: S. Southwick, 1778), p.15; Daniel M. Popek, *They '… fought bravely, but were unfortunate': The True Story of Rhode Island's 'Black Regiment' and the Failure of Segregation in Rhode Island's Continental Line, 1777-1783* (Bloomington, In.: Authorhouse, 2015).

Virginia, too, desperately needed men. Approximately half the state's soldiers' service expired before summer 1778, and many were granted early discharges to encourage reenlistments. Historian John Sellers notes that beginning 'on January 21, the older veterans left the army literally by companies. Near the end of February, more than 1,350 … had returned to their homes, [with] … 400 more … expected to follow.' Initially Virginia relied on an earlier draft law to fill its 1778 troop quota. Enacted in October 1777, the measure called for counties to provide an allotment of one-year levies from the militia, the draft lottery to be held in February 1778, and the chosen men to travel north by the last day of March. A second law, passed in the 4 May 1778 session, called for 2,000 volunteers formed into four battalions 'who are to join the commander in chief of the American army when ordered by his Excellency the Governour.' Enlistments were to be accepted until 1 August and men were to serve to 1 January 1779. No record has been found of these units taking the field.[26]

The Virginia regiments did gain a number of levies, though not enough to fully satisfy needs. A 23 May 1778 'Return of Draughts and Substitutes from the State of Virginia' lists 799 men, including 42 deserters, and 41 'left upon the Road.'[27] In an attached note General Washington informed Governor Patrick Henry,

> None of the drafts made under the first [1777] Law are comprehended in the present return, nor can I ascertain what number of them ever reached Camp. I believe it was very inconsiderable and trifling … There is certainly something wrong, the drafts do not come on, and our condition is but very little better, from any new aids we have received, than it was before.[28]

On 10 June Washington complained to his brother John, 'Out of your first and Secd. draught by which we ought to have had upwards of 3500 Men for the Regiments … we have received only 1242 in all.' At month's end the general 'received information, that the State of Virginia has determined to fill up her Regiments by Recruits,' directing two field officers to return to Virginia 'to superintend the recruiting Service.' The October 'Term of Service' return shows 796 men whose enlistments would expire by spring 1779 in three Virginia brigades. During 1778, Virginia regiments were so reduced in troop strength several were amalgamated to compensate. The downward trend continued into 1779, when in May understrength regiments were combined again.[29]

---

26 John R. Sellers, *The Virginia Continental Line* (Williamsburg: Virginia Independence Bicentennial Commission, 1978), pp.42–43, 48–49; Hening, *Statutes of Virginia*, vol.IX, 'At a General Assembly … in the City of Williamsburg, on Monday the twentieth Day of October' 1777, ('An Act for speedily recruiting the Virginia Regiments on the continental establishment'), pp.337–341, 347; Hening, *Statutes of Virginia*, 'At a General Assembly … in the City of Williamsburg, on Monday the Fourth Day of May' 1778 ('An act for raising Volunteers to join the Grand Army'), pp.445–449.

27 Library of Congress (LOC): George Washington Papers, Presidential Papers Microfilm, Washington (1961), General Correspondence, 1697–1799, series 4, reel 49, 'Return of Draughts and Substitutes from the State of Virginia,' 23 May 1778.

28 Washington to Patrick Henry, 23 May 1778, Fitzpatrick, *Writings of Washington*, vol.11 (1934), pp.438–439.

29 Washington to John A. Washington, 10 June 1778, Fitzpatrick, and Washington to Holt Richardson and Ralph Faulkner, 1 July 1778; *Writings of Washington*, vol.12 (1934), pp.42–43, 139; NA: PCC, October 1778, 'Term of Service' return.

States that Enacted a Nine-Month Levy

Five of the 11 states authorized to enact a draft did in fact do so: New Jersey, Massachusetts, Maryland, New York, and North Carolina (these states also continued to enlist men under the 1776–1777 recruiting legislation).

Massachusetts likely enjoyed the greatest success in sheer numbers of levies procured. The 20 April 1778 Massachusetts law called for raising 2,000 levies, some serving in their own battalions, the remainder to augment the state's Continental regiments. Each county was to furnish a specific quota of new recruits; each 'town or plantation' would pay a £100 fine for every man under their allotted number. One document titled 'A List of the Men Raised … in the State of the Massachusetts Bay … for the Term of Nine Months' provides names and descriptions of every man drafted in 11 of 12 counties. Out of the 1,477 men listed only 16 are noted as discharged, rejected, or never appeared, leaving a shortfall of slightly more than 500 under the number called for. The October 'Term of Service' document lists 1,172 levies in three Massachusetts Continental brigades, plus Wood's and Poor's (militia) levy regiments, 796 strong, 'inlisted for 9 M[onth]s.' Colonel Ezra Wood's levies served with Nixon's Massachusetts Continental brigade from July 1778 to January 1779, mostly in the Hudson highlands, while Colonel Thomas Poor's levy regiment, sent to West Point in July, also ended its tour of duty with Nixon's brigade.[30]

The Maryland draft law was another success; General Washington remarked on 10 June, 'I should do injustice to the States of Maryland and New Jersey, were I not to add, that they are likely to get their Regiments nearly compleated.' While the data is incomplete, the proportion of levies to longterm soldiers (possibly as high as 38 percent) rivals New Jersey numbers. The 'Act to procure troops for the American army,' passed in late March 1778, called for raising 2,742 men, the numbers to be apportioned among the state's 18 counties. Among those drafted were 'Vagrants,' defined as 'every idle person above 18 years of age, who is able bodied and hath no fixed habitation, nor family, nor any visible means of getting an honest livelihood.' These men were given the choice of serving for nine months or receiving a bounty and enlisting for three years or during the war. Like in New Jersey, the levies were to be first supplied by volunteers (or vagrants) after which a draft was to be implemented. Included under this law was the German Battalion, composed of companies from Pennsylvania and Maryland, but wholly assigned to Maryland's establishment in 1778. Records show 88 levy substitutes joining the German Battalion between 20 May and 9 June; they were apportioned only to the Maryland companies. While several September regimental returns indicate a small proportion of levies, the documents did not include 189

---

30   LOC: Jenkins, State Records, Session Laws, vol. B2, pp.16–21, 'Resolve for filling up and compleating the fifteen battalions of Continental troops, directed to be raised in the State of Massachusetts-Bay' (passed 20 April 1778); NA: Rev. War Rolls, reel 42, section 913, Massachusetts Various Organizations, 'A List of the Men Raised … in the State of the Massachusetts Bay … for the Term of Nine Months …' (The levies from the County of Barnstable are apparently missing from this list); General Orders, 22 July 1778, Fitzpatrick, *Writings of Washington*, vol.12 (1934), pp.217–218; Lesser, *Sinews of Independence*, pp.84–86, 88–90, 92–94; NA: PCC, October 1778, 'Term of Service' return.

men of the 3rd Regiment 'detain at Philadelphia,' a detachment likely including new levies. The October 'Term of Service' return shows 426 levies in the two Maryland brigades.[31]

State of the 1st, 3rd and 5th Maryland Regiments (At White Plains, New York, September 1778)

Regiment	Number of NCOs & Rank and File	Number of Levies	Proportion of Levies
1st Maryland	353	57	16.2%
5th Maryland	384	73	19.0%
3rd Maryland	502	34	6.8%

New York enacted its draft legislation on 1 April 1778. In a manner similar to New Jersey, New York militia regiments were divided into 15-man classes, each of which was to supply one man to serve for nine months in the state's Continental regiments, and, like Massachusetts, Maryland, and New Jersey, New York's efforts were relatively successful. An examination of the September 1778 2nd Regiment muster rolls reveal 367 non-commissioned officers and rank and file in eight companies; this figure includes 164 nine-month levies, 44.7 percent of the regiment's enlisted strength. The October 'Term of Service' list shows 313 nine-month levies in Brigadier General James Clinton's New York brigade.[32] Some New York levies remained in their home state, Washington informing New York recruiting commissioner Jonathan Lawrence on 6 June,

> What Men are now upon their way to Easton may be sent from thence to join their Regiments now here. Those that remain in the State may, as you advise, be delivered as they are collected to Colo. Dubois's [5th] Regiment. That Regiment was much reduced by the loss it sustained at the Storm of Fort Montgomery and Col Gansevoort's [3rd Regiment] which is at Fort Schuyler is very full.[33]

The North Carolina draft also gathered large numbers of men, though the state's Continental regiments in the north benefited little. North Carolina units serving in Pennsylvania experienced such a lack of men that at Valley Forge in June 1778 eight regiments were disbanded

---

31   Washington to John Washington, 10 June 1778, Fitzpatrick, *Writings of Washington*, vol.12 (1934), pp. 42–43; LOC: Jenkins, State Records, *Laws of Maryland Made and Passed … on the seventeenth of March [1778]*, 'An Act to procure troops for the American army'; NA: Rev. War Rolls, reels 33, 34. September 1778 returns, 1st, 3rd, and 5th Maryland Regiments, reels 130, 131, 132, German Regiment returns; Arthur J. Alexander, 'How Maryland Tried to Raise Her Continental Quotas,' *Maryland Historical Magazine*, vol.42 (1977), pp.184–196; Henry J. Retzer, *The German Regiment of Maryland and Pennsylvania in the Continental Army, 1776-1781* (Westminster, MD: Family Line Publications, 1991), p.23; NA: PCC, October 1778, 'Term of Service' return.

32   LOC: Jenkins, State Records, Session Laws, vol. B2, pp.26–28, 'An Act for completing the five Continental Battalions, raised under the Direction of this State. Passed the 1st of April, 1778'; NA: Rev War Rolls, reels 67–68, September 1778 return, 2nd New York Regiment; NA: PCC, October 1778, 'Term of Service' return.

33   Washington to Jonathan Lawrence, 6 June 1778, Fitzpatrick, *Writings of Washington*, vol.12 (1934), p.26.

and the men dispersed to the two remaining regiments. At the same time considerable numbers of men were being gathered in North Carolina, where the 14 April draft legislation had called for the raising of 2,648 new levies 'to complete the continental Battalions belonging to this State.' These new recruits were not added to existing regiments but served in their own separate organizations. The 3rd North Carolina Regiment, raised in 1776, had been disbanded in early June at Valley Forge, and Colonels James Hogun and Thomas Polk were sent south to recruit new regiments. In July Colonel Hogun returned with a reconstituted 3rd Regiment comprised solely of levies. After the men were inoculated for smallpox at Carlisle, Pennsylvania, the regiment joined the main army in New York in early autumn and set to work on fortifications at West Point. In January 1779, after leaving a small detachment at Trenton, New Jersey, Hogun's troops joined the Philadelphia garrison. They remained in the city until 20 April 1779 when enlistments for most of the men expired.[34]

The October 1778 'term of Service' roster lists 733 North Carolina soldiers; besides numbers of two and a half, and three-year enlistees, whose time was almost up, that total included 529 3rd Regiment nine-month men.[35]

3rd North Carolina Regiment (Levies)[36] (West Point, New York)

Month	NCOs and Rank and File, Fit for Duty	Detached Duty, Sick, etc.	Total	Date of Return
September 1778	424	117	541	1 October
October 1778	354	175	529	1 November
November 1778	316	196	512	

In early December 1778 about 200 nine-month levies remaining in North Carolina, ill-armed and poorly equipped, marched south to join the army under Major General Robert Howe (later superseded by Major General Benjamin Lincoln). The detachment was still some distance from Savannah, Georgia, when, on 29 December, they learned of its fall. After this setback, furloughs for all levies remaining in North Carolina were cancelled, and the men assembled to reinforce Lincoln's troops. By February 1779 the North Carolina New Levies commanded by Colonel John Ashe had 438 men in camp at Purysburg, South Carolina. Late in February many men demanded to be allowed to return home as their period of service was near termination. As a result, the American force that moved into Georgia included

---

34   LOC: Jenkins, State Records, vol. B2, pp.3–5, *Acts of Assembly of the State of North Carolina*, 14 April 1778, 'An Act for raising Men, to complete the continental Battalions belonging to this State.'; Agreeable to the 26 February 1778 Continental Congress resolution the North Carolina levies were to be collected at two locations; those men raised 'in the Districts of Halifax, Edenton, Newbern, and Wilmington, shall march … to Petersburg in Virginia, and those who shall be raised in the Districts of Hillsborough and Salisbury, shall rendezvous at Peytonsburg in Pittsylvania [Virginia]'; Hugh F. Rankin, *The North Carolina Continentals* (Chapel Hill: University of North Carolina Press, 1971), pp.146–147, reduction in the North Carolina Line Regiments; 162–163, 164–166, new levies; 178–181, 183–184; Rankin's work is invaluable, but he incorrectly names Hogun's 1778 northern levy 3rd Regiment as the 7th North Carolina.

35   NA: PCC, October 1778, 'Term of Service' return.

36   Lesser, *Sinews of Independence*, pp.84–86, 88–90, 92–94.

only 200 levies serving as light infantry. After some manoeuvring the Americans were defeated on 3 March at Briar Creek, the levies taking no part in the action. In late March Brigadier General Jethro Sumner joined Lincoln's forces at Black Swamp with 759 nine-month men returned from furlough. These men were organized into two regiments, the 4th and 5th North Carolina, participating in efforts to oust the British from South Carolina during summer 1779. At the indecisive Battle of Stono River on 20 June the North Carolina levies suffered 10 killed and 31 wounded. The remainder of their term was spent harassing British forces in the area. On 3 July 1779 the first detachment of levies, comprised of 202 'sick and weak' men, left for home; the remaining nine-month men followed on 10 July.[37]

Mustering and Joining the Regiments

A short time after the New Jersey special recruiting law was passed in April 1778, provisions for a draft were put into effect. Militia regiments were mustered the same month and divided into 18-man classes. The actual mechanics of the New Jersey draft lottery is unknown. Pennsylvania citizens chosen for militia service in 1777 were 'Serv'd with notice according to Law'; in several instances notices were given to a man's wife, 'left at his lodging,' or 'left with his Negro.'[38]

Massachusetts men drafted in 1778 were sent notifications, as follows:

> To Mr. James Cook
> Sir. With the advice of the Military Officers Select men and Committee of this Town you are Draughted to do Eight months Sarvice in the Continantal Army from this Date; and you are to furnish your Self for Camp and be in reddiness forthwith to Muster and to March When and Where Ordered or otherwise you are to pay a fine fifteen pounds in Twenty four hours from the time of your being Draughted – [39]
> New Salem April 17th 1778   William Page

Historian Paul Lutz noted that some officials were sympathetic when men gave good reason for not serving. In one case drafted New York farmer Joseph Depuy explained his failure to serve as

> solely owning to these Reasons, Viz.: He having Last Year Met with the Misfortune of Loosing his Barn by a Flash of Lightning, and with Much Difficulty and Hard Labour got the Timber for a New Barn which at the time of his being ordered out, wanted four Days work of a Carpenter … and said Carpenter Could by No Means Stay Longer with him and if did not imbrace the then oppertunity had Not the

---

37   Rankin, *North Carolina Continentals*, pp.186–209.
38   Thomas Lynch Montgomery (ed.), *Pennsylvania Archives* (Harrisburg: Harrisburg Publishing Co., 1906), 6th series, vol. I, pp.53–56; Six 1777 Philadelphia militia returns noted 'Proper Notices' delivered or attempted to the men listed. Roach, 'The Pennsylvania Militia in 1777,' p.165.
39   Paul V. Lutz, 'Greetings, or, Do I Feel a Draught?', *American Heritage*, vol.17, no.5 (August 1966), p.112.

Least prospect of Having a Barn this Season and further Says that his Wife was very ill and himself very Subject to the Rheumetism [40]

Initially Depuy was fined £15, but the court record stated, 'The Governor Considering the Case of Joseph Depuy & his late Misfortunes remits the Punishment.'[41]

After the volunteers, drafts, and substitutes were collected they were probably given a short time to put their affairs in order, after which small detachments were formed, descriptive lists compiled, and the men sent on to join their units. Militia officers were appointed to conduct the New Jersey levies to camp where they were received and signed for by the state recruiting agent. Since half of the New Jersey Brigade was at Valley Forge, Pennsylvania, and the remainder stationed in New Jersey, state authorities decided that recruits could join at either location, and in any Jersey regiment they chose.[42]

Having enrolled in one of the four New Jersey regiments, the new men were distributed among each unit's eight companies in preparation for the upcoming campaign. The 1st Regiment left Valley Forge for New Jersey on 8 May to join the 2nd New Jersey Regiment, which had been in their home state since late March. The 3rd and 4th Regiments marched from Valley Forge on the 26th, and the New Jersey Brigade was reunited at or near Mount Holly before month's end.[43]

These experiences were exciting for the men, so much so that in later years some former levy soldiers seeking pensions left vivid accounts of their 1778 service, several quite long, most brief vignettes, many giving details that would otherwise have been lost. One man, Benjamin Peachey, was 'enlisted under a Capt [Jonathan] Beasley who was a recruiting officer, and from whom he was transfered to another Capt[ain] whose name he has now forgot and from whom he was transfered to Capt Wooling [Thomas Walling, New Jersey militia?] and all the time in the Regt. commanded by Col. Isreal Shreve.' First New Jersey levy Joseph Stull 'enlisted for his class who had to furnish a man for the term by requisition'; he 'was enrolled at Somerville and joined the army at Valley Forge.' Philip Hornbaker remembered, 'A man was drafted to serve in the Militia nine months but I cannot recollect his name, I went for this man as a substitute in a company commanded by Captain John Petty … and was in the battle at Monmouth Court House,'[44] and Cornelius Rickey stated that

40   Lutz, 'Greetings', p.112.
41   Lutz, 'Greetings', p.112.
42   State Archives (NJ): Rev. War Mss. reel 5798831909, doc. #3646. 'A Descriptive Roll of Volunteers … from the first Regiment of Salem County Militia …'; Fitzpatrick, *Writings of Washington*, Washington to Israel Shreve, 23 May 1778, vol.11 (1934), p.436.
43   Locations of the four New Jersey regiments in May 1778 are discussed in the chapters titled 'Reinforcements and Alarms: The Actions of Brigadier General William Maxwell and the Remainder of the Jersey Brigade, May 7 to May 24, 1778,' <https://www.academia.edu/95630652/2nd_New_Jersey_Regiment_Section_B_20_March_to_24_May_1778_I_Expect_to_be_stationed_in_Jersey_sometime_A_Narrative_History_of_the_Second_New_Jersey_Regiment_December_1777_to_June_1779> and 'The Jersey Brigade is Reunited: May 28 to June 19, 1778,' <https://www.academia.edu/95486062/Section_C_of_I_Expect_to_be_stationed_in_Jersey_sometime_A_Narrative_History_of_the_Second_New_Jersey_Regiment_December_1777_to_June_1779> in Rees, 'I Expect to be stationed in Jersey sometime …', pp.50–55, 67–69.
44   NA: Revolutionary War Pension and Bounty-Land Warrant Application Files (Microfilm Publication

about the last of April in the year 1778 being sixteen or seventeen years old … [he] entered the service … as a substitute and a private soldier, hired for nine months by a class of eighteen, and was then living in Bernards town Somerset County, New Jersey. He joined the [3rd Jersey Regiment] … when it was stationed at Valley Forge … In about three weeks … the American army began its march to English town N.J.[45]

John Ackerman recalled enlisting

on the 18 of May [1778] with Christopher Van Deventer, Garlin Ackerman, Enoch Dunham, John Overt, George Overt, John Vreeland, Isaac Blanchard, Garret Nephis, and served in the first Jersey Regiment … he first marched after enlisting from Brunswick to Foster town near Mt Holly from thence to English town where he arrived on Saturday preceeding the Battle of Monmouth, and from thence to the Battle[46]

While the new men began joining the New Jersey regiments in early May, the greatest number (530) arrived between 21 May and 14 June; one man reached the brigade on 26 August 1778, and the last levy, William Strong, did not join until April 1779.[47]

New Jersey Brigade Tally for Joining from May to August 1778[48]
(612 levies accounted for out of 670 total)
40 levies joined between 1 May to 20 May (inclusive)
533 levies joined between 21 May and 14 June
39 levies joined between 15 June to 26 August

Levies' Prior Service

The 1778 levies' prior military service depended somewhat upon their home state, but among the new men there was a leavening of Continental Army and militia veterans. Since the draft was generally based on enrolled militia, most of that state's nine-month men had served in the militia for brief terms, including some combat experience. An examination of 266 New Jersey levy pension depositions reveals 26 former levies (9.5 percent) claiming prior service in the Continental Army. The breakdown of levies with pre-1778 non-militia military experience was 19 men who served in the 1776 New Jersey battalions (eight in the 1st Jersey, one with the 2nd Jersey, and 10 with the 3rd), two with Thompson's Rifle Battalion

M804), Records of the Department of Veterans Affairs, Record Group 15, Nos. S35552, S23953, and S2363.

45   NA: Revolutionary War Pension and Bounty Files, No. S4096.

46   NA: Revolutionary War Pension and Bounty Files, No. S16028.

47   NA: Rev. War Rolls, reels 55–62, 1st to 4th New Jersey muster rolls, 1778; NA: Revolutionary War Pension and Bounty Files, No. S33753.

48   Rees, "'The new Leveys are coming in dayly …'" <https://www.academia.edu/95432677/_The_new_Leveys_are_coming_in_dayly_The_Nine_Month_Draft_in_the_Second_New_Jersey_Regiment_and_Maxwells_New_Jersey_Brigade_1778_>.

in 1775, one each with the 3rd and 5th Pennsylvania Battalions, and one with the 1st New York Battalion, all in 1776, plus one as an artificer and one with the Pennsylvania State Navy.[49]

Twenty-three-year-old weaver Frederick Van Lew was typical, joining the 2nd New Jersey as a substitute on 28 May 1778, listed as a deserter in November, returned the next month, and discharged on 28 February 1779. In 1775 Van Lew lived on Long Island and served one month in the New York militia.[50] On a visit to his family in New Jersey he enlisted for five months in an unnamed regiment, claiming service at the Battle of Long Island where,

> we had a tight engagement and there we had to swim a tide mill pond and many of our men drowned in crossing the pond, [he] lost his rifle & coat in swimming the pond, after crossing the pond we went to Cobble hill Fort about half or three quarters of a mile distant ... and there joined the army again.[51]

Van Lew described his participation in the Battle of White Plains, and of the Fort Lee evacuation he noted being on guard and discovering,

> the River full of the boats of Brittish and as they landed deponent with his men fired and immediately run for Fort Lee, when we came to the Fort [General] Washington had left ... with his Army, for Hackinsack in New Jersey, and only about seventy men remained at the Fort of str[a]ggling appearance drinking liquor that was left by the sutlers, deponent and his men filled their Cantines & left the Fort and went after the Army[52]

Also claiming service in the Trenton and Princeton actions, Van Lew noted 'after the [Princeton] battle was over, [he] left the Army and went to his Brothers in Montgomery Township [Somerset County, New Jersey].' During 1777 he 'became attached to the Militia ... which was Classed One half went out for one month and then was relieved by the other half, and so Alternately until the Close of the War, but deponent Enlisted for nine months [in 1778] ... in the State troops and joined Washingtons Army.'[53]

Other men had interesting tales to tell. First New Jersey Regiment levy Joseph Stull said his,

> first militia service ... he thinks was in the year 1776 ... Was another tour out under Capt. [Jacob] Ten Eyck and marched to Germantown in Pennsylvania, was in the battle at Germantown. attacked a picket at Chestnut hill, near Armitage tavern ...

---

49   John U. Rees, "'From thence to the Battle ...': Gleanings from the Pension Depositions of the Soldiers of the New Jersey Brigade for 1778,' <https://www.academia.edu/95318810/_From_thence_to_the_ Battle_Gleanings_from_the_Pension_Depositions_of_New_Jersey_Brigade_Soldiers_Serving_ in_1778>.
50   NA: Revolutionary War Pension and Bounty Files, No. 23035.
51   NA: Revolutionary War Pension and Bounty Files, No. 23035.
52   NA: Revolutionary War Pension and Bounty Files, No. 23035.
53   NA: Revolutionary War Pension and Bounty Files, No. 23035.

Lieut. [John] Brokaw of the same Company was killed by deponent's side on the ground near the British picket... [He] enlisted for nine months ... in the spring of the year 1778 ... was enrolled at Somerville and joined the army at Valley Forge. He enlisted for his class who had to furnish a man for the term by requisition. [54]

Twenty-eight-year-old Elijah Holcomb (4th New Jersey) enlisted in the 5th Pennsylvania Battalion in February 1776, participated in the Battle of Long Island, and was captured at Fort Washington in November, later making 'his escape across the North River by swimming to a boat in the River.'[55] Philip Hornbaker (a.k.a. Baker, 2nd New Jersey Regiment)

enlisted at Carlisle in the state of Pennsylvania in the spring or summer of ... 1775 ... in the rifle company commanded by Capt Wm. Hendrickson [Hendricks, Thompson's Rifle Battalion] ... marched in said company from Carlisle to Boston ... remained a few months and then were marched for Quebeck in Canada under the command of Col [Benedict] Arnold and [Daniel] Morgan ... after their arrival on Abrahams plains they were joined by Genl. [Richard] Montgomery ... he was in the attack of Quebec when his captain was killed and him the said deponent received a shot in the neck and was taken prisoner and retained until the spring[56]

At least one levy, 24-year-old George Sinclair, saw sea service. In September 1776 Sinclair,

at Philadelphia ... entered the service of the United States ... to serve on board the Frigate Washington commanded by Captain Thomas Reed for ... one year as a common sailor... after [receiving a] ... discharge [he] entered ... as a common sailor to serve during one year on board the [Pennsylvania State Navy] fire ship called the Hell Cat commanded by Captain Robert French / the Hell Cat was burnt at Mud Island fort [Fort Mifflin on the Delaware River] ... [he enlisted] a few weeks after [that] ... for one year as a steward on board of the ship of war [Pennsylvania State Navy guard boat or half-galley] called the Repulse at Mud Island fort ... about two months after [he joined] ... this ship together with the remainder of the american fleet there situated were abandoned & burnt by the Americans.[57]

---

54   NA: Revolutionary War Pension and Bounty Files, No. S41654.
55   NA: Revolutionary War Pension and Bounty Files, No. S2363.
56   NA: Revolutionary War Pension and Bounty Files, No. S23953.
57   NA: Revolutionary War Pension and Bounty Files, No. S40438; Thomas Reed was appointed captain on 6 June 1776 of one of 'four ships building in Philadelphia,' his appointment to the frigate *Washington* was confirmed on 12 June 1776. The *Washington* was launched 7 August 1776, William James Morgan (ed.), *Naval Documents of the American Revolution*, vol.5 (Washington, DC: Government Printing Office, 1970), pp.397–398, 497, 1020n; John W. Jackson, *The Pennsylvania Navy, 1775-1781: The Defense of the Delaware* (New Brunswick, NJ: Rutgers University Press, 1974), pp.20, 197, 340, 343, 348.

New Jersey Levies Monmouth Battle and Subsequent 1778–1779 Service

On 28 June 1778 the opposing armies met at Monmouth Courthouse. New Jersey troops played a minor role in the battle, marching in the morning with Major General Charles Lee's advance force, and then countermarching towards Englishtown without firing a shot. Despite that, some Jersey casualties were incurred during the withdrawal and subsequent afternoon cannonade.[58]

First Jersey private David Cooper recounted Lee's advance and retreat; 'On the morning of the Battle we were marched within a Mile of Monmouth [and] there changed our direction & Marched to the ground where the battle was fought.' He recorded the New Jersey Brigade's position in the main battle line during the afternoon cannonade: 'we were placed on the extreme Left & in the rear of the first lines where we remained during the action & then we went back to Englishtown.'[59] John Ackerman, 1st Regiment, remembered,

> his regement on that day was ordered by the Colo[nel] to retreat which was effected by passing through a morass [at Spotswood Middle Brook] in which he lost his shoes – After retreating through this morass, his regement came to the road just as the troops under the immediate command of Gen Washington were passing – Gen Washington halted his troops, and the retreating Regement was immediately paraded having become disordered in retreating through the [morass] He well recollects that Gen Washington on that occasion asked the troops if they could fight and that they answered him with three cheers[60]

Among other things, James Jordan claimed to have witnessed the famous confrontation between General Lee and General Washington, recalling,

> they were led on by Maxwell to attack the left Wing of the British and had a very severe engagement / this was probably about eight or nine OClock in the morning [we] had no breakfast nor any thing to eat that day / the engagement was continued for some time when a retreat was ordered and fought all the way as they retreated back towards and past the Court House at Montmouth / After we had passed the Court House a little we were met by Gen. Washington who came up with the Main Army riding a White Horse this petitioner was within a yard of him and heard him address Gen. Lee by asking him 'What is this you have been about to day'[61]

Several men told of wounds and immediate post-battle doings. William Todd, 2nd New Jersey Regiment, stated he 'received a wound from a Musket ball in his thigh during the

---

58   John U. Rees, "'They answered him with three cheers …'": New Jersey Brigade Losses in the Monmouth Campaign, 17 June to 6 July 1778,' <https://www.academia.edu/105623113/_They_answered_him_with_three_cheers_New_Jersey_Brigade_Losses_in_the_Monmouth_Campaign_17_June_to_6_July_1778>.
59   NA: Revolutionary War Pension and Bounty Files, No. S809.
60   NA: Revolutionary War Pension and Bounty Files, No. S16028.
61   NA: Revolutionary War Pension and Bounty Files, No. W8225.

Engagement.' In a supporting deposition his brother, George, recalled that at the time of the Monmouth battle he 'was a soldier in the Militia, and understanding that his brother … was Killed in the battle he went in pursuit of him the day after and found him at English Town about one mile & a half from the Battle Ground on duty as a soldier.' Samuel Leonard did not fare so well, having 'received a severe wound in that battle the twenty eighth of June: that on account of the said wound he was Confined to the hospital for about Eight months, that on the fifth day of March [1779] … he was honorably discharged'. Muster rolls confirm Leonard was sick absent at Morristown from July 1778 to January 1779. Nathaniel Lyon, a 4th New Jersey levy, related that 'Gen. Maxwell's brigade was not much exposed during the fighting. The night of the battle [he] … was detached to assist in burying the dead, & the morning after was ordered to Princeton in charge of the sick. Remaining at Princeton about a week he went to join his company at Elizabethtown.' Frederick Van Lew was both succinct and comprehensive in his account: 'Washington Attacked them at Monmouth, and gain[ed] the victory over them it was on sunday the hotest day he ever knew remained there two days after the battle, and then left there for Elizabeth Town.' At least eight New Jersey levies were listed as casualties during the Monmouth campaign and battle – three wounded, three captured, and two missing. All five captured and missing men returned to their regiments between mid-July and October 1778.[62]

Save for British foraging operations around Hackensack in late September the remainder of the men's enlistment was relatively uneventful, spent garrisoning a line from Newark to Spanktown, with Elizabethtown at the centre. Peter Doty noted, 'a day or two after the Battle [they] Marched under General Maxfield to Elizabethtown … [and] they went into the Barrax where he remained untill his nine months expired.' James Jordan 'with his regiment, marched to Elizabeth Town … [they] lay there until Fall [when] The second regiment of the Jersey Blues … was ordered to New Ark in [New Jersey] … to Winter Quarters.'[63] Levy William Todd told of being,

> Engaged while laying [at Elizabethtown] … in one or two skirmishes with the British … remembers while there of his being selected as one who was sent over on Staten Island to take possession of a number of Guns Drums &c. of the British. After leaving Elizabeth Town marched with the Army to Hackinsack above New Ark … The British at this time had possession of New York dont recollect how long he was stationed at Hackensack but remembers while there they had several brushes with the British [64]

The majority of levies were discharged in late February or March 1779, but at the moment of their departure the British staged a surprise attack on Elizabethtown in an unsuccessful attempt to capture New Jersey Governor William Livingston. One man recalled the event in

---

62   NA: Revolutionary War Pension and Bounty Files, Nos. W6295, S554, W9510; John U. Rees, 'New Jersey Brigade Losses in the Monmouth Campaign, 17 June to 6 July 1778', <https://www.academia. edu/105623113/_They_answered_him_with_three_cheers_New_Jersey_Brigade_Losses_in_the_ Monmouth_Campaign_17_June_to_6_July_1778>.

63   NA: Revolutionary War Pension and Bounty Files, Nos. S18382 and W8225.

64   NA: Revolutionary War Pension and Bounty Files, No. W6295.

old age; Leonard Critzer was discharged at 'Elizabeth town … the last day of Feb. 1779 / on the following Morning [was] attacked by the enemy and drove them into their boats and left the service and returned home.'[65]

In an odd exception to the rule, William Strong was listed on the muster rolls as beginning his nine-month service on 1 April 1779. Strong's enlistment was delayed for some reason, as noted in his pension statement: 'he entered the Continental service under Captain [John] Hollinshead in the second Jersey Regiment … he joined the Regiment at Newwark … he was under General Maxfield and … under [Major] General [John] Sullovan he [went on] the [1779] Indian expedeten … he served nine Months.'[66]

Besides the Monmouth campaign New Jersey levies served in many capacities during their nine-month service. Levy Jabez Bigalow must have had previous musical experience, having been appointed drum major to the 3rd Jersey Regiment within three months of his enlistment, and John Vreeland stated that 'he was [a] Cattridge [cartridge] maker' when he served with the 1st Regiment. The most common occupations were guard duty and being sent 'on command' (detached service) to various locations in New Jersey. Specialized tasks included service with the flag boat at Elizabethtown used for communicating with the enemy in New York. The levies' other activities were quite varied, including doing duty 'at the Governor's' at the brigade hospital, serving with the artillery as drivers, cutting wood, assisting the forage master, working as armorers or artificers (military craftsmen), working as the bullock guard, waggoners, or making rope, 'riding for the General,' and serving as waiters to officers and staff including Reverend Andrew Hunter, New Jersey Brigade chaplain.[67]

Most New Jersey levies, 71.8 percent, were discharged at the end of their nine-month enlistment; desertions and reenlistments each accounted for 9.86 percent of the men, while 1.5 percent died in service. Of the 670 Jersey Brigade levies the fate of 37 (5.7 percent) remains unknown.[68]

New Jersey Brigade Strength, August 1778

1,690 enlisted men (670 nine-month men, 1,020 long-term soldiers) Levies comprised 39.7 percent of the whole.	
Numbers of Levies Known to Have Left the Brigade through Discharge, Desertion or Other Specific Causes	
Discharged from service	481, most in February and March 1779
Deserted	66
Died in service	10
Wounded	2, in June 1778

65   NA: Revolutionary War Pension and Bounty Files, No. S9251; NA: Revolutionary War Pension and Bounty Files, No. S43216.
66   NA: Revolutionary War Pension and Bounty Files, No. S33753.
67   John U. Rees, '"I Expect to hear the Enemy are on the Move …": The New Jersey Brigade, July 1778 to June 1779,' <https://www.academia.edu/95385503/_I_Expect_to_hear_the_Enemy_are_on_the_Move_The_New_Jersey_Brigade_July_1778_to_June_1779>.
68   Rees, 'The new Leveys are coming in dayly …,' pp.29–31, <https://www.academia.edu/95432677/_The_new_Leveys_are_coming_in_dayly_The_Nine_Month_Draft_in_the_Second_New_Jersey_Regiment_and_Maxwells_New_Jersey_Brigade_1778_>.

Missing in action	2, in June 1778
Captured by the enemy	3, in June 1778
Reenlisted in the New Jersey Brigade for three years or the war	66
Discharged in February, reenlisted for the war in March	1
Reenlisted in the light dragoons	2
Unknown	37

Reenlistment and New Jersey Post-1778 Service

Early on, Continental Army commanders entertained hopes that numbers of levies could be persuaded to reenlist for a longer term. New Jersey Brigadier General William Maxwell wrote General Washington in mid-June 1778,

> I believe we could Enlist several of the 9 Months Men during the War but considering appearances at present and what they are to receive at the end of the war, I do not think there is any advantage in the proposal; they will have 20 Dollars in hand, no more, & 100 Acres of land at the End of the war, which may possably end before their 9 months is out.[69]

In September the commander in chief wrote to Congress regarding bounties and other inducements:

> Tho' it is not expressed in the Resolution of [31 August] … that any other bounty is to be given to the Men who engage for three years or during the War, than Twenty Dollars, I shall take it for granted they are to receive the usual allowances of Cloathing and Land. There are several Continental Troops, whose time of service will expire at the end of the fall or during the Winter. I … shall direct every necessary measure to be taken to reinlist them. From the exorbitant State, Town and Substitute bounties, I am very doubtful whether Twenty Dollars will be found sufficient to engage so great a proportion, either of the Draughts or Continentals, as was at first apprehended. Our failure in the enterprise against Rhode Island will have its weight and every day, from the approach of the fall and Winter, will add new difficulties. As it is a work of the most essential importance, I will order it to be begun, the instant the Money arrives; and lest on experiment, the sum should prove too small, I would submit it to Congress, whether it will not be expedient to pass another Resolve, authorising a further bounty of Ten Dollars, to be used as circumstances may make it necessary. This can remain a secret, and will not be carried into execution, but in case of evident necessity.

---

69   LOC: GW Papers, series 4, reel 49, William Maxwell to George Washington, 14 June 1778.

I feel very much interested upon the occasion, and have submitted this mode, that there may not be the least possible delay, in attempting to engage the men under a second expedient, if the first should not succeed.[70]

Several states made efforts to retain their levies. In early November 1778 Colonel Josias Hall, 4th Maryland Regiment, sent Washington a 'Return of the Drafts and Substitutes Inlisted in the Second Maryland Brigade,' listing 10 levies, all from his unit, who had signed on for three years: one on 30 May, one in June, four in July, two in August, one in October, and one in November. Hall noted, 'Agreable to your Excellency's Instructions I have sent a Return of the Draughts inlisted in the 2nd. Brig[ade]: … None of the Regts have recruited any but the 4th and they only two since they received the Money. In recruiting we are confined to our respective Regts & the 4th have no more Draughts worth the Bounty.'[71]

The 'Octobr. 1778 Return of the Number of Men whose term of Service will expire between this time and the Spring' notes for New Jersey, 'No return but General Maxwell is supplied with money to inlist as many as possible.' Colonel Israel Shreve later recalled, 'In November 1778 at Elizabeth Town I drew money to recruit Nine months men whose times were nearly out.'[72] In the event, only 10 percent of the New Jersey men decided to reenlist; other states were no more successful.

New Jersey Nine-Month Levies Reenlisted for Three Years or the War[73]

Organization	Number of Levies Reenlisted	Percentage of Levies Who Served
1st New Jersey Regiment	2	0.78% (of 257 levies in the regiment)
2nd New Jersey Regiment	48	22% (of 218 levies in the regiment)
3rd New Jersey Regiment	11	9.33% (of 118 levies in the regiment)
4th New Jersey Regiment	5	6.50% (of 77 levies in the regiment)
New Jersey Brigade	67	10% (670 levies total)

Muster rolls testify to the presence of former levies with the Jersey Continentals until war's end. Several left accounts of their experiences. Jacob Hall, approximately 22 years old when he enlisted in 1778, served as a levy in the 4th New Jersey, reenlisted and was transferred to the 2nd Regiment in February 1779, serving 'untill the Battle of Springfield in

---

70   Washington to the President of Congress, 5 September, Fitzpatrick, *Writings of Washington*, vol.12 (1934), pp.402–403.

71   LOC: GW Papers, series 4, reel 53, Josias Hall to Washington, 3 November 1778 (with enclosure), 'Return of the Drafts and Substitutes Inlisted in the Second Maryland Brigade, Commanded by Josias C. Hall Esquire, Colonel Commandant November 3rd 1778.'

72   NA: PCC, October 1778, 'Term of Service' return; NA: Revolutionary War Rolls, reel 57, section 23, Israel Shreve to Congress, 30 December 1786.

73   Rees, 'The new Leveys are coming in dayly …,' p.33 <https://www.academia.edu/95432677/_ The_new_Leveys_are_coming_in_dayly_The_Nine_Month_Draft_in_the_Second_New_Jersey_ Regiment_and_Maxwells_New_Jersey_Brigade_1778_>.

June 1780 – was wounded in that Battle and has ever since been unable to work.'[74] Fifteen-year-old James Kirkpatrick,

> in the spring of 1778 ... joined the troops at Mount Holly ... enlisted in Capt. Patterson's company in the 3rd New Jersey in the fall of the year 1778 as a Fifer and continued to serve in that Regiment until it was reduced, when he was transferred to the first Jersey Regiment and continued to serve in it as Drummer [he became a drummer in January 1780] until he was discharged at New Burgh.[75]

Many 1778 levies went on to serve in other military capacities. Isaac Childs told of serving,

> on board of the ship called the retaliation Captain Decater from Philidelphia she carried 2 doublefortifyed 12 pounders in her bow 1 14 pounder in her waist and two swivels aft [Stephen Decatur (1752-1808) commanded the six-gun galley Retaliation, May to November 1779] / cruised on the coast between new York and Philadelphia we took a schooner call'd the Yankey Wich and another call'd the Polly Sly; We took a merchant ship from England and put a prize master on board of her at that moment a Brittish man of war hove in sight and bore down upon us and we made our escape.[76]

Soon after his enlistment expired Cornelius Rickey moved to Northumberland County, Pennsylvania, 'a frontier county' and served in 1779 and 1780 as a ranger against the British and their Indian allies. In 1780 Leonard Critzer 'again entered the service as a waggoner attached to Samuel Hunts waggon Brigade and served in that Capacity one year.' And following his discharge Peter Covert travelled south, later participating with 'a detachment of Virginia militia at York town at the siege of Cornwallis where I served three months.'[77]

Other States' Levies

Only one pension deposition of a New Hampshire levy has been found, but that man's experience mirrors several Massachusetts short-term men in that he joined his regiment after the Battle of Monmouth. John Palmer, 1st New Hampshire Regiment (one of 27 likely New Hampshire nine-month men), enlisted 26 April and,

> joined the army at a place called the White Plains in the State of New York sometime in the month of ... July ... during said time I was at Danbury & Hartford in the State of Connecticut and went into winter quarters at a place called Reding in

---

74   NA: Revolutionary War Pension and Bounty Files, No. S34909.
75   NA: Revolutionary War Pension and Bounty Files, No. W4008.
76   NA: Revolutionary War Pension and Bounty Files, No. R1918.
77   NA: Revolutionary War Pension and Bounty Files, Nos. S4096, S9251, S43340; Charles E. Claghorn, *Naval Officers of the American Revolution: A Concise Biographical Dictionary* (Metuchen, NJ: The Scarecrow Press, 1988), p.87.

that state. At the end of the nine months I received my pay and a pass to return home to New Hampshire.[78]

It is not certain whether any Massachusetts levies participated in the Monmouth campaign, though 11 of that state's regiments were with Washington's army in New Jersey. Several Massachusetts levy pensions have been discovered. Josiah Barnes enlisted in May 1778 for nine months' service,

> was mustered ... and marched to Fishkill in the state of New York where he joined the main Army – He belonged to Capt [Japhet] Daniels Company [6th Massachusetts Regiment; his entire regiment was not at Monmouth] ... He was at West Point at White Plains and at Nine Partners so called in the state of New York during said Term of service.[79]

Darius Holbrook, also with Daniels' Company, 6th Massachusetts, 'in the latter part of May 1778 at ... Mendon ... he enlisted as a soldier in the Continental line for the term of nine months and immediately marched to the town of Worcester ... and then met other troops.'[80] From there,

> he marched to the town of Fishkill ... where he was mustered & joined the army at the White Plains ... [he] served in the ... regiment commanded by Col [Thomas] Nixon, he then marched to West Point and there remained and in the vicinity guarding the lines betwixt the two armies until sometime in the month of December at which time he went into winter quarters & marched to the highlands so called at the East of West Point & there remained until February following.

Levy Caleb Holbrook, a likely relation, served in the same company.[81]

Most New York levies joined their regiments in time to participate in the Monmouth campaign and battle. Five of 18 New York levy pensioners indicate service in Major General Charles Lee's Advanced Corps of picked men, naming as commanders the Marquis de Lafayette, Charles Lee, or Colonel Henry Livingston, the latter of whom commanded a provisional battalion under Lee during the 28 June action. Second New York levy private Garret Constable's brief remark 'he was in the Battle of Monmouth ... in which he discharged twelve Rounds,' places him at the hedgerow holding action under Colonel Livingston or with Cilley's battalion at the late-day Sutfin Farm combat.[82]

---

78   NA: Revolutionary War Pension and Bounty Files, No. S41050.
79   NA: Revolutionary War Pension and Bounty Files, No. S12120.
80   NA: Revolutionary War Pension and Bounty Files, No. W1495.
81   NA: Revolutionary War Pension and Bounty Files, No. W1771.
82   NA: Revolutionary War Pension and Bounty Files, Nos. S45584, S15279, S41008, S43883. Hieronimus Mingus, Smith's Co., Livingston's 4th NY, stated he was under 'his [Col. Livingston's] Command at the Battle of Monmouth ...' Simon Nicolls noted in a supplementary deposition for Mingus that 'he was with ... Hieronimus Mingus at the battle of Monmouth ...,' Samuel Humphrey of Smith's Co., 'was in the Monmouth battle ... under the Marquis De La Fayette ...,' George Rapp stated 'he was in the battle of Monmouth being in the detachment commanded by General Lee'; and John Crawford,

Several New York levies had served against Lieutenant General John Burgoyne's British army in the 1777 Saratoga campaign and in other earlier actions. William Wattles,

> enlisted as a volunteer in september 1777 for three months … at Nine partners New York … in Col. [Morris] Graham's [militia] Regiment – marched under the ensign up the west side of Hudson river and joined Gen. [Horatio] Gates army at Bemis heights – was present at the capture of Gen. Burgoyne and was discharged at Stillwater … Next enlisted as a volunteer at Valley Forge, Pennsylvania … in Col. Henry B. Livingston's Regiment … was regularly discharged from said army at Canajoharie, New York on the river Mohawk … During this term he was in Monmouth battle.[83]

Some Maryland levies also took part in the Monmouth battle. George Dent, a 2nd Maryland levy, just missed it, but spoke of the march north, joining the standing regiments, and activities during the remainder of his enlistment.

> I … volunteered to relieve a Class out of the Charlotte Hall company in Saint Mary's County … previous to that time I never had mustered in any Militia Company - it was in … the year in which the battle of Monmouth was fought, we tried to get there in time, but could not, we heard the fireing. I was marched with I think seventy one others, some of whom were Volunteers & some drafts under the Command of Captn [Henry] Carberry as far as Annapolis … from Annapolis we were sent under charge of Sergeant King, by water to the head of Elk, there we remained some seven or eight days and Lieutenant [John] James [3rd Maryland] came from Baltimore and Marched us to head quarters in New Jersey, where we arrived the day after the battle of Monmouth, we were there dispersed to fill up the Vacancies in the deficient companies, chiefly belonging to the second Maryland Regt. Jonathan Woodburn Norman Boroughs & myself went into Capt. John Davidson's Company because Richard Hill & Henry Spaulding from our County were in that company & had been out some time … [after the battle] Our Regt. with some others was then marched to White Plains in New York, there we laid three months, I recollect my tent and Genl. Washingtons were in sight of each other / here we done much duty were frequently formed for battle & many detachments sent down to stre[n]gthen Col. Moy[l]ans [4th Continental Dragoon] Regt. then lying I think at a place calld Valentines Hill near to the British lines, our flanking parties had frequent skirmishes with the enemy, from White Plains I was marched with many others to the Fort at West-Point to stre[n]gthen that post … before I went to West-Point I was one of a guard who went to Kings Ferry under the command of Lieut. Smith, (the Brother of Genl. Sam Smith) to receive a flag ship, sent to pay Burgoyne's prisoners & had a heavy luggage to carry the box of specie to the guard-house, when we left West-Point we marched to Poukepsee on the North River, from thence to New Jersey … there we went into Winter quarters, by building huts, which we

---

4th New York, 'during the battle … was in a Detatchment Commanded by La Fayette.'
83   NA: Revolutionary War Pension and Bounty Files, No. S14795.

commenced on the day after Christmas day & I think our Mess finished ours in eleven or twelve days – I done no more service in the Maryland line, except what I done at this place & was discharged there with the others of my Countrymen, who were in the detachment with me[84]

Second Maryland levy Francis Freeman enlisted on 25 May 1778. In a June 1818 deposition 'Genl. Hezekiah Foard,' former lieutenant in the 2nd Regiment, noted that Freeman was a 'Coloured Man … belonged to the Second Regt of [the Maryland] line in the Spring of 1780 Marched With the same to South Carolina and I believe he Continued in the Service untill the Close of the War.'[85]

Only a few North Carolina levy narratives have been yet discovered, and none for the state's nine-month men who served in New York, autumn/winter of 1778-1779.

Granville County man, John Taylor, serving as a substitute for his brother,

set out with two young men of my acquaintance … We reached the army then stationed on the north side of Savannah River opposite the town of Augusta, which was then in possession of the British army … A detachment under the command of [Brigadier] General [John] Ashe [North Carolina state troops], having been ordered across the river, were directed to take their station at the point where the Briar Creek empties into the Savannah River.[86]

Taylor's company 'belonged to the detachment under General Ashe. How long we remained on duty at this post I am unable to state,' but Taylor was detailed to carry dispatches 'a few days before the attack on our detachment [3 March 1779] which proved so fatal to it.' He was vague about what occurred during the remainder of his service. John Taylor's name is in the 25 May 1778 Granville County descriptive list for levies from Captain Benjamin Wade's company; he was described as '26 years of age 6 feet high has a roguish look dark hair A planter.'[87]

Later-Life Circumstances

Most of the men who applied for pensions in the nineteenth century had fallen on hard times, a condition poignantly revealed in their statements. A supplementary deposition by Asher Hart stated that Robert Wright, former 4th New Jersey levy who had lived in Hopewell Township, Hunterdon County,

---

84   NA: Revolutionary War Pension and Bounty Files, No. S12755.
85   NA: Revolutionary War Pension and Bounty Files, No. S35951.
86   John C. Dann (ed.), *The Revolution Remembered: Eyewitness Accounts of the War for Independence* (Chicago: The University of Chicago Press, 1980), pp.205–206.
87   Dann, *The Revolution Remembered*, pp.205–206; North Carolina State Archives (Raleigh): Military Collection, War of the Revolution, Box 4, Continental Line, 1775-1778, Folder 40, 'A Descriptive List of the … men raised under the Present Act of Assembly in … Company' (fifteen sheets), Granville County, N.C., 25 May 1778.

American Revolutionary veterans were granted pensions beginning in the early nineteenth century. Their application narratives provide wartime stories and details we would otherwise would not have. George Caleb Bingham (1811-1879), 'Veteran of '76.' Lent by the people of Missouri. (Photograph courtesy of the St Louis Art Museum)

was a stone mason by trade and there are a number of stone dwellings that he put up before the Revolution now standing [1841] … during said war he [Wright] had a wife and a number of children he performed much service being of a roving disposition … many years after [Hart] heard he was found dead in the road he was a very Intemperate man.[88]

Wright's wife Ann stated his captain in both 1776 and 1778 was John Polhemus of 'Rockyhill,' that her husband 'was much attached to … Polhemus, who was his neighbour and friend.'[89] Abijah Harding, a 10th Massachusetts levy private, had an unfortunately all-too-typical tale to tell of later-life circumstances, stating in 1820 that he was 59 years old and living in Deerfield, Franklin County:

My occupation is that of an husbandman, in the Winter I occasionally make common Chairs, my health is generally poor and I am subject to epileptic fits, rheumatism and deafness I have a Wife aged fifty two years who is very infirm. I have eight children living, five of them are absent from me are without any property more than is necessary for their subsistance the three Children living with me are daughters … Julia is twenty four years of age and so sickly as to be unable to support herself / Perreratis is twenty two years old she has been for a long time unwell and for two months past been under the care of a Physician.[90]

Sixty-four year old John Seeley noted in his 1820 deposition,

I have no real or personal Estate of any description except my wearing apparel. I am by occupation a labourer, but incapable of Obtaining a livelyhood from weakness … I have no family I was a Pauper supported in the Alms house of Gloucester County N.J. I have a wife Hannah aged about 39 years who left me after I was taken to the Alms House.[91]

Like many Revolutionary soldiers, Seeley, Harding, and Wright gained nothing but pride and perhaps a small stipend from their years of Continental Army service.

Conclusion

During the war there were two views of Continental Army short-term state levies. One was consistent with what we know of the 1778 drafted men, who augmented the army at the beginning of what promised to be a crucial campaign. In this case we hear from New Jersey

---

88   NA: Revolutionary War Pension and Bounty Files, No. S7975.
89   NA: Revolutionary War Pension and Bounty Files, No. S7975.
90   NA: Revolutionary War Pension and Bounty Files, No. S32785.
91   NA: Revolutionary War Pension and Bounty Files, No. S33638; For an excellent study of veterans and pensions see, John Resch, *Suffering Soldiers: Revolutionary War Veterans, Moral Sentiment, and Political Culture in the Early Republic* (Amherst: University of Massachusetts Press, 1999), pp.47–64.

General William Maxwell when his brigade was on the front lines in early June 1778: 'There is about 450 of the new Leveys come in … [they] are coming in dayly & what adds greatly to the pleasure of their number, they are fine, likely, tractable men.'[92] On the other hand, in a garrison or winter camp when food was scarce and matters less pressing, the prospect of having short-term men galled some commanders. In March 1780, Massachusetts Brigadier General John Paterson wrote of the poor state of the army:

> Our officers [are] resigning by dozens, our men [enlisted] for during the War [are] at home waiting … for Justice, what remains are mostly composed of nine months abortions, sent here with bounties which ten times exceed those given for the war, naked, lifeless, and dead, who never saw action, [and] are now counting [the] days, hours, and minutes, they have to tarry in service.[93]

There were later efforts similar to the 1778 statutes, but none as successful. In February 1780 the Board of War unsuccessfully reiterated General Washington's recommendation for a long-term draft. The result was a one-time, six-month levy (seven months for Pennsylvania) that produced lackluster results in all but a few states. Massachusetts being the sole exception, garnering substantial numbers of levies each year from 1779 through 1782. An 18-month draft was also instituted by Virginia in autumn 1780, adding numbers of troops to that state's efforts to counter invading British forces the following year.[94]

In the end, the 1778 enlistment acts with their provisions for levying recruits were a little-known progenitor of nineteenth and twentieth century United States army conscription; the precedent they established and the levies' service both deserve proper recognition. Introduced as a stopgap measure at a time when manpower was sorely needed, the 1778 levy fulfilled its intended purpose. Although the combat effectiveness of most short-term men was never fully tested, some did see action, including those of the New Jersey Brigade in the days leading up to the Battle of Monmouth, and the New York levies with Livingston's Battalion during the 28 June combat. The untested levies probably would have acquitted themselves well in a general action when joined to the cadre of experienced soldiers already with the regiments. Most importantly, substantial numbers of new men reinforced the Continental Army, thus ensuring a more effective force of observation and deterrence during the summer, fall, and winter of 1778.

Bibliography

Primary Sources
Library of Congress, Washington, DC (LOC)
>   George Washington Papers, Presidential Papers Microfilm, Washington (1961)

---

92   LOC: Washington Papers, series 4, reel 49, William Maxwell to George Washington, 5 June 1778.
93   Massachusetts Historical Society: William Heath Papers (1774-1872), Boston (Microfilm edition, 1974), reel 15-2 (vol.15, part 2), John Paterson to William Heath, 31 March 1780.
94   John U. Rees, *They Were Good Soldiers: African Americans Serving in the Continental Army, 1775-1783* (Warwick: Helion, 2019), pp.198–199 (discussion of the Virginia 1780-1781 'Chesterfield draft').

William Sumner Jenkins (ed.), *Records of the States of the United States of America: A Microfilm Compilation* (Washington, 1949)
Massachusetts Historical Society, Boston, Massachusetts
    William Heath Papers (1774-1872), Boston (Microfilm edition, 1974)
National Archive and Records Administration, Washington, DC (NARA)
    Revolutionary War Pension and Bounty-Land Warrant Application Files (National Archives Microfilm Publication M804)
    Revolutionary War Rolls (National Archives Microfilm Publication M246), Record Group 93
    The Papers of the Continental Congress 17741789 (National Archives Microfilm Publications M247)
North Carolina State Archives, Raleigh, North Carolina
    Military Collection, War of the Revolution
State Archives, New Jersey
    Rev. War Mss.

Printed Primary Sources
Anon. (ed.), *Collections of the New-York Historical Society for the Year 1873* (New York: New-York Historical Society, 1874)
Anon., *Acts of the General Assembly of the State of New-Jersey, At a Session begun at Princeton on the 27th Day of August, 1776, and continued by Adjournments till the 11th of October 1777* (Burlington: Collins, 1777)
Anon., *Acts of the General Assembly of the State of New–Jersey … begun at Trenton on the 28th Day of October 1777* (Burlington, NJ, Collins, 1778)
Anon., *At the General Assembly … of the State of RhodeIsland … begun on the Second Monday in February* (Attleborough, MA: S. Southwick, 1778)
Anon., *Extracts from the Journal of Proceedings of the Provincial Congress of New-Jersey Held at Trenton in the Months of May, June and August, 1775* (Burlington: Collins, 1775)
Anon., *State of Rhode-Island … in General Assembly, May first session, A.D. 1778* (Attleborough, MA: S. Southwick, 1778)
Anon., *State of Rhode-Island … in General Assembly, May second session, A.D. 1778* (Attleborough, MA: S. Southwick, 1778)
Anon., *The Acts and Resolves, Public and Private, of the Province of the Massachusetts Bay* (Boston: Wright & Potter, 1886)
Anon., *The Public Records of the State of Connecticut, From October, 1776, to February, 1778* (Hartford: Lockwood & Brainard, 1894)
Anon., *The Statues at Large of Pennsylvania from 1682 to 1801* (Harrisburg, PA: William Stanley Ray, 1903)
Clark Walter (ed.), *The Colonial records of North Carolina* (Goldsboro, NC: Nash Bros, 1905)
Dann, John C. (ed.), *The Revolution Remembered: Eyewitness Accounts of the War for Independence* (Chicago: The University of Chicago Press, 1980)
Fitzpatrick, John C. (ed.), *The Writings of George Washington from the Original Manuscript Sources 1745–1799* (Washington: Government Printing Office, 1932–1934)
Ford, Worthington Chauncey (ed.), *Journals of the Continental Congress 1774–1789* (Washington: Government Printing Office, 1908)
Hazard, Samuel (ed.), *Pennsylvania Archives* (Philadelphia: Joseph Severns & Co., 1853)
Hening, William Waller (ed.), *The Statutes at Large; Being a Collection of All the Laws of Virginia, from the First Session of the Legislature, in the Year 1619* (Richmond: J. & G. Cochran, 1821)
Morgan, William James (ed.), *Naval Documents of the American Revolution* (Washington: Government Printing Office, 1970)
Thomas Lynch Montgomery (ed.), *Pennsylvania Archives* (Harrisburg: Harrisburg Publishing Co., 1906)

Secondary Sources
Alexander, Arthur J., 'How Maryland Tried to Raise Her Continental Quotas,' *Maryland Historical Magazine*, vol.42 (1977), pp.184–196

Claghorn, Charles E., *Naval Officers of the American Revolution: A Concise Biographical Dictionary* (Metuchen, NJ: The Scarecrow Press, Inc., 1988)

Fitzpatrick, Edward A., *Conscription and America: A Study of Conscription in a Democracy* (Milwaukee: Richard Publishing Co., 1940)

Jackson, John W., *The Pennsylvania Navy, 1775-1781: The Defense of the Delaware* (New Brunswick, NJ: Rutgers University Press, 1974)

Lesser, Charles H., *Sinews of Independence: Monthly Strength Reports of the Continental Army* (Chicago, IL: University of Chicago Press, 1976)

Lutz, Paul V., 'Greetings, or, Do I Feel a Draught?', *American Heritage*, vol.17, no.5 (August 1966), p.112.

Murdock, Eugene C., *One Million Men: The Civil War Draft in the North* (Madison: The State Historical Society of Wisconsin, 1971)

Popek, Daniel M., *They '… fought bravely, but were unfortunate': The True Story of Rhode Island's 'Black Regiment' and the Failure of Segregation in Rhode Island's Continental Line, 1777-1783* (Bloomington, IN: Authorhouse, 2015)

Rankin, Hugh F., *The North Carolina Continentals* (Chapel Hill: University of North Carolina Press, 1971)

Rees, John U., '"I Expect to be stationed in Jersey sometime …": An Account of the Services of the Second New Jersey Regiment, December 1777 to June 1778', (1994, unpublished typed manuscript: copy held in the collections of the David Center, American Philosophical Society, Philadelphia, PA)

    Section A. <https://www.academia.edu/95612424/Section_A_13_December_1777_to_1_April_1778_I_Expect_to_be_stationed_in_Jersey_sometime_A_Narrative_History_of_the_Second_New_Jersey_Regiment_December_1777_to_June_1779>

    Section B. <https://www.academia.edu/95630652/2nd_New_Jersey_Regiment_Section_B_20_March_to_24_May_1778_I_Expect_to_be_stationed_in_Jersey_sometime_A_Narrative_History_of_the_Second_New_Jersey_Regiment_December_1777_to_June_1779>

    Section C. <https://www.academia.edu/95486062/Section_C_of_I_Expect_to_be_stationed_in_Jersey_sometime_A_Narrative_History_of_the_Second_New_Jersey_Regiment_December_1777_to_June_1779>

Rees, John U., 'Losses in the Monmouth Campaign', <https://www.academia.edu/105623113/_They_answered_him_with_three_cheers_New_Jersey_Brigade_Losses_in_the_Monmouth_Campaign_17_June_to_6_July_1778>

Rees, John U., '"The new Leveys are coming in dayly …": The Nine Month Draft in the Second New Jersey Regiment and Maxwell's New Jersey Brigade', <https://www.academia.edu/95432677/_The_new_Leveys_are_coming_in_dayly_The_Nine_Month_Draft_in_the_Second_New_Jersey_Regiment_and_Maxwells_New_Jersey_Brigade_1778_>

Rees, John U., *They Were Good Soldiers: African Americans Serving in the Continental Army, 1775-1783* (Warwick: Helion, 2019)

Resch, John, *Suffering Soldiers: Revolutionary War Veterans, Moral Sentiment, and Political Culture in the Early Republic* (Amherst: University of Massachusetts Press, 1999)

Retzer, Henry J., *The German Regiment of Maryland and Pennsylvania in the Continental Army, 1776-1781* (Westminster, MD: Family Line Publications, 1991)

Sellers, John R., *The Virginia Continental Line* (Williamsburg: Virginia Independence Bicentennial Commission, 1978)

Smith, Jonathan, 'How New Hampshire Raised Her Armies for the Revolution', *The Granite Monthly: New Hampshire State Magazine*, vol.LIV (1922), pp.7–21.

Wright, Robert K. Jr., *The Continental Army* (Washington: Government Printing Office, 1984)

7

La Marcha Galvez: Spanish Planning, Logistics and Grit on the Road to Pensacola, 1779–1780

Joshua Provan

Origins and Plans

In May 1781, West Florida fell to the Franco-Spanish army of Bernardo de Gálvez when the garrison of Pensacola surrendered. It had been the longest siege ever recorded on North American soil to that date, and the road to get there stretched back over three long, hard years of tough campaigning in which nothing had been assured. Like all successful campaigns, the result was the consequence of planning, logistics and no little grit.

In the grand scheme of things, Gálvez was playing his part in the wider plans of his masters in Madrid. Spain's goals upon entering American War were outlined by King Carlos III's Secretary of State, and Minister of Grace and Justice, José Moñino y Redondo, conde de Floridablanca: 'Of herself Spain has no other objectives than to recover the shameful usurpations of Gibraltar and Minorca, and to cast out of the Gulf of Mexico, the Bay of Honduras, and the Coast of Campeche, those settlers which trouble her no end.'[1]

This was not just a private intention either, as the same was laid out clearly in the Treaty of Aranjuez (12 April 1779) that saw Spain formally join France in an alliance against Britain. The document itself detailed the conditions upon which Spain would enter the hostilities and the conditions upon which the Bourbon allies would end them:

> The Catholic king has the intention to acquire by war and the future peace treaty the following advantages: 1st, the restitution of Gibraltar; and, [2nd] the possession of the river and the Fort on Mobile [Bay] 3rd, the restitution of Pensacola with all the coast of Florida near the Bahama Channel, expelling from it all foreign domination; 4th, the expulsion of the British from the Bay of Honduras and the fulfilment by them of the prohibition stated in the 1763 Treaty of Paris to establish neither

---

1   Thomas E. Chavez, *Spain in the American Revolution: An Intrinsic Gift* (Albuquerque: University of New Mexico Press, 2002), pp.75–76.

there nor in any other Spanish territory any kind of settlement; 5th, the revocation of the privilege granted to the British of cutting logwood on the coast of Campeche; and 6th, the restitution of the island of Minorca.[2]

Despite enthusiasm on the part of the Continental Congress, who viewed the entrance of Carlos III's ample fleet and colonial coffers into the struggle as a guarantor of eventual liberty, Spain's position towards the Americans themselves would remain officially neutral, as the *Capitán General* of Havana, Diego José Navarro García de Valladares directed provincial governors in June 1779: 'There is no positive order or political basis for the United States to be seen or considered under any other concept but that of neutrality, since, not acting as subjects of Great Britain, they do not deserve our hostility; and not openly being friends of the Spanish nation, they should not benefit from our war efforts.'[3]

He advised governors to limit their aid to the United States to what the right of hospitality demanded. The King's effective Minister of the Indies,[4] Jose de Gálvez, wrote to the *Capitán General* in August 1779:

> The King has determined that the main objective of his arms in America during the war with the English will be to expel them from the Mexican Basin and from the banks of the Mississippi, where their settlements are harmful to our trade and to the security of our richest possessions. His Majesty desires that, without any delay, an expedition be arranged with all the land and naval forces that can be assembled to attack Mobile and Pensacola, which are the keys of the Mexican Basin, detaching, before or after, divisions that cover and clean the Englishmen from the banks of the Mississippi, which must be considered as protection of the vast empire of New Spain.[5]

The Spanish government was clear in its objectives, but it was a strategy that could only be moved forwards by aggressive, capable hands. So it was fortunate that at the outbreak of the war with Britain, the newest governor in Louisiana was Bernardo de Gálvez.

At the end of the Seven Years War, France signed over the vast territory of Louisiana to Spain in the Treaty of Fontainebleau (1762) in hopes that it would not fall prey to the British who were then in the process of amputating Canada from France. The ploy worked, and Spain reached its greatest-ever territorial extent to date despite losing the war, and losing temporary control of Cuba, Minorca and the Floridas. The sheer geographic scale of the newly acquired territory on paper was such that Carlos III wryly observed, 'My cousin is losing altogether too much.'[6]

---

2   Gonzalo M. Quintero Saravia, *Bernardo de Gálvez: Spanish Hero of the American Revolution* (Chapel Hill: University of North Carolina Press, 2018), p.144.
3   Saravia, *Gálvez*, p.145.
4   José de Gálvez, 1st Marquess of Sonora, (1720–1787) was Visitor General of New Spain, the most senior member of the Council of the Indies.
5   Saravia, *Gálvez*, p.144.
6   John Walton Caughey, *Bernardo de Gálvez in Louisiana* (Gretna: Firebird Press, 1998), p.4.

In 1768 the first Spanish governor of Louisiana, Antonio de Ulloa, was appointed. Historian Francois-Xavier Martin characterised Ulloa as a 'phantom of dubious authority'.[7] Within the year, Ulloa's administration had brought on an insurrection of the mostly French Creole gentry in New Orleans, which is sometimes called a proto-American Revolution, forcing Ulloa to flee. His replacement was *Capitán General* Alejandro O'Reilly, who arrived in 1769 with troops, money and a flotilla, restored the colony to the King's peace, and firmly established Spanish rule.

From 1769 through 1770, O'Reilly organised the establishment of a *Cabildo* (municipal council). He streamlined the defence of Louisiana, which was mostly thought of as economically useful only for the fur trade and the cultivation of indigo, and made many other economic measures besides to make the colony an asset rather than a burden. Militarily, O'Reilly had no great faith in the province being anything but a buffer between the British colonies and the frontier of New Spain. Ulloa had attempted to increase the defences on the rivers, but O'Reilly reduced the garrisons of the forts along the Missouri and Mississippi, with none being garrisoned by more than 30 men outside of New Orleans. The thinking was essentially that it would be a waste of men and time to defend such a wide border when the most valuable asset was the capital, but the effect was to render the line of the Mississippi almost devoid of regular troops. After his army of pacification was sent back to Havana only 179 regulars who volunteered to join the fixed Louisiana battalion remained, the entirety of which probably did not exceed 200. Though the regular establishment was small, O'Reilly did not think it needed to be large so long as there was a substantial militia to fill the gap. He proceeded to organise 13 militia companies totalling some 1,040 men armed by the crown and drilled by regular officers to a high standard. Thus, when O'Reilly left, the official governor, the ageing Louis de Unazaga (who had been with him the entire time and was appointed at the end of 1760, but very much in the background) was able to smoothly take the reins of a workable Spanish authority that interfered as little as possible in the lives of French and German Creoles. That being said, the flinty Irish emigre had no other use for Louisiana than to insulate the rest of Spanish America from the British colonies, which was not exactly what the Spanish government had in mind in 1779.[8]

It could be a testament to the organisation of the province that the experienced old man Unazaga saw little reason to alter what had been instituted, except to perhaps ease the grasp of Iberian control over the colony. Unazaga governed with a light touch and saw the flourishing of many initiatives that O'Reilly had implemented; but he also turned a blind eye to some he had attempted to quash. As an experienced man in colonial matters, he had sensibly allowed smuggling to resume. A tacit nod to illegal trade was common across the viceroyalties at the highest level. In some cases certain ports were so economically dependent on it that it was impossible to extinguish anyway. When the war in the British colonies broke out, (in accordance with Navarro's command to extend hospitality to neutral powers) Unazaga began supplying the Americans through local merchants, using men like Congress's agent in the south, Oliver Pollock.

---

7   Caughey, *Gálvez in Louisiana*, p.27.
8   Caughey, *Gálvez in Louisiana*, pp.41–42.

Unazaga remained in office until 1777, when the commander of the regular garrison, Don Bernardo de Gálvez, took over. Gálvez was 30 years old when he became governor. A pleasant-faced, hard-bitten, fiery and charismatic career soldier from a prominent family in Andalucia, he had been commandant of Nueva Viscaya and Sonora in 1770 and wounded in action at Algiers in 1775, where he had come to the notice of O'Reilly. Although young, he had solid military credentials and many had been keen to offer him preferment due to his good name and connections.

Now Gálvez was once again in command of a frontier, but this time he had a policy of neutrality to pursue, and he had the Apache arrow and lance wounds to remind him that such a balance was beneficial. However, it was clear that war was a possibility, and he did have a burden of intelligence and security to keep him occupied. Prior to the declaration of war, the Spanish government had sent orders that all efforts be made to gather information about the war in the British colonies. For this, Gálvez sent out his own agents and became more accommodating to Americans living and working on the Mississippi, making sure to become friends with Pollock, while still maintaining a certain pro-American neutrality.

Since relations with West Florida were quite cordial, with Gálvez sending food and supplies in times of crisis and allowing refugees shelter in Louisiana, he was able to easily deploy spies under the cover of official business. These were men like *Capitán* Jacinto Panis, whose exhaustive report in 1778 on the British gulf coast formed the basis for Galvez's future campaign plans, and the land agent Don Juan Elegio de la Puente, who used his contacts and insinuated himself into St Augustine where he wrote letters back to Havana, New Orleans and Spain. Observers and spies were also sent into the north that year; merchants from Havana appeared posing as slave traders, and experts on Florida went on fishing trips and then disappeared, only to reappear in colonial outposts far from where they were last seen. Each sent back detailed reports on military operations, from the state of fortifications in Mobile and Pensacola to news of the Battle of Saratoga, which reached Paris in December 1777 and New Orleans in the spring of the next year.[9]

It is de la Puente to whom we may first turn to in order to understand Gálvez's changing feelings regarding the defence of the colony, feelings that would in time chime with official war policy in Madrid. In 1777, Puente was certain that the English wanted the coasts of Florida 'not solely for defence against their enemies but offence', and that so long as the British held the Floridas, Louisiana was essentially forfeit.[10] The governor took note.

The British held not only the Florida peninsula but the eastern bank of the Mississippi. In a time when waterways were vital to trade, diplomacy and security, Britain's coastal possessions had the effect of shrinking the Gulf of Mexico and restricting the navigation of the Bahama channel, a vital maritime passage between Cuba and Florida that was the easiest way to the Atlantic from the Gulf. If the British were able to somewhat extend their control by taking New Orleans, then the water highway of the Mississippi River would be lost to Spain, and the vast expanse to the north would be cut off.

Gálvez could not think of the defence of his colony without considering the Mississippi and the proximity of British garrisons, information on these coming in regularly from the

9   Chavez, *Spain in the American Revolution*, p.69.
10   Chavez, *Spain in the American Revolution*, p.23.

Spanish outposts that often stood on the opposite bank. These were vital listening posts. If an attack was ever to come, these forts would act as conduction points. The largest long-term regular Spanish establishment in Louisiana seems to have never exceeded 400 men. A measure of the defensive intention of the province is to be seen when the dispute over the Falklands Islands in 1770–1771 seemed likely to spill into open conflict and Governor Unazaga planned to retreat to New Spain if he could not hold New Orleans with the regulars and militia.

Gálvez, out of respect for the wisdom of O'Reilly and Unazaga, or through his frank reading of the state of defence he had inherited, was also inclined to abandon Louisiana if he was attacked. He wrote that there were 'neither troops to defend the colony, nor forts to contain them, nor means to march on land.' This was due to the reorganisation and refinement of colonial defence strategy by O'Reilly, who had envisaged a greater reliance on the militia, not at all unusual in the colonies which could not depend on large scale mari-time defence. Indeed, entire viceroyalties such as Peru were entirely reliant on large militia establishments.[11]

It would, however, seem that the militia had gone into a decline by the time Gálvez took over, and he wrote, 'As to the militiamen, although I am confident of their good faith … we cannot count much on them because war is not their real business and they will not under-take it eagerly; and in addition, in face of danger they will always feel consideration for their families, and this will magnify dangers for them.'[12]

This is certainly the mind of a formally trained regular officer at work, but that does not mean it is unreliable, and in any event, this was what he felt on the matter. Given his doubts about the defensive capability of the colony, we have no reason to think that if he was deprived of the initiative in any conflict that he would have withdrawn first to New Orleans and then if necessary to Mexico. Then again, Gálvez saw no reason why he could not avoid that eventuality by striking first. By the time war had broken out, he had bolstered the colonial garrison to a healthy, if not aggressive, level, showing that from an early stage, he was preparing for action. Construction of gunboats had been started, and three armed oar and sail launches were also ordered, each mounting an 18- or 20-pounder. By the summer of 1779 the governor had bolstered the regular forces in New Orleans to over 659 men, and the militia to 1,510 men in 17 companies.[13] More than ample to defend New Orleans, and to act offensively.

Gálvez was a planner as well as a man of action, and he suspected that the British were also preparing for a state of war. Certainly, news of 400 troops of the Waldeck Regiment entering Manchac did not strike anyone as terribly peaceful. Such a mobilisation, he thought, 'could have no other object than that of mobilizing their forces on the river so that they would be more ready to attack us at the first news of a rupture.'[14]

On 14 May 1778, Juan de Villebeauvre, the officer commanding the Spanish defences opposite Manchac, had written to Governor Gálvez reporting suspicious activity on the

---

11   Caughey, *Gálvez in Louisiana*, p.55; Jean Descola, Michael Heron (trans.), *Daily Life in Colonial Peru 1710-1820* (London: George Allen & Unwin, 1968), pp.175–184.
12   Caughey, *Gálvez in Louisiana*, p.139.
13   Caughey, *Gálvez in Louisiana*, pp.138–139.
14   Caughey, *Gálvez in Louisiana*, p.149.

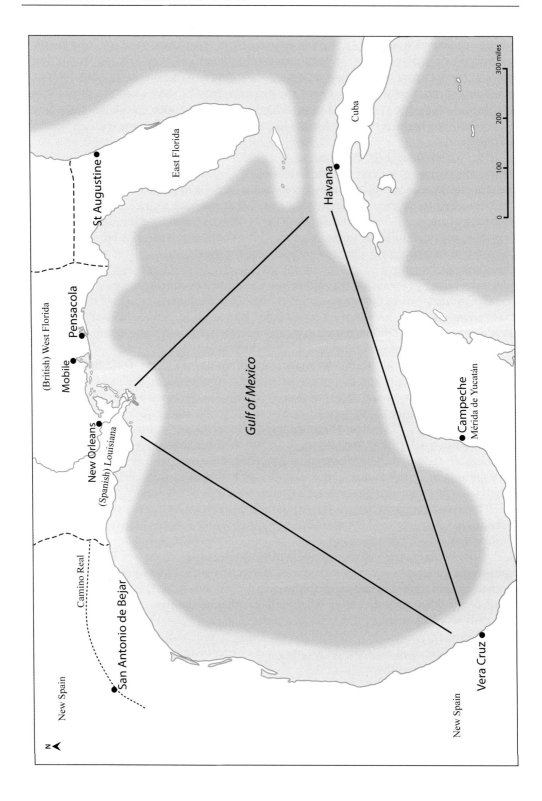

British shore, and on 6 July, he estimated from reliable sources that Lieutenant Colonel Alexander McGillivray of the British Indian Department planned to lead a force of 1,500 Choctaws, 400 Chickasaws, 300 Cherokees, and 250 Anglos supported by two frigates down the Mississippi from Natchez to New Orleans.[15]

The governor took intelligence of Muskogee and Cherokee hostility seriously, knowing that the British had a better diplomatic network in place to encourage the participation of allies, who controlled the interior of the provinces. Based on such reports, Gálvez now reasoned that if he did not go and attack the enemy's forts, then he would soon be attacked in his, and in such a scenario defeat would be likely. In assessing the weaknesses of the colony, he had observed that he was also in an excellent position to strike at the British, but all of this depended on authorisation to commence hostilities, which as yet had not reached Louisiana.

Anticipating war, Gálvez gathered a council on 13 July to discuss the defence of the colony. He laid out a map, began to explain the weaknesses of Louisiana and opened the floor to suggestions. His assembled officers all suggested fortifying New Orleans and gathering in the outlying forces, instructing frontier forts to surrender under the best possible terms. All except *Coronel* Esteban Miró agreed that the best approach was to follow the dictum of O'Reilly. The *coronel* suggested constructing redoubts below Manchac and using it as a place to gather troops to take the fight to the British.

This meeting was as much about gauging the resolve of his officials and officers as actually planning a defence strategy, and one can almost imagine the gleam that came to Gálvez's eye when Miró spoke up. This was much more in line with what the governor wanted. Not having any mandate to plan an offensive, however, he noted those upon whom he could rely when the time came and pretended to heed the call to caution. Meanwhile, under the pretence of preparing to defend the colony internally, he instructed Minister of War Juan Antonio Gayarré to gather boats and supplies for an irresistible offensive against the British based on the Mississippi, keeping even the arrival of the official declaration of war secret until it suited him.

Logistics

In general terms the logistics involved were both daunting and quite simple. The territory of Louisiana then encompassed most of the Midwest of the current United States, though practically, firm European control ended at St Louis, and was sketchy across northern Texas. But even along the more navigated stretches of the Mississippi, forts and posts were scattered widely. The back country of Georgia, West Florida and Louisiana was controlled by Native American confederacies, principally those of the Muskogee nations and the Cherokee. The terrain of swamps and forests was challenging, with few roads, and offered sparse means of subsistence for large groups. The commercial land route between Louisiana and Mexico, the Camino Reale de Tejas, was slow, dangerous, and barely a collection of well beaten trails in

---

15   Jack D.L. Holmes, 'Juan de La Villebeauvre: Spain's Commandant of Natchez During the American Revolution', *Journal of Mississippi History*, vol.27, no.1 (1975), pp.97–129.

some stretches, used for driving cattle. British West Florida was no better connected from Pensacola to Mobile, making rivers and coastlines vital for both commerce and conflict.

Weather also played an important role. The warm, moist air created by the Gulf of Mexico acts as a conductor for a multitude of increasingly severe meteorological events through the year, which could interrupt travel and business, and contribute to the spread of disease amongst dense populations.

The Mississippi river provided the easiest way to move supplies, but this. and the gulf coast in general, was tricky in terms of navigation. Coupled with often poor weather, this meant that it was challenging for naval forces to shadow an army as it marched, or to transport it totally. Likewise, the wagon road that ran in places between the main posts was no quicker or more reliable, and still required water access to New Orleans, a convenient bay, or an anchorage on the gulf.

In late August 1779, Navarro and the head of the Audiencia of New Spain, Francisco Roma y Rosell, were in earnest communication over the supply of food, gunpowder and money to Havana and New Orleans, which more or less laid out the triangulation of supply in Spanish American maritime strategy. Havana had the political and royal authority to requisition the wealth of Mexico for distribution to Louisiana, Guatemala and Campeche, and the defensive material for the other islands as well. A glance at the map reveals why this was the case, as Vera Cruz sits at the bottom edge of the Mexican basin, with ships having to round the Yucatan to get out. Havana was a logical port in which to stop, being in some sense the gateway to the Caribbean from the west and directly proximate to the Bahama Channel.

In terms of munitions, the old powder factory of at Chapultepec, outside Mexico City in New Spain, was the sole supplier of gunpowder and munitions to the Spanish empire in North America since the Bourbon reforms created a government monopoly in 1766.[16] It had already been shipping thousands of pounds of gunpowder through the magazines of Cuba to the other colonies, so much so that by 1777 the manufacture of powder needed to be expanded in Mexico City in anticipation of higher demand.

Louisiana was the clearing house for munitions headed for the depots of the Continental Army, and of course now began to shift towards being a central part of Spain's war effort. The Audiencia promised cargos of dried vegetables and flour, large quantities of powder, and a new factory for munitions production at Santa Fé. Newly cast cannons were to be sent out from the foundry at Vera Cruz, which Navarro called the 'General depot of military supplies'; the city became one of the most important places in Spanish America for the remainder of the war.[17]

Gálvez's preparations drew on practically every resource available to him, and this included seeking out supplies of fresh meat for his troops from an innovative place. He had knowledge of the northern frontier, and he knew the *ranchos* and missions of San Antonio

---

16   See: James A. Lewis, 'The Royal Gunpowder Monopoly in New Spain (1766–1783): A Case Study of Management, Technology, and Reform under Charles III', *Ibero-Amerikanisches Archiv, Neue Folge*, vol.6, no.4 (1980), pp.355–372.

17   Lawrence Kinnaird (ed), *Annual Report of The American Historical Association for The Year 1945: Volume II Spain in the Mississippi Valley* (Washington: Government Printing Office, 1949), pp.352–355.

were a rich source of cattle; and that between the hard-bitten Presidiales and the Rancheros, there existed the means of getting cattle to Villa Bucareli, the old capital of Texas near the Louisiana border.[18]

In 1778, frontier diplomat Athanase de Mézières was sent on a tour of inspection and reported on the plentiful cattle on the Béxar and La Bahía *ranchos*, estimating tens or hundreds of thousands of animals being bred for hides, tallow and meat.

The next year, Gálvez despatched Francisco García with a letter for the governor, Domingo Cabello, requesting cattle. García arrived in Béxar on 20 June 1779 and this triggered a flurry of activity from the governor to requisition a large herd. He was aided by Fray Pedro Ramírez de Arellano of Mission San José, the Father President of the Texas missions, and by August 2,000 head were ready to drive. Overall, the ranches of Texas would supply 10,000 to 15,000 head of cattle between 1779 and 1782 for Gálvez. Additionally, on 17 August 1780 Carlos III issued a decree requesting voluntary donations from the colonies. In Texas this amounted to a collection of 1,659 pesos. This was tallied into the treasury of New Spain and sent to Vera Cruz to bolster the 500,000 pesos of government funds delivered to the King's agent, Francisco de Saavedra, in the critical period of late 1781. This was only the initial sum, which was actually funnelled to French *Lieutenant Général des armées navales* de Grasse to pay his fleet arrears. Another 1,000,000 pesos was forwarded to *Lieutenant Général* Rochambeau in order for him to progress against Yorktown. The ingenuity of Saavedra and the immense wealth of Mexico did not seem to have an end as a further 9,000,000 pesos was earmarked for the abortive invasion of Jamaica.

War was officially declared on 21 June 1779, rewarding Gálvez's foresight, but copies and instructions had been sent out before that time which matched perfectly with his own intentions to strike before the British could prepare. The news reached Havana on 17 July. Navarro then wrote out instructions for war to governors who were 'to direct all our efforts … to drive the British forces out of Pensacola, Mobile, and the other posts they occupy on the Mississippi.'[19] By mid-August Gálvez had overcome all his organisational challenges and was nearly ready to move. He was preparing a public appeal where he would announce his recent confirmation as governor, the declaration of war, and his plan to defeat the British before they could strike, but as it happened, nature struck first. On 18 August, as Gálvez was planning the start of his campaign, a hurricane swept through New Orleans causing massive destruction to both private and civic property and to the stores and transportation of the expeditionary force.

Gálvez was apparently unfazed by such obstacles, and he had capable lieutenants who had gifts for organisation. Within a week of the hurricane hitting, he had given his public appeal, reconstituted and rearmed the flotilla, and assembled a small army to take the war to the British.

---

18   Robert H. Thonhoff, *The Vital Contribution of Texas in the Winning of the American Revolution: An Essay on a Forgotten Chapter in the Spanish Colonial History of Texas* (Karnes City: Published by the author, 2006), p.4.
19   Caughey, *Gálvez in Louisiana*, p.149.

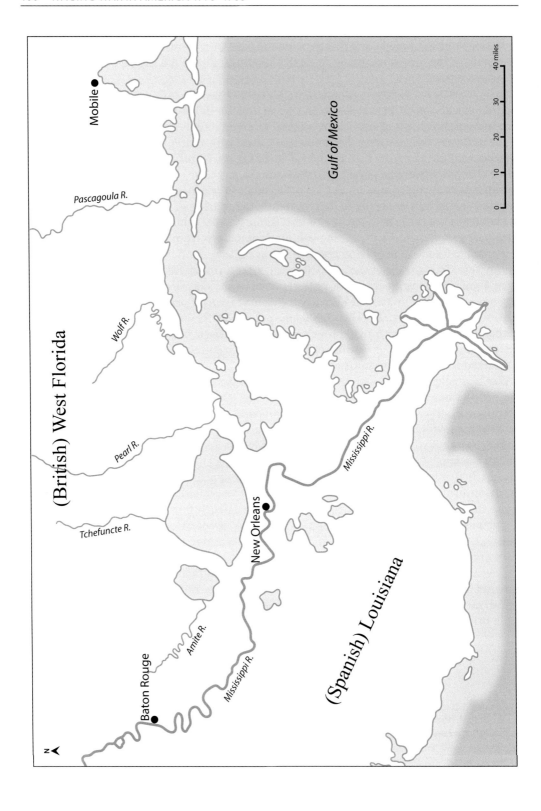

Grit

The first target was Fort Bute on Bayou Manchac. On 16 August, Gálvez had notified military posts of the declaration of war in secret. A week later, with the ravages of the storm still being dealt with, *Comandante* Debreuil of the fort opposite Manchac reported that the English seemed to be fortifying their defences. Gálvez wanted to move quickly, while the British, still ignorant of the declaration of war, would consider Louisiana insufficiently recovered from the hurricane to be a threat. His army was small, made up of 'men of all conditions, nations and colours,' but the governor was satisfied with it.[20]

There were 170 veteran regulars, including officers such as Esteban Miró and Jacinto Panis, 339 regular recruits from Mexico and the Canaries, 20 carabiniers, 60 militiamen and habitants, 80 free Blacks, and seven Anglo[21] volunteers including, Congress's agent in Louisiana, Oliver Pollock who acted as aide de camp, for a total of 667 men and an estimated 10 cannon, but without a single engineer and only one ailing artillery officer. To bolster this, Gálvez hurried ahead and mustered the militia of the Acadian and German coasts to bring his total force to 1,427 men, including 160 Native Americans.

The initial march of 35 leagues began on 27 August and was completed in 11 days. Gálvez had taken secrecy to new levels, maintaining a friendly correspondence with the British commander at Pensacola, Major General John Campbell, arresting British officials that entered Louisiana, and keeping the declaration of war even from his own troops until they were before Manchac. The British were suspicious but completely in the dark, with distances and poor translations of Spanish documents delaying perception of what was going on, in some cases until September.

Gálvez came in sight of Manchac on 6 September, and he now addressed his men, about a third of whom had fallen sick on the march, informing them that they were at war with Britain and that they were going to seize the British forts.

Manchac was a trading post of a few sturdy houses, tents, and simple shacks, defended by a stockade. The main fortification, Fort Bute, was deemed indefensible and was held by only a token force of around 20 men, Lieutenant Colonel Alexander Dickson having chosen to retreat to Baton Rouge after discovering he was to be attacked. Gálvez therefor decided to season his militia, who stormed Manchac on 6 September with no casualties. The governor specifically mentioned that the Acadian militia were ever eager to fight the British, as they had come to Louisiana after being driven from their homes in Canada by the British in the French and Indian War.[22]

Gálvez had made preparations to prevent, slow, or give warning of a British attempt to relieve the Mississippi via lakes Pontchartrain and Maurepas, which lie just to the north of New Orleans. A local Creole named Vicente Rieux, apparently of the militia or a volunteer, was sent with an armed brig to blockade the passage that connected the lakes. He and his

---

20   Saravia, *Gálvez*, p.149
21   The use of Anglo here is to identify British American supporters of Congress, as to the Spanish the
      term American was insufficient to specify citizens of the United States.
22   Gilbert C. Din (ed.), *The Louisiana Purchase Bicentennial Series in Louisiana History Vol II: The
      Spanish Presence in Louisiana 1763–1803* (Lafayette: Centre for Louisiana Studies University of
      Southwestern Louisiana, 1996), pp.192–193.

crew captured a ship carrying a detachment of Waldeckers on 7 September. This was one of a number of successful small ship actions which essentially cut off the British forts on the Mississippi from help by water. On 10 September, Captain William Pickles of the American frigate *Morris* (formerly the *Rebecca*) outfitted by Gálvez, entered Lake Pontchartrain to seek out and capture the British five-gun brigantine *West Florida*, which was then in command of the lake. Pickles, successfully boarded and seized the *West Florida* on 10 September. The prize was renamed *Gálvez* and given to the governor.[23]

Meanwhile, the Spaniards who had waited five days at Manchac pressed on the 15 miles to Baton Rouge with 200 men of the Louisiana regiment as an advance guard. Unlike at Manchac, the defences of Baton Rouge were new; Lieutenant Colonel Dickson had feared a rebel assault and had been prioritising the settlement. Gálvez's inspection of the enemy works on 12 September revealed that the redoubt, named Fort New Richmond, finished in only six weeks from 30 July, was positioned on cleared plantation land, with an 18-foot-wide, nine-foot-deep ditch and an earthen wall, protected by a palisade of felled timber, defended by 13 guns. The approaches were open and the smell of freshly turned soil and newly cut wood was probably thick in the air, already suffused by campfire smoke.

Dickson would not surrender without a fight, and he had 400 regulars in the garrison, drawn from the Royal Artillery, the 16th and 60th Regiments of Foot, and the 3rd Waldeck Regiment, in addition to 150 settlers, armed slaves and freemen.[24]

Gálvez had no time for a regular siege. His men, including his chief artillery officer Julian Alvarez, were getting sick and the garrison opposing them was strong. Although he had cut it off, he had every expectation that the fort could hold out for more than enough time for help to arrive. Nor did he have the men or the political support to sanction a costly assault. Gálvez would have been aware that taking the fortifications with a needless slaughter among his force, composed mostly of Louisiana volunteers, would cause justifiable outrage in New Orleans.

Gálvez surveyed his objective carefully, and this reconnaissance identified two things. First, that there were some buildings that could provide cover for his artillery, and second, that there was a prominent grove of trees reaching out towards the fort that had not yet been cleared. This was the most obvious place to attack from, and for this reason, the governor decided that the British probably thought so too.

On 20 September, Gálvez sent a mixed force of militia with his Native American allies to occupy and fortify the grove; they were encouraged to make a lot of noise in doing it. The garrison took the bait, and the next morning the British found that Spanish guns had been entrenched a musket shot away on the opposite side of the fort, hidden by a garden wall until it was too late. The fort surrendered in the middle of the afternoon on 21 September after a three-hour bombardment. The terms of capitulation included orders for Fort Panmure at Natchez to surrender as well, and the trusted Villebeauvre was sent to receive its surrender. The first stage of the plan had been a stunning success. Offsetting difficult supply lines, small numbers, and limited assistance, Gálvez had stopped a British attack on Louisiana in its tracks. The campaign lasted just about a month, and ended with the capture of three

---

23   Din, *Spanish Presence in Louisiana*, pp.196–197.
24   Albert W. Haarmann, 'The Spanish Conquest of British West Florida, 1779–1781', *Florida Historical Quarterly*, vol.39, no.2 (1960), pp.111–112.

forts, 550 regular prisoners and another 500 militia who were released upon taking a loyal oath. The cost to the Spanish was entirely in those who fell sick on the march and less than three killed and wounded by enemy action.

News of the setback reached Mobile in October. Settlers and officials sensed Mobile was next to be attacked, but when Brigadier General Campbell heard of the fall of the Mississippi forts, he ordered the strengthening of Pensacola, and seemingly left Mobile to fend for itself.[25]

With the lower Mississippi secured, Gálvez now had to face the challenge of opening two new fronts, one against the British-held Gulf coast and the other against the *capitán general* at Havana.

Navarro is often painted as the archetypal antagonist to the heroic figure of Gálvez, and he was indeed reluctant to give Gálvez the support he requested, even knowing that the King and his ministers mostly supported him and his plan. However, it was more Navarro's preference to dispense with taking Mobile and to press on against Pensacola immediately that drove his resistance.

Gálvez asked for 2,000 men to capture Mobile, which he saw as a vital post for diplomacy with the Chickasaws and Creeks, and also an important part of the supply chain to Pensacola which could not be allowed to remain in enemy hands. On 2 January 1780, Gálvez gave orders to prepare to attack Mobile, having sent an emissary to hurry reinforcements from Havana, and specifying that all be ready to embark on the night of the 10th. His diary states he had been given indications that an expedition from Havana would be at sea but would be dispatched only after careful consideration of the propitious moment. This, however, was so much padding for consumption in Spain. He was to await the confirmation of Francisco Xavier de Navias of the Real Cuerpo de Ingenieros. Whether or not Gálvez simply lacked the patience to wait, or it was as he said in his diary to avoid any further delays that might be caused by Navias becoming ill or delayed, he gave orders to his officers, placing Gironimo Girón de Moctezuma, Marquis de las Amarillas (a direct descendant of the last Mexican Tlatoani) as second in command. The message was clear: Navarro could either support him or not, but Gálvez was going to Mobile with or without official permission from Havana.

By the afternoon of 11 January, Gálvez had embarked the Regimiento de España, detachments of the Principé, the Regimiento Fijo de Havana, the Fijo de Louisiana, artillerymen, Carabineros, the Blanco, Pardo and Moreno, Libre Milicia (of New Orleans), and a number of enslaved men. His force, amounting to about 700 men on 11 ships at New Orleans, was ready to go.[26]

Although all was ready, it was far from the ideal armada Panis had advised. Adverse conditions delayed sailing until 14 January at 9:00 a.m., on which day the flotilla travelled eight leagues. It was hard going through the winding channels of the Mississippi delta, resting the troops ashore, lightening the ships when necessary, and sending *Sub Teniente* Juan Antonio de Riaño, Gálvez's 22-year-old brother-in-law and commander of the King's Galleot *Valenzuela*, ahead as the chief pilot to scout the best channel through to the gulf.[27]

25   Haarmann, *Conquest*, pp.113–115.
26   *Suplemento a la Gazeta de Madrid del Martes 20 de Junio de 1780*, p.435, <https://www.boe.es/diario_gazeta/comun/pdf.php?p=1780/06/20/pdfs/GMD-C-1780-49.pdf>, accessed 28 March 2023.
27   Eric Beerman, "'Yo Solo' Not "Solo": Juan Antonio de Riano', *Florida Historical Quarterly*, vol.58, no.2

The east channel was selected, but continual bad weather forced the convoy to anchor in the lee of a small island until the 27th. At 9:00 a.m. on the 28th the frigate *Volante* signalled for the fleet to make sail and exited the Mississippi that day.

A lack of wind now delayed sailing. The ships beat round the mouths of the Mississippi to the east, until a breeze sprang up on 4 February allowing better progress to be made. By the 6th this breeze had backed strongly from the southwest, and the horizons had darkened ominously. After travelling 20 leagues, the *Volante* signalled that the convoy needed to keep to the cape in order to use the land as shelter. Curtains of rain came first, followed by peals of thunder and hail. The worst moment came when a tell-tail feather of curling cloud began to fall out from the heavens like the stinger of a wasp, thickening in frightening swirls of vapour until it met the water and surged towards the helpless convoy in the form of a what Gálvez called a whirlwind. This term is unsatisfactory as it can be used to describe several kinds and sizes of weather vortexes, but as he noted that it caused several ships to founder and that it was only when the wind changed to blow from the east that they found relief, it is likely that they were struck by a powerful waterspout caused by the storm.

On the 7th in the morning, despite the bad night, the ships were still together, their storm sails set, but the wind continued to blow strongly all day. The next morning, Gálvez found himself alone with only his own brig and four other small boats, two of which would be blown away in the course of the day, and all reported taking on water. On the 9th the scattered elements of the convoy sailed east independently with fair weather until they reached the mouth of the Perdido River, and to everyone's great relief, the closer they came to Mobile the more of the convoy they could spot. By noon the *Volante* had been sighted with four other ships, but the wind dropped, and they could only reunite at dusk.

At long last the Spaniards had reached their goal, and as a reward a British ship was sighted in the channel of the bay. Gálvez made arrangements to attack it at once. The *Valenzuela*, which carried a 24-pounder bow chaser, and some of the armed boats were detailed for the mission. Before they had cleared for action, the British ship had taken fright after her hails to the *Volante* had gone unanswered, so Riaño was sent in a fast launch to chase it down. Riaño returned at 9:30 p.m. with a small Guairo which he had captured inside the bay.[28] The second officer and five men were his prisoners. They informed the Spanish that a frigate of 16 guns (mounted and swivels) with a crew of 20 (making it more likely to be a sloop of war) was in Mobile Bay, having left Pensacola five days before to deliver messages. Riaño took his Galleot and three armed launches to attack the vessel, but after three attempts to get across the bar in the failing light, he gave up the enterprise. The wind changed to blow from the southwest and strengthened on the 10th; the sea rose and became troublesome for the already leaking ships damaged in the storm. In these conditions, the *Volante* and *Gálvez* attempted to force the bar and attack the enemy vessel, which upon spotting the Spaniards, was run aground and abandoned. The *Volante* crossed first with relative ease, followed by the *Gálvez*. However, the *Volante* sent back her pilot to help the other vessels over the bar and soon went aground itself. One by one, *Gálvez* and four others grounded too, all too distant from each other to help. The crew of the *Volante* worked all day to free their vessel

---

(1979), p.177.
28   Guairo: A Cuban word for a small coastal vessel.

but failed. The crew of the *Gálvez* worked feverishly from noon until 1:00 a.m. when finally, it was freed, shipping nine inches of water per hour. Only two of the others managed to escape. The other two craft had to be abandoned and called for help to get the troops and as many supplies as possible rescued before they sank.[29]

The weather stayed troublesome on the 11th and prevented aid from being given to the stranded ships. Gálvez felt he had no choice but to begin disembarking his troops and supplies. Though few men were reported lost while crossing the bar and landing on the deserted beach at the point of the bay, which took place between the 12th and 17th, the operation was such a fiasco, and so much was lost, that Gálvez, looking at his destitute and in his words, half-naked, army, contemplated abandoning his guns and retreating over-land. While he considered his options, he made sure to keep his men's minds on fighting the enemy rather than their predicaments, and he was cheered to see them eagerly set to salvaging wood from the damaged vessels of the convoy to make siege ladders. On the other side, the entire episode gave the British the impression that most of the Spanish naval force had been sunk and that up to 700 men had drowned, and this in itself caused a great complacency in the garrison which could have potentially done considerable damage to the invaders; indeed, it is not without the bounds of possibility that they could have forced the enemy to surrender.

Gálvez had been in too many tough spots like this to give up while he still had a measure of hope, and the British, content in their fort, did not seem half so daunting as the fortifica-tions of Algiers in 1775, or the Apaches he had faced when he was riding with the Dragones de Cuera in 1770. Then he had been led into the trackless wastes along the Rio Pecos in search of his quarry; cut off and starving, he had addressed his discontented company of riders and his words to his men at that time must have echoed in his ears 10 years later:

> Alone I would go without having anyone to accompany me; and I will either take a scalp to Chihuahua and perform my duty or pay with my life for the king's bread that I have eaten. There is the road from our land, follow it those of you who have faint hearts; but follow me those of you who wish to take part in my glorious hard-ships, follow me on the assumption that I can give you nothing but thanks for this fineness, but that it will live always in my memory and recollection.[30]

Little did he know that his optimism and grit would be rewarded. His agent and friend in Havana, José de Ezpeleta, had convinced Navarro to release 567 men of the Regimiento de Navarra and these sailed on 10 February. Until that time Gálvez, sitting in his beach-front camp, knew the situation was serious. The second in command of the army, *Coronel* Geronimo Girón, wrote in his report, which bears out Gálvez's diary:

> … the troops found themselves ashore without arms or ammunition, naked and with nothing to eat in a land surrounded by enemies. There they remained for twelve days without tents or food other than the rice arrived from Havana. But far

---

29   *Suplemento a la Gazeta de Madrid del Martes 20 de Junio de 1780*, p.436.
30   Caughey, *Gálvez in Louisiana*, p.63.

from being disheartened with these misfortunes, when the reinforcements arrived they were found to be making ladders, which they were to carry on their shoulders the long distance that still separated them from the enemies' stronghold, where they were certain to find every thing they needed in the enemies' stores.[31]

These reinforcements, accompanied by the loyal Ezpeleta, landed at Mobile on 20 February, and with fresh troops Gálvez rallied his men with such encouraging words as he had used on the Pecos. The governor was popular amongst the soldiers and volunteers; he radiated confidence, shared their dangers, ate their rations, and spoke to them in words they could understand, so when he told them they were going to march on Fort Charlotte, they listened and obeyed. On 28 February, Spanish troops crossed the Dog River and made camp. The next day shots were fired from the fort at a scouting party, officially opening the hostilities.[32]

Gálvez's spy, Panis had written on the defences at Mobile in 1778:

[they] are in very bad condition; they consist of a regular square, built of brick, and … with breastworks, trench, and glacis … situated very near the barracks and at the shore of the bay for defence by sea, as on land by Indians. Its walls are going to ruin. Almost all the artillery is dismounted, and the trenches in some places are choked up. The barracks are in equally bad repair; in the front and side sections are housed the small garrison of forty-five soldiers, commanded by a captain, lieutenant, and sergeant; the other side, the northeast, is uninhabitable, for nothing but its walls remain, the rest having been consumed by a fire.[33]

The British had not been idle in those two years however, for though the 62-year-old local brick and oyster shell lime of the old French fort had been allowed to fall into disrepair, the materials were sturdier than the mouldering wood and earth defences on the Mississippi and so with extra entrenchments, it was in a defensible state as of 1779.

On 1 March, Gálvez sent a letter into Fort Charlotte, addressed to Captain Elias Durnford, of the Royal Engineers, which in courteous but firm tones plainly stated the disparity of the forces at each other's disposal and the necessity for all parties concerned to avoid the trials of a costly siege, which could be dispensed with by the prompt and honourable surrender of the fort.

Elias Durnford commanded just over 300 men, consisting of an understrength battalion of the 60th, a Royal Artillery company and contingents of the Pennsylvania Loyalists and the Maryland loyalists. Durnford was an engineer and had served at Havana and as commanding engineer and surveyor general for the province of West Florida, even stepping in to act as interim lieutenant governor on one occasion. The emissary that Gálvez sent was an old acquaintance of Durnford's, *Teniente Coronel* Francisco de Bouligny, who was invited to share a meal in the fort. The conversation in the headquarters building was companionable but both men made sure to get their relative points across. From this exchange both commanders gained a small insight into the capabilities of the other.

---

31   Saravia, *Gálvez,* p.166.
32   Haarmann, *Conquest,* p.117.
33   Caughey, *Gálvez in Louisiana,* p.146.

As was entirely proper, Durnford, though certainly outnumbered, felt unable to simply concede a post while he had the means to defend it, and, indeed, while he had a logical hope of relief from Pensacola. He replied the same day with the sentiment that he would defend his post 'until I am under conviction that resistance is in vain.'[34] Durnford had up to this point been under the impression that Gálvez had lost hundreds of men to shipwreck, and revealed a second consideration for refusing the summons to surrender in the letter he sent off to Major General Campbell after his guest left:

> During our conversation I found that the Report of the Shipwreck was true; he acknowledged that they had undergone great hardships, but would not allow to have lost any men, and informed me that they were about 2500 men, but by trusty Indians who were sent by me into the camp in the morning, I learned that a great number were negroes and mulattoes and that they had landed no cannon ... As soon as Colonel Bolyny left me I drew up my Garrison in the square, read to them Don Gálvez's summons, and then told them that if any man among them was afraid to stand by me that I should open the gate and he should freely pass. This had the desired effect, and not a man moved. I then read to them my answer to the summons in which they all joined in three cheers and then went to our necessary work like good men. I really believe their (the enemy's) force is greatly magnified.[35]

Durnford would not surrender, and though aware of the size of his enemy's force, seemed to feel it was exaggerated, and lay great store in the idea that there was a large contingent of Black troops with them. The course of the siege was straightforward but never a foregone conclusion, as Campbell indeed did stir himself and replied to Durnford that he would come to his aid. Between 5 and 6 March, Durnford and Gálvez continued to correspond on the subject of how best to preserve civilian property. This included a genteel exchange of presents which served the dual purpose of keeping an uncivil situation civil, and giving the impression that neither side was in any sort of difficulty. Durnford especially had cause to hope that his indications of tranquillity in his fort would be as well rewarded as Gálvez's unearned optimism on the beach, as the first elements of the relief force had marched from Pensacola on the 5th. However, it was 72 miles of bad roads, thick forest, and swampland between Mobile and help. Campbell, who had pulled together what resources he could on very short notice, had only been able to muster 522 men, and it took until the 6th for the main body to leave Pensacola.

Gálvez was ready to start excavations on 9 March, and he did so with customary verve. Drawing up the 300 guards and 200 workers selected for the task, he gave them a speech and then sent them to work, opening the first trench that night. Durnford had been watching closely and siting his guns. The next morning, with only minor adjustments the cannon of Fort Charlotte roared to life, killing six men and wounding another five, prompting an end to the work until night once more returned. By this time Spanish scouts had discovered

34   Haarmann, *Conquest*, p.116.
35   Haarmann, *Conquest*, p.116

Campbell's force encamped in two places at a spot called Tensa,[36] 30 miles above the fort, building rafts for the crossing of the eastern channel of the Mobile River.

Bad weather once again added to the anxieties of the Spanish general as he listened to the reports of the scouts on the 11th. Work on the batteries had been postponed, and he had to assume that Campbell would be upon him within the next few days. What was worse, Gálvez had either a very imprecise understanding of the size of the relief force, or he was being overly dramatic in his report to his uncle José when he wrote:

> His [Campbell's] vanguard was in sight before we had finished opening the trenches; because, having lost most of the launches in the shipwreck, we consequently had to use those that remained to carry supplies for our subsistence and had transported munitions too slowly. You can understand our situation, on the verge of having our food give out, with very little munitions (for the greater part was lost in the ship-wreck), with 1,100 men in sight from whose muskets their general had removed the flints in order to attack us with cold steel, with 300 in the fort, who with those of General Campbell totalled 1400, a number equal to ours, and with the country on their side, and the protection of a fort.[37]

The Spanish work parties toiled all through the day of 12 March, and by dawn of the next day, eight 18-pounders and a 24-pounder had been emplaced, with not a moment to lose. These guns opened fire and battered the walls of Mobile until nightfall when two breaches began to appear. On 14 March, after some straightforward negotiations, Durnford's small garrison marched down the breach and surrendered to the Spanish.

Gálvez summed it up for his uncle: 'For eight days he [Campbell] was a witness of the valour and courage of our troops, with which, having changed his mind, he broke camp to return to Pensacola with his army, from whose rear guard one of our parties took prisoner a captain and twenty men.'[38]

Campbell was not an aggressive officer and can be criticised for not pressing ahead to relieve the fort. However, his forces were not as large as Gálvez reported, and caution seemed the best option to prevent the combined 800 men from falling into a disastrous defeat.

On 17 March Spanish scouts reported the retreat of Campbell's force, which regained Pensacola two days later. Durnford was not the only one to be disappointed by those who had promised to assist him. As a result of lack of further aid from Cuba, Gálvez put Ezpeleta into Mobile with a garrison and sent the rest of the army to New Orleans, angry he could not press on in pursuit of Campbell.

'I cannot give expression to the sentiments with which all the individuals of my small army saw the retreat of General Campbell without coming to grips with us,' wrote Gálvez to his uncle:

---

36   The Tensaw River. In fact, Campbell would report that only his scouts actually came in sight of Mobile, the rest remained here, preparing boats.

37   Caughey, *Gálvez in Louisiana*, pp.183–185.

38   Caughey, *Gálvez in Louisiana*, p.184.

nor could we reflect without sadness that if the expedition from Havana had arrived to join with us we could have succeeded over the English the same as at Saratoga, And so that you may know whether this belief is well or ill founded, I Would have you know that General Campbell got out with only enough bread for eight days and the meat which was to be found in the houses, counting on arriving at the fort before it was taken, that the road by which they are returning is seven leagues longer than the one we would have taken to cut off the retreat and block the crossing of the Perdido River, indispensable for their return to Pensacola.[39]

Although a valid point, Gálvez was here attempting to blame Havana for not supporting him fully from the start. For as we have seen it was the vital contributions of the Regiment de España and timely food convoys that saved the Spanish from disaster and allowed Gálvez to maintain the initiative. The governor of Louisiana was speaking of an expedition that had never been agreed to.

Despite this, by the end of 1780, all the territory from the Mississippi River to the Bay of Mobile had been taken by the Spanish, every British gun had been taken between Natchez and Pensacola with 1,300 men taken prisoner. Gálvez's use and understanding of intelligence and logistics had allowed him to plan effective campaigns, and despite difficulties derived from the notorious late summer weather in the Gulf of Mexico, and strategic differences with Havana, he was able to deliver two decisive blows against important targets at short notice. The planning and preparation were essential, as the terrain and climate of West Florida required that ambitious plans be built on impressive foundations. Undoubtedly, he had been fortunate, having provided for as many eventualities as he could. Nature was unbeatable, and at Mobile, not even Gálvez's careful calculations would have saved him if the British had attacked or had a squadron of their ships been in the Gulf. The torpor of his enemies was a bonus that Gálvez was only too pleased to take advantage of, and it is this grit to see his plans through, and improvise new ones, which makes the campaigns of the Mississippi such a fascinating study in the annals of American and eighteenth-century warfare.

The campaign of Gálvez on the Gulf is not a well-known theatre of the American Revolution. For many decades this army was side-lined in popular retellings of the war, dismissed as a war within a war, or in a paragraph that mentions how the Spanish took Pensacola, all of which gives the distinct impression that this was a mostly un-American event. Yet for all that, the army that Gálvez brought through the lower Mississippi to Mobile, and eventually to the trial of the siege of Pensacola, made up of all conditions, nations, and colours, was nothing if not more recognisably American to us today than even George Washington's, because here we can see the Americas on the march, rather than just the America of the United States.

---

39   Caughey, *Gálvez in Louisiana*, p.184.

Select Bibliography

Beerman, Eric, '"Yo Solo" Not "Solo": Juan Antonio de Riano', *Florida Historical Quarterly,* vol.58, no.2 (1979), pp.174–184

Caughey, John Walton, *Bernardo de Gálvez in Louisiana* (Gretna: Firebird Press, 1998)

Chavez, Thomas E., *Spain in the American Revolution: An Intrinsic Gift* (Albuquerque: University of New Mexico Press, 2002)

Descola, Jean, Michael Heron (trans), *Daily Life in Colonial Peru 1710-1820* (London: George Allen & Unwin Ltd, 1968)

Din, Gilbert C. (ed.), *The Louisiana Purchase Bicentennial Series in Louisiana History Vol II: The Spanish Presence in Louisiana 1763–1803* (Lafayette: Centre for Louisiana Studies University of Southwestern Louisiana, 1996)

Haarmann, Albert W. (1960) 'The Spanish Conquest of British West Florida, 1779–1781,' *Florida Historical Quarterly*, vol.39, no.2 (1960), pp.107–134

Holmes, Jack D.L., 'Juan de La Villebeauvre: Spain's Commandant of Natchez During the American Revolution', *Journal of Mississippi History*, vol.27, no.1 (1975), pp.107–137

Kinnaird, Lawrence (ed.), *Annual Report of The American Historical Association for The Year 1945: Volume II Spain in the Mississippi Valley* (Washington: Government Printing Office, 1949)

Lewis, James A., 'The Royal Gunpowder Monopoly in New Spain (1766–1783): A Case Study of Management, Technology, and Reform under Charles III', *Ibero-Amerikanisches Archiv, Neue Folge*, vol.6, no.4 (1980), pp.355–327

Saravia, Gonzalo M. Quintero, *Bernardo de Gálvez: Spanish Hero of the American Revolution* (Chapel Hill: University of North Carolina Press, 2018)

Thonhoff, Robert H., *The Vital Contribution of Texas in the Winning of the American Revolution: An Essay on a Forgotten Chapter in the Spanish Colonial History of Texas* (Karnes City: Published by the author, 2006)

8

L'expédition particulière and the American War of Independence, 1780–1783

Robert A. Selig

The Defeat of 1763 as the Reason for French involvement in the War of Independence

On 6 February 1778, His Most Christian Majesty Louis XVI, By the Grace of God, King of France and Navarre, &c &c entered into an alliance with the self-proclaimed United States of America, a polity that was in a state of rebellion against his fellow monarch George III, By the Grace of God, King of Great Britain, France, and Ireland. For years, absolutist France had already bankrolled a government that claimed to 'derive its just powers from the consent of the governed' based on the seditious idea that 'all men are created equal' and endowed with 'certain unalienable rights' such as 'life, liberty, and the pursuit of happiness.'

In retrospect it is hard to imagine two allies more different than France and the United States. Their alliance was not based on shared values or the ideology of the revolutionaries. In March 1776, the King told his Foreign Minister Charles Gravier, comte de Vergennes, how much he 'disliked the precedent of one monarchy giving support to a republican insurrection against a legitimate monarchy.' Only after Vergennes had convinced him that the goal was 'not so much to terminate the war between America and England as to sustain and keep it alive to the detriment of the English, our natural and pronounced enemies' did the King release funds in support of the Americans.[1] A 1783 memorandum, 'Motifs de la Guerre', asserted that 'France fought the war to assure that independence, to assure the liberty of the seas, and to attain the weakening of English power.'[2] 'Weakening of English power' meant detaching Britain from her Continental American colonies and forcing her to refocus her foreign policy eastward onto Continental Europe and the Ottoman Empire. Concurrently this 'weakening of English power' would re-establish the equilibrium among

---

1   Quoted in General Fonteneau, 'La période française de la guerre d'Indépendance (1776-1780)', *Revue historique des armées* vol.3, no.4, (1976), p.48.

2   Beinecke Rare Book and Manuscript Library, Yale University (BRBML): Rochambeau Papers, Gen Mss 308, Box 1, folder 39.

the five great European powers which had been upset by Britain's victory in the Seven Years War.

Preparations for the next Anglo-French war began in February 1762 already, a full year before the conclusion of the First Peace of Paris. Étienne François, duc de Choiseul-Stainville, France's chief minister during negotiations in 1762, declared that after the end of that war, he would pursue 'only one foreign policy, a fraternal union with Spain; only one policy for war, and that is England.'[3] There was much posturing behind France's official resentment of the loss of her colonial possessions in India and in the New World, where Canada became British and Louisiana was given to Spain. All that was left were St Pierre and Miquelon, the sugar islands of Martinique and Guadeloupe and the fever-infested swamps of French Guyana. Choiseul, however, had almost insisted that Canada be given to Britain. He realized that giving up Canada freed French foreign policy in North America. British negotiator John Russell, Duke of Bedford, anticipated Choiseul's dreams. He saw an alarming mirage emerge across the Atlantic, wondering 'whether the neighborhood of the French to our North American colonies was not the greatest security for their dependence on the mother country, which I feel will be slighted by them when their apprehension of the French is removed.'[4] In 1776 Bedford's fears and Choiseul's hopes became reality. As London reminded her colonists of their obligations to, and dependence on, the mother country, they responded with a *Declaration of Independence* that stressed their differences rather than commonalities.

French Army reforms 1763–1776

Before the next war could be waged, however, France's armed might had to be rebuilt. The defeats of the Seven Years War had laid painfully bare the backwardness of her army and navy.[5] The infantry was 'still basically functioning as in the days of Louis XIV', the artillery in a state of disarray.[6] Beginning in 1762, the war ministry issued dozens of ordonnances which synchronized the organizational structure of the infantry regiments, standardized personnel records, equipment, and training, centralized recruiting, and forbade officers from taking their servants from the ranks. Captains were relieved of the administrative burdens for their companies, which were placed under direct governmental control.[7] By the

---

3   BRBML: Rochambeau Papers, Gen Mss 308, Box 1, folder 39. See also John Singh, 'Plans de Guerre français 1763-1770.' *Revue historique des Armées* vol.3, no.4 (1976), pp.7–22.

4   Quoted in W. J. Eccles, 'The French Alliance and the American Victory' in John Ferling (ed.), *The World Turned Upside Down. The American Victory in the War of Independence* (Westport, CT: Greenwood Press, 1976), p.148.

5   As Secretary of State for the Navy from 10 April 1766 to 24 December 1770, Choiseul initiated the equally urgent reform and rebuilding of the French navy.

6   René Chartrand and Francis Back, *The French Army in the American War of Independence* (London: Osprey, 1991), pp.6–14; the quote is taken from page 6.

7   Rafe Blaufarb, 'Noble Privilege and Absolutist State Building: French Military Administration after the Seven Years War', *French Historical Studies*, vol.24, no. 2 (Spring 2001), p.230 *et passim*. See also Julia Osman, 'Ancient Warriors on Modern Soil: French Military Reform and American Military Images in Eighteenth-century France' *French History*, vol.22, no. 2 (June 2008), p.183.

early 1770s, *Maréchal* de Saxe's dream of the 1740s that some day the French army would march in step was coming true. Reforms were pushed further in 1774, when Louis XVI succeeded to the throne of France. For decades the crown had raised revenue through the sale of offices, titles of nobility, and officer commissions, many of them to young men from wealthy families who had little or no interest in the military profession.[8] The army was over-burdened with generals and colonels. The *Etat militaire de la France* of 1774 lists 11 *Maréchaux de France* and 913 generals, one for every 160 soldiers, and some 900 colonels for 163 regiments. Claude Louis, comte de Saint-Germain, Louis XVI's Minister of War from October 1775 to September 1777, forbade the sale of officers' commissions, retired hundreds of generals, 865 colonels and thousands of company-grade officers. With the savings he added personnel to each company. He abolished the King's Guards, the Horse Grenadiers, and the famous Musketeers as too expensive. In March and April 1776, all regiments (except the Guards and the Régiment du Roi) were reduced to two battalions; regiments with four battalions saw their 2nd and 4th battalions organized into new regiments.[9]

The structure of two-battalion regiments with five companies each plus an auxiliary company of variable strength set up in the *ordonnance* of 25 March 1776, was further clarified on 1 June 1776. Each regiment had one grenadier company in the first battalion consisting of six officers, 14 non-commissioned officers, one *cadet gentilhomme*, one surgeon's assistant, 84 grenadiers and two drummers for a total of six officers and 102 men. Each of the four companies of fusiliers had the authorized strength of six officers, 17 non-commissioned officers, one *cadet gentilhomme*, one surgeon's assistant, 116 fusiliers and two drummers for a total of six officers and 137 men. The newly created chasseur, or light infantry, company of the same strength served in the second battalion. The regimental staff consisted of 12 men: the colonel, the second colonel, one lieutenant colonel, one major, one quarter-master treasurer, two ensigns, one adjutant, one surgeon-major, one chaplain, one drum-major, and one armourer. At the eve of the French departure for America the authorized strength of a regiment stood at 67 officers and 1,148 men (excluding the auxiliary company), but for bookkeeping purposes the strength was fixed at 1,003 men for French, and 1,004 men for foreign, infantry.[10]

The debacles of the Seven Years War had also revealed the urgent need for modernizing the French artillery. Though there had been more French than Prussian cannon at Rossbach in November 1757 (130 to 80) and Minden in August 1759 (246 to 230), but France lost both battles. Haphazard replacement of lost artillery pieces meant that by early 1764, the artillery of Victor François de Broglie's army consisted of seven different makes and models.[11]

---

8   Blaufarb, 'Military Administration', p.228.

9   The best-known of the new regiments is the Gâtinois, whose grenadiers and chasseurs stormed Redoubt No. 9 before Yorktown on 14 October 1781.

10   Including the two *portes-drapeaux* (flag-bearers) and the *quartier-maître trésorier* (pay/quarter master). The strength of a regiment is taken from Lee Kennett, *The French Forces in America, 1780–1783* (Westport, CT: Greenwood Press, 1977), p.22, the regimental organization from Chartrand and Back, *French Army*, p.9. In 1780 the French infantry consisted of 79 French and 24 Foreign Line Regiments. Michel Pétard, 'Les Étrangers au service de la France (1786)', *Tradition*, 32 (September 1989), pp.21–29.

11   Pierre Nardin, *Gribeauval, lieutenant des armées du roi (1715–1789)* (Paris: Fondation pour les études de défense nationale, 1982), p.112.

The task of modernizing the French artillery fell to Jean Baptiste Vaquette de Gribeauval, appointed Inspector General of the Artillery in April 1764. The cornerstone of Gribeauval's reforms was the *ordonnance du Roi* dated 13 August 1765. It established the Royal Corps of Artillery and organized it into four categories based on tactical use. Siege, fortress, and coastal artillery – the stationary artillery – had 12-, 16- and 24-pounders. Also included in this group were the 12-inch and 8-inch *mortiers*. The campaign artillery was equipped with 12-, 8- and 4-pounders and 6-inch howitzers, all of them lighter and more mobile than the old Vallière guns. To maintain secrecy the ordonnance was not printed; copies only were distributed to the inspector-generals and the commanders of the artillery schools.

By the Spring of 1777, the French artillery consisted of seven regiments of two battalions each. Each battalion had 10 companies: four *cannonier* companies equipped with two 12-pounder field guns each, three *cannonier* companies with four light 4-pounder guns per company, and two *bombardiers* companies, each with two 6-inch howitzers. The tenth company were sappers. The strength of each company was uniformly set at one captain, three lieutenants, and 71 non-commissioned officers and enlisted men, including 24 *cannoniers* and 32 assistants, but the number of guns per company was proportional to the number of men needed to maintain and fire them; while five bombardiers were needed for a 6-inch howitzer and eight men were sufficient for a 4-pounder, 15 men were needed to work each 12-pounder. A staff of 24 officers brought the total strength of an artillery regiment to 774 officers and men.[12]

These reforms, necessary as they were, brought St Germain numerous and powerful enemies in the officer corps and at court, but it was the introduction of the universally hated Prussian-style drill and uniform that caused his downfall in September 1777. His successor Alexandre Marie Eleonor of Saint-Mauris, prince of Montbarrey, was forced to resign in December 1780 just after French forces had entered winter quarters in New England.[13]

The Troops of the *Expédition Particulière*

Decision to send troops to the United States came in late January 1780. On 2 February the King approved a plan code-named *expédition particulière*, which sent a force large enough to decide the outcome of the war to America. On 1 March 1780, the King appointed Jean-Baptiste Donatien de Vimeur, comte de Rochambeau, to command the forces of the 'Special Expedition.' He was free to select the units he wanted to take with him from the

---

12   Howard Rosen, *The Système Gribeauval. A study of technological development and institutional change in eighteenth century France* (Thesis (Ph.D.), University of Chicago, 1981), p.41.

13   The highly unpopular uniform of 1776 was not officially replaced until February 1779. Uniforms were replaced in three-year cycles, which suggests that Rochambeau's troops may have worn two different kinds of uniforms. Anticipating difficulties in supplying replacement uniforms, Montbarey appropriated funds 'à l'achat des effets nécessaires pour un habillement complet neuf pour toutes les troupes.' J. Henry Doniol, *Histoire de la participation de la France a l'Établissement des États-Unis d'Amérique*, 5 vols. (Paris: Imprimerie Nationale, 1886-1892), vol.5, pp.322–323. Some units kept parts of their old equipment – the grenadiers of the Soissonnois Regiment wore their bearskin hats on parade through Philadelphia on 3 September 1781.

regiments assembled around Brest for the aborted 1779 invasion of Great Britain.[14] The Bourbonnois Regiment stood under the command of 33-year-old Anne Alexandre, marquis de Montmorency-Laval, but Rochambeau's son, 25-year-old Donatien Marie was *mestre-de-camp-en-second*, second in command, which may have influenced the decision. Soissonnois' *mestre de camp*, Jean-Baptiste Félix d'Ollière, comte de Saint Maisme, was all of 19 when he took command of the regiment in June 1775. St Maisme's second in command, 24-year-old Louis Marie, vicomte de Noailles, was a son of *maréchal* the duc de Mouchy, an influential courtier, and brother-in-law of Gilbert du Motier, marquis de Lafayette. He received his new position on 8 March 1780. Adam Philippe, comte de Custine, the 38-year-old *colonel* of the Saintonge Regiment of Infantry, was by far the oldest (and most difficult) of these regimental commanders. Since his second in command, 24-year-old Armand de la Croix, comte de Charlus, also appointed to the position in March 1780, was the son of the navy minister, the decision to take the regiment may not have been Rochambeau's alone.

Rochambeau had been given blank commissions and quickly found himself pressed by applicants anxious to join his force or looking for employment for family members, friends, and acquaintances. The best known among them is probably 26-year-old Axel von Fersen, favourite of Queen Marie Antoinette, who became an aide-de-camp to Rochambeau. Antoine Charles du Houx, baron de Vioménil, Rochambeau's second in command, secured appointments for about a dozen of his comrades from the Polish campaigns. He also brought along his brother, a cousin, a son-in-law, and two nephews, as well as his eldest son, 13-year-old Charles Gabriel, who served as *aide-de-camp* to his father. Besides his son Rochambeau took his nephew, the comte de Lauberdière, as one of six *aides-de-camp*.[15] Custine's kinsman Jean Robert Gaspar de Custine became a *sous-lieutenant* in the Royal Deux-Ponts on 4 April 1780, three days after his 16th birthday and barely a day or two before embarkation in Brest. Quarter-Master General de Béville took his two sons as members of his staff. It was not just French officers who sought appointments. Friedrich Reinhard Burkard Graf von Rechteren used his descent from Charlotte de Bourbon, his great-great-great-great-great-grandmother who had married William of Orange in 1574, to secure an appointment as *cadet-gentilhomme* in the Royal Deux-Ponts on 11 March 1780.[16] Armed with a Letter of Recommendation from Clemens Wenceslaus, Archbishop and Elector of Trier and uncle of King Louis XVI, Ferdinand von La Roche secured a commission as *sous-lieutenant* in the Royal Deux-Ponts on 4 March.[17]

Rochambeau's instructions from the marquis de Jaucourt, the officer in charge of the operational planning for the *expédition particulière*, stipulated that one third of his troops

---

14   Alain Boulaire, 'Le comte de Rochambeau et ses troupes à Brest, au printemps 1780', *Actes du Colloque international : Victoire de Yorktown et naissance de l'amitié franco-américaine. Bulletin de la Société Archéologique Scientifique & Littéraire du Vendômois* (2022), pp.83–90.

15   Noman Desmarais (trans. and ed.), *The Road to Yorktown: The French Campaigns in the American Revolution, 1780–1783, by Louis-Francois-Bertrand du Pont d'Aubevoye, comte de Lauberdiere* (El Dorado Hills, CA: Savas Beatty, 2021).

16   Jane A. Baum, Hans-Peter Baum, and Jesko Graf zu Dohna (eds), *The adventures of Friedrich Reinhard count of Rechteren-Limpurg in the Mediterranean and the American War of Independence 1770–1782* (bi-lingual) (Baunach: Spurbuchverlag, 2016).

17   Robert A. Selig, 'Friedrich Franck von La Roche (1757–1805)', *German Life*, vol.29 no.1 (June/July 2022), pp.10–19.

consist of German-speaking soldiers. Jaucourt argued that such units could be kept at full strength by recruiting 'deserters from the troops that the English have drawn from Germany, and even prisoners, if any are taken.'[18] Rochambeau chose the Royal Deux-Ponts, which he described to Montbarey on 27 March 1780, as a regiment *que je regarde comme aussi solide par sa composition qu'aucun régiment français et dans le meilleur état* ('which I consider as solid in its make-up as any French regiment and in a better condition').[19] Politics, however, may also have influenced the selection of the regiment. Charles II August of Zweibrücken, a member of the House of Wittelsbach and *colonel propriétaire* of the regiment, ruled an important duchy on France's eastern border. He was also next in line to inherit the vast Wittelsbach territories in Bavaria and elsewhere, which would make him one of the most powerful rulers of the Holy Roman Empire.[20]

Rochambeau also needed light troops. Louis Armand de Gontaut, duc Lauzun, wanted to accompany Rochambeau to America, but lacked troops to command. Created on 5 March 1780 expressly for Lauzun, the Volontaires-étrangers de Lauzun solved both problems. Dissolving the incomplete Second Legion of the Volontaires étrangers de la Marine created in 1778 for the duc de Lauzun and gathering up whatever other personnel was available around Brest, Lauzun's Legion consisted of one company of light infantry, a company of grenadiers, an artillery company and two squadrons of 150 hussars each; light cavalry with roots in the borderlands of south-eastern Europe. Two companies of fusiliers had to remain in France when no shipping space could be found. Around 600 men strong in the American campaign, Lauzun's Legion used German as its language of command, was part of the French Navy, and included a sort of bodyguard for Lauzun in the First Squadron of Hussars.[21] A Hessian spy report from White Plains, New York, in mid-July 1781 stated that 'Thirty-five men are armed with Lances, wear fur Caps, [and] are the best mounted. The whole Legion a fine body of men, and their accoutrements for horses and men very good.'[22] On 6 April 1780, barely four weeks after its creation, the Legion boarded transport vessels in Brest.[23]

Rochambeau's campaign artillery consisted of the reinforced Second Battalion of the Auxonne Regiment of Artillery, around 500 artillerists with eight 12-pounder guns, sixteen 4-pounder guns and six 6-inch howitzers.[24] Lauzun's Legion added two 1-pounder guns *à la Rostaing*.[25] Rochambeau's siege artillery consisted of twelve 24-pounder guns, eight

---

18   Quoted in Kennett, *French Forces*, p.23.

19   Rochambeau's correspondence prior to his departure until 9 December 1781 is published in Doniol, *Histoire*, vol.5, pp.313–590, the quote is on p.331. The complete correspondence is in the Rochambeau Papers MSS 38067 in the Library of Congress, Washington, DC.

20   He died in 1795; his younger brother Maximilian Joseph became the first King of Bavaria in 1806.

21   For a history of Lauzun's Legion see Robert A. Selig, *Hussars in Lebanon! A Connecticut Town and Lauzun's Legion during the American Revolution, 1780–1781* (Lebanon, CT: Lebanon Historical Society, 2004).

22   'Sir Henry Clinton's Original Secret Record of Private Daily Intelligence', *Magazine of American History*, vol.12, no.2 (August 1884), pp.170–171.

23   Samuel F. Scott, *From Yorktown to Valmy: The Transformation of the French Army in an Age of Revolution* (Niwot: University Press of Colorado, 1998), is an indispensable history of the *expédition particulière*.

24   The reinforcement added four 4-pounder guns and two howitzers to the armament of the battalion.

25   In the 1750s Philippe Joseph, comte de Rostaing developed a compact, lightweight carriage for 1-pounder guns used to support infantry.

16-pounder guns, four 8-inch and seven 12-inch mortars and two 8-inch howitzers.[26] A few dozen *mineurs* and engineers, rounded out Rochambeau's combat troops.[27] A quartermaster staff under Pierre François de Béville, a medical department of about 100 under Jean-François Coste,[28] a commissary department headed by Claude Blanchard,[29] a provost department under Pierre Barthélémy Revoux de Ronchamp, rounded out the first division.[30] It consisted of 459 officers (20 more arrived between July 1780 and November 1783[31]) and 5,218 non-commissioned officers and enlisted men. In June 1781, 660 reinforcements arrived from France, and 160 men were recruited in America, for a total of 6,038 men who served in Rochambeau's forces.[32] On 17 April 1780 Rochambeau boarded the *Duc de Bourgogne*, one of five 80-gun vessels in the French navy. On 2 May the convoy of 32 transports and cargo ships protected by seven ships of the line, four frigates, four flutes, a cutter and a schooner under the command of *Chef d'escadre* Charles Henry Louis d'Arsac, chevalier de Ternay, sailed out of Brest.

Living as allies in a foreign country: Military-Civilian Relations

The coast off Rhode Island was sighted on 9 July 1780. On 11 July the convoy sailed into Narragansett Bay; from 13 to 16 July the troops debarked. During the crossing Rochambeau began his record of general orders, *Livre d'ordres contenant les ordres donnés depuis le débarquement des troupes à Newport en Amérique septentrionale 1780*. In his first, undated entries, he copied some of the rules for contact of his forces with the Continental Army

---

26 These are the numbers in a table dated 1 March 1782. Service Historique de la Défense, Château de Vincennes, Vincennes, France (SHD), Guerre d'Indépendance d'Amérique, 3W148.

27 The engineers stood under the command of Colonel Jean Nicolas Desandrouïns. Fragments of his diary are published in Charles Nicholas, *Le Maréchal de Camp Desandrouïns* (Verdun: Renvé-Lallemant, 1887), pp.341–368. The *mineurs* were commanded by Joseph Dieudonné de Chazelles. See Ambassade de France, *French Engineers and the American War of Independence* (New York: 1975).

28 Louis Trenard, 'Un défenseur des hôpitaux militaires: Jean-François Coste', *Revue du Nord*, vol.75, no.299, (January 1993), pp.149–80, and Raymond Bolzinger, 'À propos du bicentenaire de la guerre de l'Indépendance des États-Unis 1775-1783 : Le service de santé de l'armée Rochambeau et ses participants messins', *Mémoires de l'Académie Nationale de Metz*, 4/5 (1979), pp.259–284.

29 Thomas Balch (ed.), *The Journal of Claude Blanchard, Commissary of the French Auxiliary Army sent to the United States during the American Revolution* (Albany: Munsell, 1876), and Jean des Cilleuls, 'Le service de l'intendance à l'armée de Rochambeau', *Revue historique de l'Armée*, no.2, (1957), pp.43–61.

30 Trentinian provides slightly different numbers, i.e., 5,062 non-commissioned officers and men, 183 civilian employees, 232 domestic servants, 23 women and two children plus 467 men 'à la table des capitaines' Jacques de Trentinian, *La France au Secours de l'Amérique* (Paris : Editions SPM, 2016), p.170. The second division, which was to consist primarily of the regiments Anhalt and Neustrie and additional artillery, never came to America. Only the two companies of fusiliers of the Volontaires étrangers de Lauzun, some 410 men strong, who had been left behind in 1780, sailed for the Caribbean in October 1781.

31 Samuel F. Scott, 'The Army of the Comte de Rochambeau between the American and French Revolutions', *Proceedings of the Annual Meeting of the Western Society for French History*, vol.15, (1988), p.144. Twelve non-commissioned officers were promoted to officer rank during the campaign.

32 Samuel F. Scott, 'Rochambeau's Veterans: A Case Study in the Transformation of the French Army', *Proceedings, the Consortium on Revolutionary Europe 1750-1850* (Athens, 1979), p.157.

and civilian American authorities he had received from the King on 1 March 1780.[33] Countersigned by Montbarey, their overriding purpose was winning the hearts and minds of the Americans. George Washington, the President of Congress, and all governors were to be accorded the honours of a *maréchal de France*, of which there were only a dozen in 1780, including eight created by Louis XVI in 1775. At equal rank and date of commission, Continental Army officers took precedence, and French forces were always to yield the place of honour on the right. Of his own authority Rochambeau ordered French troops to add a black tie, the colour of the United States, to their cockades as an outward sign of the Franco-American alliance.[34] Throughout the stay in the United States 'la discipline la plus exacte et la plus sévère' (the most exact and severe discipline) would be observed, but all issues of discipline were to be adjudicated by French military authorities. Marauding was expressly forbidden – no piece of wood, no bundle of straw, no kind of vegetable was to be taken unless by mutual agreement and paid for. Rochambeau meant what he said: on 17 July 1780, already, he ordered an officer's servant who had been arrested the previous day for taking a small amount of fodder without paying for it to receive 25 *coups de baton*.

Louis XVI's instructions to Rochambeau aimed at keeping relations with the Americans as smooth as possible. On the level of field-grade officers, inter-army relations went smoothly enough. Accounts of French officers are full of praise for General George Washington and Rochambeau never challenged Washington's position as commander-in-chief. On the level of company-grade officers and the rank-and-file, Rochambeau succeeded primarily by keeping his forces away from the Continental Army. From July 1780 to June 1781, French forces were posted in Newport, Rhode Island.[35] During the six-week encampment in Greenburgh, New York, the troops set up their tents in widely separated camps.[36] Road conditions and issues of supplying the armies placed them on separate routes and marching schedules on the march to Virginia in August and September 1781.[37] It was during the siege of Yorktown that an altercation occurred between French and American forces when Captain Patrick Duffy was court martialed 'for abusing a French soldier.' Duffy was sentenced to be discharged.[38] While the Continental Army returned north in October and

---

33   The instructions are printed in Doniol, *Histoire*, vol.5, pp.324–326, the secret instructions on pp.327–328.

34   'Les troupes françaises ajouteront à leurs cocardes du noir qui est la couleur des Etats-unis d'Amérique', Armée de Rochambeau, *Livre d'ordres contenant les ordres donnés depuis le débarquement des troupes à Newport en Amérique septentrionale 1780*. Archives départementales de Metz: call number E 235, (unpaginated). The livre d'ordres were published by Arnaud Blondet, *Jeux de Guerre, L'Histoire de L'Armee de Rochambeau Au Secours des États-Unis 1780-1781 Tome 1* (Monfaucon: Éditions Jean-Jacques Wuillaume, 2023).

35   Robert A. Selig, *The Washington-Rochambeau Revolutionary Route in the Commonwealth of Rhode Island, 1781-1783. An Historical and Architectural Survey* (Providence, RI: Washington-Rochambeau Revolutionary Route Association of Rhode Island and Providence Plantations, 2015).

36   Robert A. Selig, *The Franco-American Encampment in the Town of Greenburgh, 6 July–18 August 1781: A Historical Overview and Resource Inventory* (Greenburgh, New York: Town of Greenburgh, 2020).

37   In March 2009, the United States Congress designated the land and water routes taken by the allied armies to and from Yorktown as the Washington-Rochambeau Revolutionary Route National Historic Trail. Background information, resource inventories and site surveys are available at <https://w3r-us.org/>.

38   William Feltman, *The Journal of Lieut. William Feltman, of the First Pennsylvania Regiment, 1781–82*

November 1781, French forces spent the winter in and around Williamsburg and did not set out for New York until July 1782. Following a brief joint encampment at Verplanck on the Hudson River in September 1782, the armies went their separate ways, the Continental Army to Newburgh, French forces eventually to Boston, from where they sailed for the West Indies on Christmas Day 1782.

French officers were impressed the one time they saw the Continental Army. While encamped at Greenburgh, 'General Washington invited our headquarters staff to come to see it.' On 9 July 1781, Baron Closen was in for a surprise. 'I had a chance to see the American army, man for man. It was really painful to see these brave men, almost naked with only some trousers and little linen jackets, most of them without stockings, but, would you believe it? Very cheerful and healthy in appearance. A quarter of them were negroes, merry, confident, and sturdy.'[39] Artillery *Lieutenant* Jean-François Louis, comte de Clermont-Crèvecœur, wrote that 'in beholding this army I was struck, not by its smart appearance, but by its destitution: the men were without uniforms and covered with rags; most of them were barefoot. They were of all sizes, down to children who could not have been over fourteen. There were many negroes, mulattoes, etc.'[40] To Cromot du Bourg, the Continental Army seemed 'to be in as good order as possible for an army composed of men without uniforms and with narrow resources.' Like Closen, who called the Rhode Island Regiment 'the most neatly dressed, the best under arms, and the most precise in its maneuvres', du Bourg mentioned that 'The Rhode Island Regiment, among others, is extremely fine', and added to the 'great number of negroes in the army;' he estimated the overall strength of Washington's army at 'four thousand and some hundred men at the most.'[41] The comte de Lauberdière observed that a 'glance gave me great pleasure not because of the appearance and uniform of the regiments, for, at present, and since the beginning of the war, they are practically all naked. But I remember their great accomplishments and I could only see, with a certain admiration, that it was with these same men that General Washington so gloriously defended his country.'[42]

In the absence of court martial records or regimental orderly books, reconstruction of discipline issues is dependent on sources such as the *contrôles*, the enlistment records of Rochambeau's soldiers. Sometime after 25 September 1781, during the march from Williamsburg to Gloucester Court House, one of Lauzun's chasseurs killed a Virginian. On 1 October, 25-year-old Jacques Bergeot was executed for *assassinat* – murder. The case was hushed up and no information on the victim, or the time and place of the murder, has been found.[43] Entries in diaries and journals also provide glimpses of tensions between French soldiers and the civilian population. On 28 July 1782, Judge George Lindenberger informed Maryland Governor Thomas Sim Lee that 'a most audacious and Bloody Riote

---

(Philadelphia: Historical Society of Pensylvania, 1853), p.19.

39   Evelyn Acomb (ed.), *The Revolutionary Journal of Baron Ludwig von Closen, 1780-1783* (Chapel Hill: University of North Carolina Press, 1958), pp.90–92.

40   Jean-François Louis, comte de Clermont-Crèvecœur, *Journal* in Howard C. Rice Jr. and Anne S. K. Brown (eds), *The American Campaigns of Rochambeau's Army 1780, 1781, 1782, 1783* (Princeton: Princeton University Press, 1972), vol.1, pp.33–34.

41   Marie-François baron Cromot du Bourg, 'Diary of a French Officer, 1781', *Magazine of American History*, vol.4 (April 1880), p.299.

42   Desmarais, *The Road to Yorktown*, p.105.

43   Archives Nationales de France, Paris, *Contrôles* of Lauzun's Legion, catalogue number D 2c 32.

was Comitted Last Thursday by a number of Sailors on some French Soldiers.' Two soldiers and a hussar had been in a tavern at Fell's Point when a brawl broke out. The sailors 'took the Swords from 2 Soldiers, drawed the Swords through the Soldiers hands and cut them; a Light horse men of the French when seeing the Soldiers disarmed, … drew his Sword … but 2 of the Sailors with their Swords struck with the Swords at the L. Horse men.'[44] A few days later, Robert Guillaume Dillon, *colonel-en-second* of Lauzun's Legion, galloping through Baltimore, knocked down a child. A hussar riding behind Dillon got into an argument with the father, a crowd gathered and almost beat the hussar to death.[45]

Except for a three-sentence addition to the 'Ordonnance du Roi pour régler l'exercice de ses troupes d'infanterie' of 1 June 1776 concerning firing in two ranks and an equally short addition to Title 20 of the *Règlement provisoire sur le service de l'infanteris en campagne* of 1778 concerning picket posts, Rochambeau did not order any alterations to military manuals. During their 30 months in the United States, Rochambeau's forces found themselves in but a handful of small, traditional combat situations. French infantry never debarked during the naval expedition under Jean François de Galaup, comte de Lapérouse, to Virginia in March 1781. An amphibious operation on 12 July 1781 against English forces at Fort Franklin on Lloyd's Point in Huntington, Long Island, New York, carried out by some 500 French troops, failed. Equally unsuccessful was a surprise attack on Morrissania Manor carried out by Lauzun's Legion in cooperation with American forces under General Benjamin Lincoln in the early morning hours of 4 July 1781. That leaves the Battle of the Hook in Gloucester County, Virginia, between Lauzun's hussars and Lieutenant Colonel Banastre Tarleton's dragoons on 3 October 1781, and the siege of Yorktown, which was conducted along the traditional lines outlined a century earlier by Sébastien Le Prestre de Vauban.[46]

Most of the time the French officers were bored. In September 1780, Lafayette's brother-in-law the vicomte de Noailles expressed the frustration of many when he wrote that the 'gallant Frenchmen' had come to America 'to deliver America entirely from the yoke of her tyrants', but all they seemed to be doing was waste time and money in their less than comfortable winter-quarters in Newport.[47] Frustration caused by forced inactivity resulted in at least three duels among officers in Newport.[48] Questions of honour and promotion also proved a fertile ground for tensions in the officer corps. As the Saintonge regiment prepared for departure in the spring of 1780, the position of *major* became open. *Capitaine* Pierre Rezard de Wouves had hoped to receive the position, but it went to Teissedre de Fleury instead. With the compliance of other officers who resented the appointment of an outsider

---

44   '1782 Depositions regarding a riot between French soldiers and American sailors, July 27, 28 at Fell's Point', Maryland Center of History and Culture, Baltimore, MS 1814. The sailors escaped before they could be arrested.

45   Jean-Baptiste-Antoine de Verger, *Journal*, in Rice and Brown, *American Campaigns*, vol.1, p.161.

46   Jerome A. Greene, *The Guns of Independence: The Siege of Yorktown, 1781* (El Dorado Hills, CA: Savas Beatie, 2005).

47   In a letter to Vergennes of September 1780, quoted in Kennett, *French forces*, p.87.

48   For details see Gilbert Bodinier, *Les officiers de l'Armée royale combattants de la guerre d'Indépendance des États-Unis de Yorktown à l'an II* (Vincennes: Service Historique de l'armée de Terre, 1983), pp.189–201. Bodinier lists eight duels during the stay in the United States; six of them involved officers of Lauzun's Legion.

to this coveted position, Wouves tried to make Fleury's life miserable until he was court-martialled and sent to prison late February 1781. Upon release he resigned his commission on 4 April 1781, sailed to Martinique, and entered Spanish service. After the victory at Yorktown, William de Deux-Ponts returned to France and resigned his commission as *colonel-en-second. Lieutenant-colonel* Baron Ludwig Eberhard von Esebeck 'had much reason to hope for and even some rights to this position', but the appointment of 27 January 1782 went to Axel von Fersen instead, who 'was too well liked at Court!!!'[49]

On campaign in 1781, discipline broke down on at least one occasion as French forces went on a rampage. In the afternoon of 22 July, during the Grand Reconnaissance of British fortifications around New York City, the grenadiers and chasseurs of the Soissonnois and Saintonge regiments cooperating with Lauzun's Legion were pursuing Loyalist 'cowboys.' During a rest,

> some alarmed poultry took flight and our grenadiers got ready to chase them. The chevalier de Brie who commanded them was about to stop them but the comte de C[harlus], our *colonel-en-second*, told him: 'Hey young man, leave them be, that's faire game!' These few words did not fall onto the ground, they were heard and spread with amazing speed. Lauzun's Legion, which did not need to be encouraged to engage in pillaging swept our troops along. It lost all cohesion, spread out into remote houses, and helped themselves to everything that caught their eyes. The boldest soldiers dared to go up to the rear of the enemy. Some of them, searching meticulously, found trunks, clothing, silverware, which the inhabitants of the countryside had hidden, and then, greed knows no boundaries: everywhere where the soil had been moved, they searched, they saw gold everywhere, they always believed to find rich loot, and coming across an area where there had been fighting, they finished by exhuming a pile of dead bodies, which afterwards almost brought the plague into the country.[50]

Saint-Cyr's comment that Lauzun's Legion 'did not need to be encouraged to engage in pillaging' points to the one constant component in virtually all the trouble both within the French army and with the civilian population. Quickly thrown together in the Spring of 1780 and replenished with equally quickly deserting volunteers from among German prisoners of war, the Legion lacked cohesion and *esprit de corps*. An equally fractious officer corps only aggravated the situation. Losses reflect the fragile structure of the Legion: six

---

49   Acomb (ed.), *The Revolutionary Journal of Baron Ludwig von Closen*, p.242.
50   Georges Cyr Antoine de Bellemare de Saint-Cyr, *Extrait des Mémoires du chevalier de Bellemare de Saint-Cyr, lieutenant-colonel d'infanterie [Régt. de Saintonge] régié par lui-même en 1815.* David M. Rubenstein Rare Book & Manuscript Library, Duke University, Durham, North Carolina, Warrington Dawson Collection, Collection no. 1424. The incident is mentioned in other journals as well, viz. the *Journal of Robert Guillaume Dillon,* Society of the Cincinnati, Washington, DC, MSS L2015G152 M. Dillon encountered 'Unfortunate women [who] had been stripped up to the kerchiefs they had at their throats, and God knows everything that had been done and that I did not see.' Captain Jean Georges Anne Prosper du Rieu de Madron de Brie commanded the company of chasseurs of the Saintonge Regiment during the American Campaign. Charlus' letters to his father are in SHD: call No. A13 722; they do not mention this incident.

of its soldiers were executed, five of them for desertion, while only two hussars were killed in combat on 3 October 1781, and three men are known to have died of combat-related wounds. Another five were expelled for various offenses and one sentenced to the galleys.[51]

Adjusting to social norms in America posed its own challenges. Americans knew as little about their allies as the French knew about the people that had come to assist. The process of getting to know each other began the moment Rochambeau's contingent stepped ashore into a culture deeply imbued with anti-French, anti-Catholic sentiments. Reflecting on his journey to England in the 1750s, Louis Charles Fougeret de Monbron informed his French readers,

> We are the only nation in the universe that the English do not despise. They rather do us the honour of hating us with all the heartiness possible. Their aversion against us is a sentiment with which they are inculcated from the cradle. Before they know that there is a God to worship, they know that there are Frenchmen to be detested.[52]

These sentiments had travelled with the settlers from the British Isles to New England and been reinforced in decades of warfare, most recently in the French and Indian War. Twelve years of uneasy friendship since the Peace of Paris had done little to eradicate old prejudices rooted in a long tradition of Puritan and *emigré* Huguenot anti-Catholicism.[53] In May 1779, more than a year after the signing of the Franco-American alliance of February 1778, the Reverend James Dana reminded the state legislators that 'the preservation of our religion depends on the continuance of a free government. Let our allies have their eyes open on the blessings of such a government, and they will at once renounce their superstition. On the other hand, should we lose our freedom this will prepare the way to the introduction of popery.'[54] Americans saw Frenchmen as 'adherents of a despicable and superstitious religion, as the slavish subjects of a despotic and ambitious prince, as frivolous dandies lacking in manly virtues, as physical and moral inferiors whose very dress and eating habits evidenced this inferiority.'[55]

Upon arrival, Rochambeau's officers expected a heartfelt welcome, but a disappointed William de Deux-Ponts remarked upon landing in Newport that the French had 'not met with that reception on landing which we expected and which we ought to have had.'[56] Clermont-Crèvecœur added that 'the local people, little disposed in our favour, would have preferred, at that moment, I think, to see their enemies arrive rather than their allies.' He

---

51   For more detail see Robert A. Selig, 'Hessians Fighting for American Independence? German Deserters recruited for Lauzun's Legion in America, 1780–1782', *Journal of the Johannes Schwalm Historical Association*, vol.7, no.4 (2004), pp.39–51.

52   Jean-Louis Fougeret de Montbron, *Préservatif contre l'Anglomanie* (A Minorque, 1757), p.52.

53   See Gayle K. Brown, '"Into the Hands of Papists": New England Captives in French Canada and the English Anti-Catholic Tradition, 1689–1763', *The Maryland Historian*, vol.21 (1990), pp.1–11.

54   James Dana, *A Sermon Preached before the General Assembly of the State of Connecticut at Hartford on the Day of the Anniversary Election, May 13, 1779* (Hartford: Hudson & Goodwin, 1779), p.15.

55   Samuel F. Scott, 'Foreign Mercenaries, Revolutionary War, and Citizen Soldiers in the Late Eighteenth Century.' *War and Society*, vol.2 (September 1984), pp.42–58.

56   William de Deux-Ponts, Samuel Abbot Green (ed.), *My Campaigns in America* (Boston: J.K. Wiggin & W.P. Lunt, 1868), p.91.

thought the British were to blame. They 'had made the French seem odious to the Americans … saying that we were dwarfs, pale, ugly, specimens who lived exclusively on frogs and snails.'[57] French history had followed the soldiers of Louis XVI across the Atlantic. For the rest of her life seven-year-old Eliza Susan Morton remembered the summer day in August 1781 when French troops on their way to Yorktown stopped opposite her house in Basking Ridge, New Jersey to refresh themselves. She and her family

> were all in raptures at the sight of their new allies coming to fight their battles and ensure victory. Every one ran to the doors and windows, except Mrs. Kemper, who retired to her apartment with my grandfather. The cruel conduct of the French soldiers in Germany could not be forgotten by these emigrants from their 'father-land.' They refused to be comforted and bewailed with tears the introduction of these allies.[58]

Like thousands of Germans, 'Mrs. Kemper' and 'my grandfather' had sought refuge in the New World from the devastation caused by French forces along the Rhine during the War of the Austrian Succession (1740-1748). Even some of their fellow French-speakers wanted little to do with Rochambeau's soldiers. *Sous-lieutenant* Nicolas François Denis Brisout de Barneville thought that the negative image of the French had at least partly been formed 'by numerous French refugees', (Huguenots) who had settled in America after the revocation of the Edict of Nantes in 1685.[59]

Nevertheless, French forces were welcomed by local populations even in New England for the simple reason that they, or rather their purchasers, paid goods in specie rather than in worthless Continental Dollars. On 31 December 1781, John Jeffrey wrote to Jeffrey Whiting from Hartford, 'Money is very scarce among the People in General, their daily Prayers are that the French Army may return soon to the part of the World that Money may again circulate amongst them.'[60] The impact of Rochambeau's gold and silver on the economy of the United States was enormous. Lee Kennett estimates that between public and private funds, 'French forces may well have disbursed 20 million livres in coin', possibly doubling the amount of specie circulating in the 13 states.[61] French wealth in turn occasionally lead to friction with American supply officers who found themselves priced out of the market once French purchasers appeared. On 21 August 1781, Deputy Quartermaster James Hendricks in Alexandria complained:

---

57   Clermont-Crèvecœur, *Journal*, p.17. These views were not confined to New England. Following Cornwallis's surrender, Colonel William Fontaine of the Virginia militia wrote on 26 October 1781 that 'the French are very different from the ideas formerly inculcated in us of a people living on frogs and coarse vegetables.' Quoted in Henry P. Johnston, *The Yorktown Campaign and the Surrender of Cornwallis 1781* (New York: Harper & Brothers, 1881), p.178.

58   Eliza Quincy, *Memoir of the Life of Eliza S. M. Quincy* (Boston: J. Wilson and Son, 1861), pp.39–40.

59   'Journal de Guerre de Brissout de Barneville. Mai 1780-Octobre 1781', *The French-American Review*, vol.3, no. 4 (October 1950) p.242.

60   Connecticut Historical Society, Hartford, CT: Wadsworth Papers Box 39, folder 10: Wadsworth and Carter Correspondence, July 1781–February 1782.

61   Kennett, *French forces*, p.68.

Lord knows what will be done for provisions! Colo. Wadsworth & Carter, the French Agents have their Riders all round the Country, buying flour & beef with specie, this will effectively prevent the Commissioners from procuring any, as there is not a probability of the People letting the State Agents have an Ounce on Credit while they can get the French Crowns & Louis, I wish the Executive wou'd fall on some method to get the Cash from the French, and furnish the Supplies, without some method or other is fell on, the American Army will be starved.[62]

French officers knew little about their allies, their customs and society.[63] Rochambeau's staff contained a small number of 'American' veterans such as Fleury who had served in the Continental Army. Denis Jean Florimont de Langlois, marquis du Bouchet had fought at Saratoga but returned to France in 1779, reclaimed his commission, and returned with Rochambeau.[64] These men provided important points of contact between Washington and Rochambeau, greatly facilitating cooperation between the two armies.[65] Few of the other officers spoke English or knew much about the United States. High-ranking officers imbued with the ideals of the Enlightenment expected virtuous people fighting selflessly for high ideas. Their perception of the *Mirage in the West* of an idealized America as a *tabula rasa* had been created by *philosophes* rather than by reality.[66] This world was peopled by noble savages and settlers living in lone outposts of civilization in the American wilderness. Citizen-soldiers had risen in a spirit of patriotism and sacrifice against perfidious Albion – an image that could not survive the test of reality when the two worlds met.[67]

'Reality' meant that Americans seemed to primarily care about money. Rochambeau felt himself 'at the mercy of usurers.'[68] Axel von Fersen told his father in January 1781,

---

62 National Archives and Records Administration (NARA): Revolutionary War Records, Miscellaneous Numbered Records, Record Group 93, microfilm reel 92, No. 26743. American officers repeatedly bemoaned the fact that they could not invite their French counterparts to dinner because they simply did not have the funds.

63 Robert A. Selig, 'Old World Meets New: Franco-American Encounters and the *expédition particulière*, 1780-1782', *The Brigade Dispatch. Journal of the Brigade of The American Revolution*, vol.37, no.1 (Spring 2007), pp.2–11.

64 Du Bouchet's *Journal d'un emigré; ou cahier d'un etudiant en philosophie* is located in the Rare Books and Manuscripts Division of Cornell University Library. See Robert A. Selig, 'A French Volunteer who lived to rue America's Revolution: Denis Jean Florimond de Langlois, marquis Du Bouchet', *Colonial Williamsburg. The Journal of the Colonial Williamsburg Foundation*, vol.21, no.3 (June/July 1999), pp.16–25.

65 Thomas Antoine de Mauduit du Plessis had served as a captain in the Continental artillery and distinguished himself at Redbank in 1777. In 1779, he returned to France but joined Rochambeau in 1780 as *aide-major* of artillery.

66 Durand Echeverria, 'Mirage in the West: French *Philosophes* rediscover America', in Charles W. Toth (ed.), *Liberté, Egalité, Fraternité: The American Revolution and the European Response* (Troy, NY: Whitston Publishing, 1989), pp.35–47.

67 Jean-Jacques Fiechter, 'L'aventure américaine des officiers de Rochambeau vue à travers leurs journaux' in Michèle R. Morris (ed.), *Images of America in Revolutionary France* (Washington, DC: Georgetown University Press, 1990), pp.65–82, and Gilbert Bodinier, 'Les officiers du corps expéditionnaire de Rochambeau et la Revolution française', *Revue historique des armées*, vol.3, no.4 (1976), pp.139–164.

68 Quoted in Samuel F. Scott, 'Strains in the Franco-American Alliance: The French Army in Virginia,

the spirit of patriotism only exists in the chief and principal men in the country, who are making very great sacrifices; the rest who make up the great mass think only of their personal interests. Money is the controlling idea in all their actions ... Their greed is unequalled, money is their God; virtue, honour, all count for nothing to them compared with the precious metal.[69]

Unaccustomed to a market economy based on the laws of supply and demand, the French noble officer corps largely lived in a world of its own where demand, their demand, was all that mattered. If they felt that Americans were taking advantage of them, they partly had themselves to blame. Thomas Lloyd Halsey of Providence explained that high freight costs 'might have been lower had they even had asked a day before they wanted but they never would or did. They commonly sent to me at Sunsett to obtain what they wanted for the Morning, which is no way of taking the advantage of Business.'[70]

The most serious tensions between Americans and French troops arose during winter quarters in Virginia. Virginians were convinced that French officers were stealing enslaved people by claiming them as their servants.[71] Besides Rochambeau, other French officers such as Ludwig von Closen, Jean-François Coste, Robert Guillaume Dillon, and Mathieu Dumas had either purchased enslaved people or hired free black as servants. There is evidence, however, that some French officers, especially in the confusion following the surrender at Yorktown, did indeed spirit Blacks on board some of de Grasse's ships for transportation to the West Indian sugar plantations.[72] Once again Lauzun's Legionnaires appear prominently in the written record. On 22 March 1782, Colonel Thomas Read informed the governor of Virginia from the Legion's winter quarters in Charlotte Courthouse that 'there is a number of negroes with the Troops' and unless they were quickly reclaimed, 'those who have Property of that kind in the vicinity of the Camps will suffer by their going off.'[73] In May 1782, William Dandridge complained that one of his enslaved people, a 'very likely and valuable fellow' was employed by a French *major* who refused to turn him over since the man claimed to be a freeman, and he had therefore a right to employ him. Since then

1781–82' in Richard A. Rutyna and Peter C. Stewart (eds), *Virginia in the American Revolution* (Norfolk: Old Dominion University, 1983), p.91.

69   'Letters of Axel de Fersen, Aide-de-Camp to Rochambeau written to his Father in Sweden 1780-1782', *Magazine of American History*, vol.3 (1879), p.371.

70   Thomas Lloyd Halsey to Peter Colt, 23 October 1781, in Connecticut Historical Society, Hartford, Connecticut: Jeremiah Wadsworth Papers, Original Correspondence July 1781 to February 1782.

71   The issue is discussed in detail in Scott, 'Strains' and *Yorktown to Valmy*, pp.79–80.

72   Joachim du Perron, comte de Revel, *Journal Particulier d'une Campagne aux Indes Occidentales (1781–1782)* (Paris: Chez Henri Charles-Lavauzelle, 1898), p.176. Dupleix de Cadignan, *Lieutenant colonel* of the Régiment d'Agenois, indirectly confirmed Perron's observations when he entered into his journal on 16 November 1781 that 'a few negroes taken at York had brought the small-pox onto the Ville de Paris.' Jean-Baptiste de Dupleix de Cadignan, *Journal des differentes campagnes que j'aÿ fait soit par terre ou par mer, depuis que je suis entré au service, ainsi que des principaux evenements qui se sont passés dans les differents climats que j'aÿ parcouru*, vol.2, p.277. MSS L2018F24f [Bound], Society of the Cincinnati, Washington, DC.

73   Anon., *Calendar of Virginia State Papers and other Manuscripts* (Richmond, VA: James E. Goode, 1883), vol.3, p.107.

that slave had disappeared only to be replaced by another runaway.[74] When the *major*, Jean Ladislas Pollerescky, wanted to return to Europe after the victory at Yorktown, the Legion's *Lieutenant colonel* Claude Hugau placed him under arrest. Among the more serious charges in the 20-count indictment was that of running a horse-theft ring, but as the complaint by Dandridge indicated, he also seems to have traded in enslaved people.[75]

Rochambeau's officers had brought much cultural baggage with them. New England society was a society composed largely of equals. In 1782, Hector St. John de Crèvecœur observed that 'the rich and poor are not so far removed from each other as they are in Europe.' He defined an American as someone who had left 'behind him all his ancient prejudices and manners', who saw no reason to defer to someone because he wore epaulettes or had a title of nobility.[76] French peasants had no right to question a nobleman's actions. In America the rules of warfare were different. The chevalier de Coriolis informed his father,

> Here it is not like it is in Europe, where when the troops are on the march you can take horses, you can take wagons, you can issue billets for lodging, and with the aid of a gendarme overcome the difficulties the inhabitant might make; but in America the people say they are free and, if a proprietor who doesn't like the look of your face tells you he doesn't want to lodge you, you must go seek a lodging elsewhere. Thus the words: 'I don't want to' end the business, and there is no means of appeal.[77]

The vicomte de Tresson, a captain in the Saintonge, told his father disgustedly: 'Here they have more respect for a lout than they have for a duke in France.'[78] Could it be that a colonist had pointed out to de Tresson that in America we 'have no princes for whom we toil, starve and bleed'?[79]

Recruitment and Desertion

By the time they moved into winter quarters in November 1780, Rochambeau's units had lost almost 200 men.[80] Jaucourt's assumption that Hessian prisoners in Pennsylvania and Maryland would need but little encouragement to take French service proved correct.[81]

---

74   Anon., *Calendar of Virginia State Papers*, vol.3, p.183.
75   Gérard-Antoine Massoni, *Détails intéressants sur les événements arrivés dans la guerre d'Amérique. Hyver 1781 à 1782. Hampton, Charlotte et suitte. Manuscrit de Claude Hugau, lieutenant-colonel de la Légion des Volontaires Etrangers de Lauzun* (Besançon: Université de Franche-Comté, 1996), pp.71–79.
76   Hector St. John de Crèvecœur, *Letters from an American Farmer* (New York: E.P. Dutton, 1957), p.36.
77   'Lettres d'un officier de l'Armée de Rochambeau: le chevalier de Coriolis', *Le correspondant*, no.326 (25 March 1932), p.818.
78   Quoted in Lee Kennett, 'L'expédition Rochambeau-Ternay: un succès diplomatique', *Revue historique des armées*, vol.3, no.4 (1976), p.100.
79   Crèvecœur, *Letters*, p.36.
80   Samuel F. Scott, 'The Soldiers of Rochambeau's Expeditionary Corps: From the American Revolution to the French Revolution' in Claude Fohlen and Jacques Godechot (eds), *La Révolution Américaine et l'Europe* (Paris: Centre national de la recherche scientifique, 1979), p.570.
81   Hessian is used as a generic term to denote all of Britain's German-speaking auxiliaries.

When news of the landing of French forces in Newport reached Pennsylvania, Hessian deserters approached Anne-César de La Luzerne, the French minister in Philadelphia, offering to serve either in Lauzun's Legion or in the Royal Deux-Ponts. Only two weeks after Rochambeau's arrival, Luzerne on 25 July 1780 contacted Joseph Reed, President of the Supreme Executive Council of Pennsylvania, who saw no legal obstacle to French recruitment of Hessian volunteers. The next day Luzerne told Rochambeau to send recruiters to Philadelphia.[82] By mid-August 1780, advertisements appeared in newspapers in New England and in the Mid-Atlantic States calling on 'all German deserters from the armies of Great-Britain' to enlist 'in the hussars, commanded by the Duke of Lauzun, who is in Rhode Island at the head of a Legion, or in the German regiment called Zweybrück or Royal Deuxponts, commanded by the Count of Deuxponts.' Concurrently, *sous-lieutenant* Charles de Kilmaine of the Hussars was sent to Philadelphia to head recruiting stations at 'the Barracks' on Fifth and Green Streets and at 'Mr. Peter Hays's, in Third-street, near Race-street.'[83]

On the surface the recruitment of Hessian deserters appears to have been successful. Kilmaine and the recruiters from the Royal Deux-Ponts quickly signed up 160 men; 92 for Lauzun's Legion and 67 for the Royal Deux-Ponts.[84] The Royal Deux-Ponts had lost 12 men during the transatlantic crossing; from September to 1 November another 57 soldiers died. Without having fired a shot the regiment was 69 men short by the time it went into winter quarters.[85] The 67 recruits made up these losses, but the benefits the regiment derived from them were mixed at best; 35 men deserted before the regiment sailed out of Boston for the West Indies on Christmas Day 1782, and 46 men from Lauzun's Legion abandoned the colours before the Legion sailed from Philadelphia for France in May 1783. When a whole patrol of hussars rode into the woods of Connecticut from its winter quarters in Lebanon in mid-December 1780, Rochambeau on 22 December 1780 ordered Lauzun 'not to [further] taint yourself with the business of recruiting Hessian deserters, of whom as you know I have never had a good opinion.'[86] After that recruitment slowed down but never ceased completely; as late as November 1782, a new recruit joined the Legion.[87]

The inclusion of the Royal Deux-Ponts and the German-speaking *volontaires étrangers* in Rochambeau's little army proved a mistake. Most of the Royal Deux-Ponts had been recruited in the Palatinate, home of most of the German settlers in Pennsylvania. Georg Daniel Flohr, an enlisted man in the regiment, wrote that during the march through

---

82   Luzerne to Rochambeau with insert of Reed's letter. BRBML: Rochambeau Family Papers, Gen Mss 146, Box 2.

83   The advertisement is dated Philadelphia, 29 August 1780, and quoted as printed in the *New-Jersey Gazette* (Trenton), 27 September 1780. Rochambeau was not allowed to recruit among the American population. Jean Folmer of Pennsylvania who joined the Second Squadron of Hussars on 5 November 1780 is the only American-born soldier known to serve in any of Rochambeau's units. Enlisted only for the duration of the war, he was discharged on 1 May 1783.

84   See Scott, 'Rochambeau's Veterans', p.155. A single soldier enlisted in another unit.

85   All data based on the Royal Deux-Ponts *côntroles* are SHD: 1 Yc 869 (1776–1783 and 4 February 1784 to 1786).

86   Rochambeau to Lauzun, 22 December 1780, Library of Congress: Rochambeau Papers, vol.7.

87   Contrôles of Lauzun's Legion, Archives Nationales de France: catalogue number D 2c 32 (March 1780–1783).

Philadelphia 'one can justly say that the third part of the regiment met fellow countrymen. Among them were also very many brothers and sisters who met and who had not seen each other for many years [because] they had emigrated to go to this New Country.'[88] There were German immigrants in most states, providing German-speaking deserters a built-in support network. Even their religious affiliation worked to their advantage. 'French' regiments were almost exclusively Catholic, but 269 (22.8 percent) of the men of the Royal Deux-Ponts were Lutheran, another 180 (15.2 percent) Reformed Christians whose presence posed no threat to the souls of Americans. The 104 deserters from Royal Deux-Ponts and 131 men from Lauzun's Legion, provided 75 percent of the 316 deserters of Rochambeau's forces.[89] The three 'French' regiments and the artillery accounted for the remaining 81 deserters, many of whom deserted at crucial moments such as just prior the departure from Newport in June 1781, from Williamsburg following winter quarters in 1781–1782 or the embarkation in Boston, when a decision had to be made. Besides deserters Rochambeau lost 600 men, 30 of them to combat or combat-related wounds, 140 men were discharged, another 31 officers and 14 enlisted men retired with military pensions.[90]

Conclusion

France had entered the war in part to assist the United States in gaining their independence. With the victory at Yorktown that goal was achieved. Following winter quarters in 1780–1781 in Newport and Lebanon, French forces united with the Continental Army on 6 July 1781 in Westchester County. *Lieutenant Général des armées navales* de Grasse's missive that he was sailing for the Chesapeake reached the Odell House on 14 August. Four days later, the allied armies, around 2,350 Americans, their officers and around 50 women and children, and around 4,300 French soldiers and 312 company-grade officers accompanied by 1,000 or more servants, two dozen women and children, some 1,500 horses and a wagon train of over 300 wagons pulled by six oxen each, were on their way. The roughly 650-mile deployment across a thinly populated country – towns such as Trenton had but 500 inhabitants – was a major logistical achievement. Sailing down the Chesapeake from Plum Point near Elkton, Fell's Point in Baltimore, and Annapolis, the allied armies landed at College Creek in late September and marched to Williamsburg. On 28 September the siege of Yorktown began; three weeks later the British army there surrendered. French forces spent the winter of 1781–1782 in Virginia. The march to the northward began on 1 July and took them to Boston by early December. On Christmas Day the troops sailed out of Boston for the West Indies; only Lauzun's Legion remained behind in Wilmington, Delaware, and sailed for France in May 1783. His mission accomplished Rochambeau departed from Annapolis for

---

88   *Reisen Beschreibung von America welche das Hochlöbliche Regiment von Zweybrücken hat gemacht zu Wasser und zu Land vom Jahr 1780 bis 84*. Médiathèque André Malraux, Strasbourg, France: Fonds Patrimoniaux MS 15. See Robert A. Selig, 'A German Soldier in America, 1780–1783: The Journal of Georg Daniel Flohr', *William and Mary Quarterly*, vol.50, no.3 (July 1993), pp.75–90.
89   Scott, 'Rochambeau's Expeditionary Corps', p.570.
90   Scott, 'Rochambeau's Veterans', p.156.

France on 14 January 1783. By November 1783, the last remnants of the *expédition particulière* had reached France as well.

Bibliography

Primary Sources
Archives départementales de Metz
  Armée de Rochambeau, *Livre d'ordres contenant les ordres donnés depuis le débarquement des troupes à Newport en Amérique septentrionale 1780*
Archives Nationales de France, Paris
  Contrôles of Lauzun's Legion
Beinecke Rare Book and Manuscript Library, Yale University, New Haven, CT (BRBML)
  Rochambeau Papers
Connecticut Historical Society, Hartford, CT
  Jeremiah Wadsworth Papers
Cornell University Library
  Journal d'un emigré; ou cahier d'un etudiant en philosophie
David M. Rubenstein Rare Book & Manuscript Library, Duke University, Durham, North Carolina
  Warrington Dawson Collection
Library of Congress, Washington, DC
  Rochambeau Papers
Maryland Center of History and Culture, Baltimore
  '1782 Depositions regarding a riot between French soldiers and American sailors, July 27, 28 at Fell's Point'
Médiathèque André Malraux, Strasbourg, France
  Fonds Patrimoniaux
National Archives and Records Administration, Washington, DC (NARA)
  Revolutionary War Records, Miscellaneous Numbered Records
Society of the Cincinnati, Washington, DC
  Journal of Robert Guillaume Dillon

Printed Primary Sources
Abbot Green, Samuel (ed.), Deux-Ponts, William de, *My Campaigns in America* (Boston: J.K. Wiggin & W.P. Lunt, 1868)
Acomb, Evelyn (ed.), *The Revolutionary Journal of Baron Ludwig von Closen, 1780-1783* (Chapel Hill: University of North Carolina Press, 1958)
Anon., *Calendar of Virginia State Papers and other Manuscripts* (Richmond, VA: James E. Goode, 1883)
Balch, Thomas (ed.), *The Journal of Claude Blanchard, Commissary of the French Auxiliary Army sent to the United States during the American Revolution* (Albany: Munsell, 1876)
Baum, Jane A., Hans-Peter Baum, Jesko Graf zu Dohna (eds), *The adventures of Friedrich Reinhard count of Rechteren-Limpurg in the Mediterranean and the American War of Independence 1770–1782* (bilingual) (Baunach: Spurbuchverlag, 2016)
Chinard, Gilbert, 'Journal de Guerre de Brisout de Barneville. Mai 1780-Octobre 1781', *The French-American Review*, vol.3, no.4 (October 1950), pp.217–278
Contenson, Ludovic de, 'Lettres d'un officier de l'Armée de Rochambeau: le chevalier de Coriolis', *Le correspondant*, no.326 (25 March 1932), pp.807–828
Crèvecœur, Hector St John de, *Letters from an American Farmer* (New York: E.P. Dutton, 1957)
Cromot du Bourg, Marie-François baron, 'Diary of a French Officer, 1781', *Magazine of American History*, vol.4 (April 1880), pp.293–308
Dana, James, *A Sermon Preached before the General Assembly of the State of Connecticut at Hartford on the Day of the Anniversary Election, May 13, 1779* (Hartford: Hudson & Goodwin, 1779)

Desmarais, Noman (trans. and ed.), *The Road to Yorktown: The French Campaigns in the American Revolution, 1780–1783, by Louis-Francois-Bertrand du Pont d'Aubevoye, comte de Lauberdiere* (El Dorado Hills, CA: Savas Beatty, 2021)

Doniol, J. Henry, *Histoire de la participation de la France a l'Établissement des États-Unis d'Amérique* (Paris: Imprimerie Nationale, 1886-1892)

Emmet, Thomas Addis, 'Sir Henry Clinton's Original Secret Record of Private Daily Intelligence', *Magazine of American History*, vol.12, no.2 (August 1884), pp.162–175

Feltman, William, *The Journal of Lieut. William Feltman, of the First Pennsylvania Regiment, 1781–82* (Philadelphia: Historical Society of Pensylvania, 1853)

Fersen, Axel de, 'Letters of Axel de Fersen, Aide-de-Camp to Rochambeau written to his Father in Sweden 1780-1782', *Magazine of American History*, vol.3 (1879), pp.369–376

Massoni, Gérard-Antoine, *Détails intéressants sur les événements arrivés dans la guerre d'Amérique. Hyver 1781 à 1782. Hampton, Charlotte et suitte. Manuscrit de Claude Hugau, lieutenant-colonel de la Légion des Volontaires Etrangers de Lauzun* (Besançon: Université de Franche-Comté, 1996)

Montbron, Jean-Louis Fougeret de, *Préservatif contre l'Anglomanie* (A Minorque, 1757)

Revel, Joachim du Perron, comte de, *Journal Particulier d'une Campagne aux Indes Occidentales (1781–1782)* (Paris: Chez Henri Charles-Lavauzelle, 1898)

Rice, Howard C., Jr. and Anne S. K. Brown (eds), *The American Campaigns of Rochambeau's Army 1780, 1781, 1782, 1783* (Princeton: Princeton University Press, 1972)

Secondary Sources

Ambassade de France, *French Engineers and the American War of Independence* (New York: 1975)

Blaufarb, Rafe, 'Noble Privilege and Absolutist State Building: French Military Administration after the Seven Years War', *French Historical Studies*, vol.24, no.2 (Spring 2001), pp.223–246

Bodinier, Gilbert, *Les officiers de l'Armée royale combattants de la guerre d'Indépendance des États-Unis de Yorktown à l'an II* (Vincennes: Service Historique de l'armée de Terre, 1983)

Bodinier, Gilbert, 'Les officiers du corps expéditionnaire de Rochambeau et la Revolution française', *Revue historique des armées*, vol.3, no.4, (1976), pp.139–164

Bolzinger, Raymond, 'A propos du bicentenaire de la guerre de l'Indépendance des États-Unis 1775-1783: Le service de santé de l'armée Rochambeau et ses participants messins', *Mémoires de l'Académie Nationale de Metz*, 4/5, (1979), pp.259–284

Boulaire, Alain, 'Le comte de Rochambeau et ses troupes à Brest, au printemps 1780', *Actes du Colloque international: Victoire de Yorktown et naissance de l'amitié franco-américaine. Bulletin de la Société Archéologique Scientifique & Littéraire du Vendômois* (2022), pp.83–90

Brown, Gayle K., '"Into the Hands of Papists": New England Captives in French Canada and the English Anti-Catholic Tradition, 1689–1763', *The Maryland Historian*, vol.21 (1990), pp.1–11

Chartrand, René and Francis Back, *The French Army in the American War of Independence* (London: Osprey, 1991)

Cilleuls, Jean des, 'Le service de l'intendance à l'armée de Rochambeau', *Revue historique de l'Armée*, no. 2, (1957), pp.43–61

Eccles, W. J., 'The French Alliance and the American Victory' in John Ferling (ed.), *The World Turned Upside Down. The American Victory in the War of Independence* (Westport, CT: Greenwood Press, 1976), pp.147–163

Echeverria, Durand, 'Mirage in the West: French *Philosophes* rediscover America', in Charles W. Toth (ed.), *Liberté, Egalité, Fraternité: The American Revolution and the European Response* (Troy, NY: Whitston Publishing, 1989), pp.35–47

Fiechter, Jean-Jacques, 'L'aventure américaine des officiers de Rochambeau vue à travers leurs journaux' in Michèle R. Morris (ed.), *Images of America in Revolutionary France* (Washington, DC: Georgetown University Press, 1990), pp.65–82

Fonteneau, General, 'La période française de la guerre d'Indépendance (1776-1780)', *Revue historique des armées*, vol.3, no. 4, (1976), pp.47–77

Greene, Jerome A., *The Guns of Independence: The Siege of Yorktown, 1781* (El Dorado Hills, CA: Savas Beatie, 2005)

Johnston, Henry P., *The Yorktown Campaign and the Surrender of Cornwallis 1781* (New York: Harper & Brothers, 1881)

Kennett, Lee, 'L'expédition Rochambeau-Ternay: un succès diplomatique', *Revue historique des armées*, vol.3, no.4 (1976), pp.87–105

Kennett, Lee, *The French Forces in America, 1780–1783* (Westport, CT: Greenwood Press, 1977)

Nardin, Pierre, *Gribeauval, lieutenant des armées du roi (1715–1789)* (Paris: Fondation pour les études de défense nationale, 1982)

Nicholas, Charles, *Le Maréchal de Camp Desandrouïns* (Verdun: Renvé-Lallemant, 1887)

Osman, Julia, 'Ancient Warriors on Modern Soil: French Military Reform and American Military Images in Eighteenth-century France' *French History*, vol.22, no. 2 (June 2008), pp.175–196

Pétard, Michel, 'Les Étrangers au service de la France (1786)', *Tradition*, vol.32 (September 1989), pp.21–29

Quincy, Eliza Susan Morton, *Memoir of the Life of Eliza S. M. Quincy* (Boston: J. Wilson and Son, 1861)

Rosen, Howard, *The Système Gribeauval. A study of technological development and institutional change in eighteenth century France* (Thesis (Ph. D.), University of Chicago, 1981)

Scott, Samuel F., 'Foreign Mercenaries, Revolutionary War, and Citizen Soldiers in the Late Eighteenth Century.' *War and Society*, vol.2 (September 1984), pp.42–58

Scott, Samuel F., *From Yorktown to Valmy: The Transformation of the French Army in an Age of Revolution* (Niwot: University Press of Colorado, 1998)

Scott, Samuel F., 'Rochambeau's Veterans: A Case Study in the Transformation of the French Army', *Proceedings, the Consortium on Revolutionary Europe 1750-1850* (Athens: University of Florida Press, 1979), pp.155–163

Scott, Samuel F., 'Strains in the Franco-American Alliance: The French Army in Virginia, 1781–82' in Richard A. Rutyna and Peter C. Stewart (eds), *Virginia in the American Revolution* (Norfolk: Old Dominion University, 1983), pp.80–100

Scott, Samuel F., 'The Army of the Comte de Rochambeau between the American and French Revolutions', *Proceedings of the Annual Meeting of the Western Society for French History*, vol.15, (1988), pp.143–153

Scott, Samuel F., 'The Soldiers of Rochambeau's Expeditionary Corps: From the American Revolution to the French Revolution' in Claude Fohlen and Jacques Godechot (eds), *La Révolution Américaine et l'Europe*, (Paris: Centre national de la recherche scientifique, 1979), pp.565–578

Selig, Robert A., 'A French Volunteer who lived to rue America's Revolution: Denis Jean Florimond de Langlois, marquis Du Bouchet', *Colonial Williamsburg. The Journal of the Colonial Williamsburg Foundation*, vol.21, no.3 (June/July 1999), pp.16–25

Selig, Robert A., 'A German Soldier in America, 1780–1783: The Journal of Georg Daniel Flohr', *William and Mary Quarterly*, vol.50, no.3 (July 1993), pp.75–90

Selig, Robert A., 'Friedrich Franck von La Roche (1757–1805)', *German Life*, vol.29, no. 1 (June/July 2022), pp.10–19

Selig, Robert A., 'Hessians Fighting for American Independence? German Deserters recruited for Lauzun's Legion in America, 1780–1782', *Journal of the Johannes Schwalm Historical Association*, vol.7, no. 4 (2004), pp.39–51

Selig, Robert A., *Hussars in Lebanon! A Connecticut Town and Lauzun's Legion during the American Revolution, 1780–1781* (Lebanon, CT: Lebanon Historical Society, 2004)

Selig, Robert A., 'Old World Meets New: Franco-American Encounters and the *expédition particulière*, 1780-1782', *The Brigade Dispatch. Journal of the Brigade of The American Revolution*, vol.37, no.1 (Spring 2007), pp.2–11

Selig, Robert A., *The Franco-American Encampment in the Town of Greenburgh, 6 July–18 August 1781: A Historical Overview and Resource Inventory* (Greenburgh, New York: Town of Greenburgh, 2020)

Selig, Robert A., *The Washington-Rochambeau Revolutionary Route in the Commonwealth of Rhode Island, 1781–1783. An Historical and Architectural Survey* (Providence, RI: Washington-Rochambeau Revolutionary Route Association of Rhode Island and Providence Plantations, 2015)

Singh, John, 'Plans de Guerre français 1763-1770.' *Revue historique des Armées*, vol.3 no.4 (1976), pp.7–22

Trenard, Louis, 'Un défenseur des hôpitaux militaires: Jean-François Coste', *Revue du Nord*, vol.75, no.299, (January 1993), pp.149–180

Newspapers

New-Jersey Gazette [Trenton], 27 September 1780

Lessons from the Courts: What Trial Proceedings Tell about Warfare in America

Don N. Hagist

Most information about individual battles and skirmishes during the American War comes from accounts written by officers to their superiors, and letters and journals written by participants. These typically give a single perspective, recording the aspects of events that the writer thought most important for the reader. Rarely, if ever, do we find more than one account by people in the same specific location who wrote of the same specific aspects of an engagement – and always we are left wanting more detail about the actions and experiences of individuals.

On rare occasions, British officers were brought to trial for their behavior on the battlefield. Trial proceedings are unique in that they contain accounts by many individuals about very specific aspects of a battle. As such, they enhance our understanding of the action concerned in the trial, and also provide an assortment of operational details seldom recorded anywhere else. Often the most interesting bits of information are details that were casually mentioned in testimony, rather than being of great significance to the charges being considered.

What follows is information on five battles that took place in America, gleaned from seven trials of officers charged with some form of misconduct or other misbehavior that occurred during, or as a result of, the engagement.

Cornet Henry Evatt at the Battle of Princeton, 3 January 1777

The Battle of Princeton, New Jersey is famous enough that a detailed discussion of it is not needed here. To recap, on the morning of 3 January 1777 a British column moving along a road in one direction came upon a much larger American column on a parallel path heading in the opposite direction. The two forces deployed – the British to their right and the Americans to their left – and engaged each other. After an initial British push, the overwhelming size of the American force became apparent. With an enemy strong enough to form a line of battle in front and also send substantial numbers around the flanks, British forces had no choice but to withdraw, some after nearly being surrounded.

When formed for battle as the engagement unfolded, the centre of the British force consisted of seven companies of the 17th Regiment of Foot, and a composite company composed of soldiers recently recovered from wounds or illness who were on their way to rejoin their regiments elsewhere. Protecting their flanks were troopers of the 16th Light Dragoons, mounted cavalry on the left flank, dismounted men operating as skirmishers on the right flank. Almost two years after the battle, a general court martial convened in the city of New York to hear charges against Cornet Henry Evatt of the 16th Light Dragoons; he was accused by fellow officer Lieutenant Simon Wilmot of 'Disobedience of Orders and Misbehaviour before the Enemy' during the Battle of Princeton. The case had taken so long to come to trial because Wilmot was captured during the battle and was only able to formally present the charges after he was exchanged and back in British-held territory.

At the time of the battle, Evatt was one of the most junior officers in his regiment, having been commissioned as a cornet barely a year before, on 28 December 1775. But he was not young or inexperienced. Born in Ireland in 1746, he had joined the 4th Regiment of Horse and was appointed quartermaster of a troop in that corps in 1766.[1] When the 16th Light Dragoons was ordered to America, it was augmented to more than twice its peacetime size, including the addition of one cornet to each of its six troops (equivalent to companies in infantry regiments).[2] Evatt obtained one of those cornetcies and embarked with his regiment in the summer of 1776, arriving in New York in late October and quickly joining the ongoing campaign that drove rebel forces out of New York and New Jersey.

The Battle of Princeton, the culmination of a 10-day series of actions that re-established the American rebels' determination to fight, may have been Evatt's first major action. The proceedings of the trial describe a number of important details about how the dismounted dragoons were employed in the early stages of the battle, and also give a sense of the uncertainty and confusion that occurs in combat.[3]

On the morning of the battle, as the British force marched in column on a road, Cornet Evatt commanded a flanking party. He claimed to have been the first to notice unidentified flankers from another column in the distance but 'could not be certain who they were, whether the Enemy or Hessians.' Borrowing a 'spying Glass' from another officer, 'looking thro' it he perceived their Colours.' The flags were white. Evatt 'was therefore very certain that they were Rebels.'

From the testimony of various witnesses, it is clear that the dismounted contingent of the 16th Light Dragoons consisted of about 70 men divided into four divisions, each division commanded by an officer. Three were commanded by cornets, the fourth by a lieutenant; all three of the cornets, including Evatt, had been commissioned at the same time, about a year before. When the 17th Regiment of Foot turned off the road, formed a line and advanced towards the enemy, the four divisions of dismounted dragoons formed to their right, also in a line facing the enemy. Evatt's division was on the far right. Lieutenant Wilmot had overall command of the four divisions and appears to have posted himself in the centre of

---

1   The National Archives (TNA): WO 25/210: Succession books, 1764-1771.
2   TNA: WO 12/1246: Muster rolls, 16th Light Dragoons.
3   TNA: WO 71/84: Trial of Henry Evatt, pp.343–361. All information in this section is from these trial proceedings, unless otherwise stated.

them. The term 'division' is used consistently in the trial, and nowhere do the terms 'troop,' 'company' or 'platoon' appear.

'The whole detachment was formed in a line behind a rail,' recalled one witness, 'at the open distance light Troops generally form.' Wilmot directed a sergeant 'to go along the Line and inform the men they were not to fire a Shot, till such time as he gave the Order.' Cornet Evatt was heard to 'bid the men to behave Cool and not to waste or throw away their ammunition, and to be attentive to the Officer who Commanded them.' One private soldier recalled being the 'right hand man of the rear rank' in Evatt's division; given that each division had only 17 or 18 men and there was 'not ten yards' between divisions, forming in two ranks, even at 'at the open distance' suggests a total front of 200 feet or so for the four divisions of dismounted dragoons.

As rebel forces worked their way around the British right flank, Evatt ordered his division 'to the right about and follow him' in retreat. The other three sections of dismounted dragoons followed; according to one non-commissioned officer, 'They retreated by files from the right; there was some Confusion, and he Cannot say that their files were quite regular.' One dragoon observed of the enemy, 'there were many of their party laying down and others kneeling and keeping up a constant fire.'

The focus of the trial was that Cornet Evatt had retreated without orders, and had not responded to Lieutenant Wilmot's orders to halt. Wilmot testified that the dismounted dragoons had withheld fire until the advancing rebels were quite close, and that upon delivering a volley of musketry the enemy retreated; Wilmot was preparing to order a charge when he was surprised to see that Evatt's division was retreating. Wilmot called to Evatt to halt, and directed a sergeant to do the same, but to no avail. Within moments the other dragoon divisions followed suit and filed off to the rear.

Several witnesses corroborated that there was no order to retreat, but emphasized that, when Evatt's division retreated, the enemy on Evatt's flank was putting all of the dismounted dragoons in danger. No one could say whether it was possible for Evatt to hear Wilmot's orders over the noise of gunfire. Moreover, the 17th Regiment and their supporting artillery had already begun to retreat, leaving Wilmot's skirmishers behind; far from being in a position to charge the enemy, Wilmot's men were in danger of being cut off. Some witnesses at the trial saw an infantry captain waving his hat, motioning for the dragoons to retreat, 'calling out, come off, or you will be all cut to pieces.' No one gave any indication that Evatt had misbehaved in any way. Another cornet told the court, 'Cornet Evatt shewed as much presence of mind as any person could have done, and behaved like an Officer.'

Even as the battle raged, Wilmot 'came up with Cornet Evatt, and asked him how he came to retreat without any Order for it.' Evatt answered that Wilmot 'had injured his Character, he therefore should demand satisfaction,' and Wilmot 'told him that he should have satisfaction given him by a Court Martial.' Soon after, Wilmot was wounded and captured. He recovered in captivity and was exchanged about 18 months later. Evatt, meanwhile, fought in several other significant engagements with no accusations of misbehaviour. One might think the affair at Princeton would soon be forgotten, but soon after Wilmot finally returned to British lines in the summer of 1778 he received a letter from Evatt: 'Sir, I understand that you have censured my Conduct on the 3rd January 1777, when engaged with the rebels; any thing that you have to say on that Subject, I beg that you will commit immediately to the Commanding Officer of this Regiment, in order that it may be cleared up immediately in the most public manner.' This letter led to the general court martial that convened on 22 October 1778 in the garrison town of Brooklyn, adjacent to the city of New York.

The court heard testimony for two days, then acquitted Cornet Evatt of both charges.

Major John Vatas and Captain Richard Blackmore, Province Island, 11 October 1777

British forces successfully seized Philadelphia in September 1777, but there was much work to be done before the city could be truly secure. Philadelphia's connection to the sea, and therefore to sustainability, was the Delaware River. Rebel forces had constructed a series of defences along this river between the city and the sea, including Fort Mifflin on the Philadelphia side and Fort Mercer on the opposite bank, both a few miles downstream of the city. The forts held out for two months, commanding a protracted British effort to reduce them and open the vital waterway to shipping that would sustain the city through the winter. The story of American defence of the Delaware River is well-chronicled, but details of an incident that was part of it come to us only through a court martial.

Fort Mifflin was built on an island aptly named Mud Island. Adjacent to it were Province Island and Carpenter's Island, which the British referred to collectively as Province Island. All three were low, marshy plateaus of silt subject to flooding by the wide and meandering river. Province Island was a poor location for any sort of fortification, but it was the closest land to Fort Mifflin, prompting British engineers to direct construction of an artillery battery designed to pummel the American fort.

A ferry took men 200 yards across the narrow waterway between the mainland and Province Island. A ferry house stood on the island, from which a road led to a nearby farm. Turning left there, it was about a mile walk to the battery under construction on the river side.[4] Building and manning the battery was gruelling, tedious work. Throughout the month of October detachments of soldiers laboured to construct the earthen walls and wooden platforms required to mount heavy guns that could bear on the enemy position. Rain fell heavily, flooding the works and the roads to them, forcing men to wade up to their waists 'for miles' according an officer, just to arrive at the batteries where they toiled in knee-deep water.[5] On the morning of 11 October about 200 from the 10th Regiment of Foot, the 2nd Battalion of Grenadiers, and some German troops were working on the island, commanded by Major John Vatas of the 10th Regiment. The battery was almost complete. It was too small for all 100 British and German soldiers working there to fit within its ramparts, so some were outside while others worked within. Proceedings from two trials provide the only detailed accounts of the subsequent events on the island.[6]

---

4   Douglas W. Marshall and Howard H. Peckham, *Campaigns of the American Revolution: an Atlas of Battlefield Maps* (Ann Arbor, MI: The University of Michigan Press, 1976), pp.60-61.

5   Ira D. Gruber (ed.), *John Peebles American War: the Diary of a Scottish Grenadier, 1776-1782* (Mechanicsburg, PA: Stackpole Books, for the Army Records Society, 1998), pp.141–146.

6   TNA: WO 71/87: Trial of John Vatas, pp.355–380; WO 71/87: Trial of Richard Blackmore, pp. 381–97. All information in this section is from these trial proceedings, unless otherwise stated. Vatas's name is spelled 'Vattas' on the regiment's muster rolls, and 'Vatass' in published army lists; the spelling used

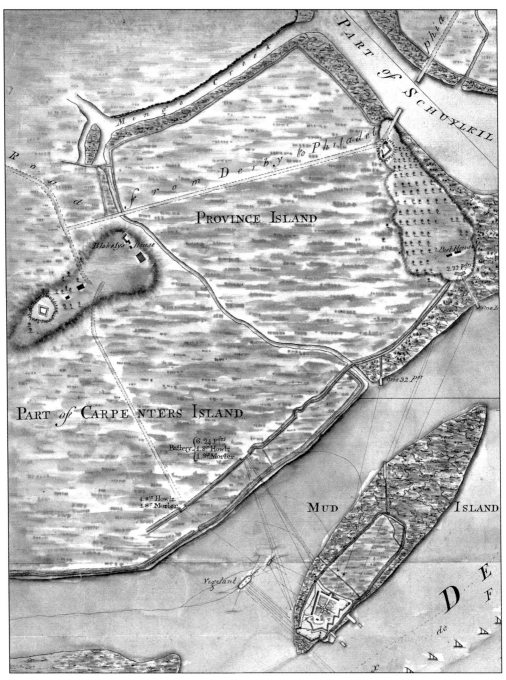

Province Island and Mud Island; although Carpenter's Island is named separately on this map, those who described the attack in October 1777 referred only to Province Island. The ferry and ferry house are at upper right, the farmhouse at centre left, and the British battery at lower centre. Detail from 'A Plan of the Attacks Against Fort Miflin on Mud Island.' (Library of Congress)

At around 7:00 a.m., after spending 'a night of fatigue, in wet and dirt up to the waist,' the soldiers took cover behind the rampart or embankments when American batteries opened fire from Mud Island. Soon, three whaleboats mounting swivel guns and carrying about 70 rebel soldiers pushed in close to the shore. The only cannon yet mounted in the battery, a 12-pounder, was positioned to fire against Mud Island and could not be brought to bear against the boats. The rebels landed about a half mile away and took cover behind trees and embankments while the British troops remained pinned in their position.

The troops in the battery were commanded by Captain Richard Blackmore of the 10th Regiment. With him were Lieutenant William Finch of the 27th Regiment's grenadier company, and Ensign Richard Hankey of the 10th Regiment. Their situation seemed tenuous, being 'much fatigued and wet and dirty by the fatigue of the Night,' and 'not very well covered by an unfinished work, which was constantly giving way, covering us with dust & dirt every Shot.' Seeing the rebels take position, and one British soldier killed and another wounded in the hail of cannon fire, Ensign Hankey said to Captain Blackmore, 'what shall we do, we shall be all killed, if you don't strike or put up a flag of distress.' Blackmore ignored his young subordinate, but Hanky persisted, and finally 'he took out his handkerchief and tied it either to a ramrod or a piece of stick.' Blackmore then asked an enlisted man – a matross in the Royal Artillery – if the enemy had landed and were advancing (which suggests that Blackmore was unwilling to expose himself to look). The matross responded that the enemy had in fact landed, but 'were not many in number,' and that because there was a formation of Hessian troops in sight the rebels probably would not attempt to storm the battery. Ensign Hanky continued to argue for hoisting up the white handkerchief, but the matross asserted that there was no danger. 'Some were for putting it up,' remembered the matross, 'and others were against it'; then, remarkably, 'Capt. Blackmore asked the men in general, what they thought of it.' Someone gave the handkerchief to a grenadier and demanded that he hoist it. When the matross snatched it away, 'Ensign Hankey call'd out, is there no Grenadier or other Man here, that will shoot that Artillery man?'

Either Hanky or Blackmore gave the ramrod holding the handkerchief to the grenadier and ordered him to climb onto the cannon and wave it. Seeing this signal, several rebel boats put ashore in front of the battery, and men came to take the British soldiers prisoner. They complied and began filing down to the waiting boats, led by Ensign Hanky with the handkerchief.

Meanwhile, at the onset of the attack a few men had managed to flee the battery and make their way across the island to the ferry house where Major Vatas was. They reported to Vatas that the battery was under attack. Captain James Moncrieffe of the Corps of Engineers, after consulting with Vatas, took 100 Hessians and hurried to relieve the detachment at the battery. Some time passed, and individual soldiers 'drop'd in from the battery,' their ammunition rendered 'useless from the several Creeks and ditches they had to cross between it & ferry house, being frequently above their waists in water or mud.' They brought news that the battery had surrendered, Moncrieffe and his men were defeated and captured, and the rebels possessed the 12-pounder gun. Vatas decided that the island was untenable given the few men remaining at the ferry house. He ordered a cannon to be positioned on the wharf

---

here is the spelling in the trial proceedings.

to cover a retreat; a Hessian lieutenant volunteered to take 17 men into the ferry house and defend it from the windows.

As these preparations proceeded, Captain William Brereton of the 17th Regiment of Foot came onto the island; he happened to be in the area and, hearing gunfire, came over to see what was going on. Major Vatas, who had apparently been near the ferry the entire night and was not in a position to directly observe the situation at the battery, explained that the island was not worth defending and he intended to abandon it. Brereton argued that 'the Island was a place of great consequence, and that if they once left it, they might find difficulty in retaking it'; that there was a 6-pounder gun nearby on the mainland that could be brought over, and that there were enough men to defend the place long enough for relief to come. Vatas equivocated. Brereton finally volunteered to lead the defence himself, to which Vatas consented. Then Vatas left the island.

Back at the battery, the engineer Captain Moncrieffe arrived with his 100 Hessians to find the British officers and soldiers there filing onto boats at the shoreline. Rebels in the fort 'instantly fled,' so he called to the British would-be prisoners to move aside so he could fire on the boats. In the ensuing confusion, Captain Blackmore and many of the soldiers were rescued. Lieutenant Finch, Ensign Hanky and 56 other ranks already in boats were rowed off as prisoners,[7] but the battery was retaken, and the island was secure; no further attacks came. Major Vatas, in the meantime, after consulting with another officer on the mainland, returned to the island and finally took charge of preparing the area around the ferry house for a defence that was no longer needed.

Just five days after the near-debacle, Major John Vatas and Captain Richard Blackmore were brought to trial, 'accused of having Misbehaved themselves before the Enemy, on the 11th day of October, 1777.' Vatas was tried first. Six officers, including Captains Moncrieffe and Brereton, testified against him, all speaking in various ways to his ambivalence, equivocation and general lack of decisiveness and leadership throughout the affair. In his defence, Vatas focused primarily on the confused and exaggerated reports he received from individuals straggling in from the battery, in particular the false news that Moncrieffe's relief force had surrendered, as well as 'the unaccountable panick which had seemingly seized the Soldiers.'

Vatas also told the court some things that may have done more to incriminate than defend himself. He pointed out that, until Captain Brereton arrived, 'the Hessian Officer excepted, I had not a person to consult or advise with,' and that 'had I had any British Officer to advise with, I should not perhaps have meditated a retreat' – even though that Hessian officer testified that he had volunteered, with only a small detachment, to make a stand, and there was also a Royal Artillery officer on the scene. He said that he was told by stragglers that 'numbers of Rebels were imagined to be seen advancing towards the Ferry house,' but 'I could not myself discern a Single one, 'though as I am very near sighted, it might have been otherwise.' He attributed his departure from the island to a desire 'to reconnoiter the situation of the opposite Shore,' and said he returned to the island because he 'gave into Captain Brereton's way of thinking after a little consideration & adopted it so far

---

7   William Bradford, Sr., and John Hazelwood to George Washington, 11 October 1777, in Philander D. Chase and Edward G. Lengel (ed.), *The Papers of George Washington, Revolutionary War Series, vol.11, 19 August 1777–25 October 1777* (Charlottesville: University Press of Virginia, 2001), pp.482–484.

as to agree to maintain the Island with his farther assistance.' As for the delay in accepting Brereton's proposals, 'I had not then the pleasure of a very particular acquaintance with the Gentleman.' He closed by pointing out to the court that although he had been in the army for over 31 years, 'my Services have extended very little beyond Garrison duties, those of the field I have been acquainted with only since the breaking out of the Rebellion.'

Captain Blackmore, tried next, attributed his actions to the general panic that prevailed when the fort came under withering fire. He called upon several soldiers to confirm their fatigue and fear, even telling Blackmore that they 'would not stay in the works, to be murdered for him or any other person.' He asserted that more rebel troops had landed than any witness had testified. He placed blame for much of the panic, and the idea of surrender which spread among his men, to Ensign Hanky, who he called an 'unhappy youth.' Richard Hanky, not quite 18 years old, had arrived in America less than five months before the battle after spending his first year in the army on recruiting service in Great Britain.[8] Blackmore testified that Hanky's 'young mind (enervated by an effeminate education & not long enough in the Service to acquire that temper & firmness, of which I am persuaded it is capable &, which it may attain) was too soon infected by the general panic,' and that Hanky's 'repeated instances to surrender, exciting my compassion, gave additional weight to those circumstances, which finally induced me to consent to do so.'

The officers of the court were not impressed with either Vatas's or Blackmore's defences. Both officers were found guilty for 'a breach of the first part of the 13th Article of War of the 14th Section.' Both were sentenced to be cashiered, that is, put out of the army without receiving the value of their commissions, a substantial loss of equity that would otherwise fund their retirement. In an act of compassion, the commander-in-chief approved the verdict but allowed the men to retire, selling their commissions rather than forfeiting them.[9]

Richard Hanky spent several months as a prisoner of war, returning to service after being exchanged in 1778. He soon returned to Great Britain and recruiting but retired from the army in September 1780.[10] He returned to the family business of banking and became active in London society. His role in the American Revolutionary War had been short and undistinguished, but he was unwittingly connected with a significant contribution to American history. Around 1784 he became president of a social music club called the Anacreontic Society, a role he retained for a decade. A song that came out of that society, *To Anacreon in Heaven*, became popular in the ensuing years, so much so that in 1814 it was used as the tune for a new American song – *The Star Spangled Banner*.[11]

---

8   Richard Hanky was commissioned in May 1776, embarked for America in March 1777 and landed in New York at the end of that May. TNA: WO 65/26: 1776 printed annual army list; University Library, University of Durham: Journal of Viscount Cantilupe.

9   'British Army Orders,' in Anon. (ed.), *Collections of the New York Historical Society for the year 1883* (New York: New York Historical Society, 1884), p.452.

10   TNA: WO 12/2750: Muster rolls, 10th Regiment of Foot; WO 65/30: 1780 printed annual army list, p.78.

11   William Lichtenwanger, 'The Music of "The Star-Spangled Banner": From Ludgate Hill to Capitol Hill', *The Quarterly Journal of the Library of Congress*, vol.34, no.3 (July 1977), pp.156, 169n.

Lieutenant Daniel McGuin, Rhode Island, 29 August 1778

One of the war's biggest battles was so strategically inconsequential that it is easy to over-look entirely. From December 1776 through October 1779 a British garrison occupied the two largest islands in Narragansett Bay in today's state of Rhode Island. The town of Newport is near the southern end of the larger island, at the time itself called Rhode Island; the rest of the island, 15 miles north to south but only five miles wide at the widest point, was farmland. Because the mainland was very close to the island's eastern shore and north end, Rhode Island was a front line where raids and skirmishes were frequent during the three-year British presence.

In August 1778 a large American force supported by a French fleet attempted to dislodge the British garrison. The British, German and Loyalist troops, outnumbered about three to one, withdrew into defensive lines around Newport, taking advantage of a valley that cut across the island and provided a measure of natural defence. For three weeks the garrison was under siege, but a number of factors caused the Americans to abandon the effort. During the night of 28–29 August they withdrew from their siege lines to the northern end of the island, where the complex operation of ferrying thousands of troops to the mainland would begin.

Seeing an opportunity, at dawn British troops sallied out of their lines hoping to disrupt the American withdrawal, perhaps cutting off their escape entirely and achieving a dramatic victory after being on the brink of defeat. A column of German troops advanced up the island's west side, skirmishing with rebel rear guards, while a British column pursued on the east side. But the topography of the island's north end favoured defence, and the American troops concentrated there remained organized and stubborn. After a day of hard fighting, the battle devolved into an artillery duel across a valley; during the night and the following day the Americans effected their escape from the island.

On the battlefield today, a monument commemorates the heroic efforts of the American 1st Rhode Island Regiment, composed largely of African-American and Native American men, in repelling repeated assaults by Hessian regiments. It was not only Germans, however, that attacked in this area. Supporting the three Hessian regiments was the King's American Regiment, composed of Loyalists mostly from New York and Connecticut; contemporary accounts often referred to it as Fanning's Regiment after its commanding officer, Colonel Edmund Fanning. Seven weeks after the 29 August battle one of the regiment's officers, Lieutenant Daniel McGuin, was brought to trial for 'Disobedience of Orders in leaving his platoon, and for behaving in a manner unbecoming the Character of an Officer.'[12]

The charges arose because, during the battle, a platoon commanded by McGuin was ordered to take position at a stone wall. They were under heavy fire from the enemy, and several officers and soldiers saw McGuin 'creeping under a stone wall, and lay down on the Ground.' One witness 'did not see him rise up during his stay there which was above an hour, or give any orders to the men,' another attested that 'he lay under the wall, and trembled very much,' and a third recalled that McGuin 'lay still and did not shew his head where

---

12   TNA: WO 71/87: Trial of Daniel McGuin, pp.404–14. All information in this section is from these trial proceedings, unless otherwise stated.

a ball flew.' When the regiment retreated from this forward position, McGuin was nowhere to be seen. It was not until a half-hour or so later, when the regiment was regrouping in a safe location, that McGuin appeared with several other straggling soldiers.

The trial record brings out two significant details about the King's American Regiment and its role in the battle. Officers testified that on the morning of 29 August, when the regiment was preparing to march out to face the enemy, the commanding officer ordered the regiment 'to be told off into Platoons, and for the Officers and Non Commissioned Officers to be posted accordingly.' One would expect that that the arrangement of platoons and officers commanding them would already be well established and regularly practiced, rather than something organized on the morning of an impending engagement. Whether this is an indication that the regiment was so well trained that the men adapted readily to ad-hoc organization, or that the regiment was so poorly managed that no one had thought to create an order of battle ahead of time, is a matter of interpretation. Most likely this telling off into platoons was simply refining an already-established formation, based on exactly which men were fit for service on that day. A return taken on 10 August put the strength of the King's American Regiment at just under 400 other ranks, which – assuming 10 companies and that a platoon was half of a company – puts the strength of McGuin's platoon at about 20 men including a sergeant and a corporal.[13]

By comparing witness testimony to a map of Rhode Island published in 1777, it is possible to discern, with some certainty, where the King's American Regiment was at its closest approach to the enemy.[14] An American force made a stand on Turkey Hill, and a British officer wrote that they were 'attacked with great spirit' by two Hessian corps and the King's American Regiment, and that 'the weight of the action this day fell on' two British battalions on the east road and 'Huyne's and Fannings Regiment in driving them out of the Swamp in front of Turkey Hill.'[15] One witness in McGuin's trial mentioned going through the swamp, and McGuin's platoon taking position at 'a stone wall with a corner at the end of which there was a very thick Bush.' The 1777 map clearly shows the stream that flows east to west just south of Turkey Hill, with a swampy area where it drains into the bay. On the north side of the creek is a network of stone walls, two of which have right-angle corners. Both locations are on the west side of Turkey Hill, near the south end of this oblong eminence. The King's American Regiment was probably on the left flank of the Regiment von Huyn, which most likely advanced on or adjacent to the road that ran up the hill.

Accused of cowardice by his fellow officers, Lieutenant Daniel McGuin put up an able defence. With supporting testimony from several soldiers and the regiment's surgeon, he explained that he had been ill for some time before the day of battle, and only with great effort mustered the strength to march with the regiment. He lay down not only because the stone wall afforded little cover at his location, but from fatigue; that his trembling was caused not by fear, but from a bout of ague (malaria) that overcame him.

13   Frederick Mackenzie, *The Diary of Frederick Mackenzie* (Cambridge, MA: Harvard University Press, 1930), p.346.
14   Library of Congress, Washington, DC: A topographical chart of the bay of Narraganset in the province of New England, Engraved & printed for Wm. Faden, 1777,< https://www.loc.gov/item/74692134/>, accessed 1 November 2023.
15   Mackenzie, *Diary*, pp.382–383.

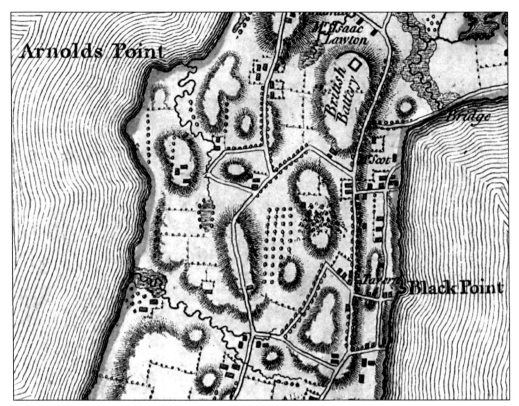

The creek and marshy area, centre left, and the network of stone walls just north of it at the base of a hill. This is where the King's American Regiment fought in the Battle of Rhode Island on 29 August 1778. Detail from *A topographical chart of the bay of Narraganset in the province of New England*, engraved & printed for Wm. Faden, 1777. (Library of Congress)

The court accepted his defence, and acquitted McGuin of both charges. He returned to his duty, but his reputation may have suffered irreparable damage; for reasons unknown, he left the army in the second half of 1779.

Lieutenant Colonel Henry Johnson, Stony Point, 15–16 July 1779

About 40 miles north of Manhattan, a craggy point of land juts from the western shore into the Hudson river. Aptly named Stony Point, its heights offer a commanding view of the river. The British army in New York opened the 1779 campaign season by seizing Stony Point and adjacent Verplanck's Point on the opposite shore and building fortifications. Rocky outcrops dictated the irregular shape of earthen ramparts, but British engineers positioned cannon of various calibres to cover approaches from both the land and water. Armed ships in the river provided additional security. By mid-July the fort was incomplete but generally secure, at least it seemed to be. Nonetheless, on the night of 15–16 July 1779, American troops stormed the fort and overwhelmed the garrison of some 600 men, killing and wounding almost 100 and capturing almost all the rest. Also lost was a substantial quantity of artillery pieces, ammunition, and other military stores.

The fort's commander, Lieutenant Colonel Henry Johnson of the 17th Regiment of Foot, was brought to trial for 'Having suffered the Post of Stoney Point, with the troops in Garrison, the Artillery and Stores to fall into the Hands of the Enemy.'[16] The trial did not take place until 18 months after the event, when the prisoners had been exchanged, allowing the participants to appear at the trial. During seven weeks in January and February 1781, the court in New York heard testimony about the fort's design and the state of its construction, the disposition of artillery and alarm posts of the garrison, and the specific events on the night it was attacked. The trial proceedings provide rich details on exactly which troops and guns were posted where, and how individuals behaved during the roughly half-hour battle that took place in pitch darkness. There is far too much information to relate here, but the testimony in over 100 manuscript pages includes many interesting details about military operations during the war.

The court asked many questions about procedures at the fort in the days leading up to the attack. From the responses they learned that 'The time for giving out the usual Orders of the day, was always notified by beat of Drum' upon which officers on duty went to the garrison adjutant's tent to receive them. If there were 'after orders,' that is, additional orders given later in the day, the adjutant sent a message to report to his tent. The commander of the Royal Artillery mentioned that he might send the sergeant major of the artillery to the sergeant major of the infantry to receive the after orders. A non-commissioned officer testified that 'we used to relieve our Sentries in general by the Ship Bells, but it blew so hard that Night, that I could not hear them.'

Procedures were in place at Stony Point to, in the event of an attack, notify the ships and the British position across the river. The signal for an attack was to fire three rockets; 'Nails were Accordingly drove into the frame of a Hut, to the left of the Magazine, for fixing them on.' Artillerists were also prepared to illuminate the night sky by firing 'a Composition of Mealed Powder & other Materials, made up so as to serve for a light ball.' When the attack did come, things happened so quickly that neither of these signals were put into use. One officer did hail the biggest ship in the river, a simple and frequent means of communication.

Lines of abbatis – felled trees arranged with their branches pointing outwards, creating a tangle of timber to impede attackers – were a key component of the fortifications. Their placement was not questioned, but the court asked if they were properly pinned down to prevent them being pushed aside. An engineer asserted that they were pinned down or, in places where they rested on rock, were chocked. The method of chocking was not described, but the engineer seemed confident that it was sufficient.

Gaps in the abbatis, necessary to allow outer guards and others to enter and exit, were prepared for defence in various ways. A howitzer placed to cover one entrance did not have stakes or anything else fixed 'in order to bring the Howitzer to point at the same Object again, after the Natural & Common Alteration that might have been occasioned by every Recoil.' An artillery officer assured the court that 'had it been necessary to fire Shells to 150,

---

16   TNA: WO 71/93: Trial of Henry Johnson, pp.1–137; also published in Don Loprieno, *The Enterprise in Contemplation: the Midnight Assault of Stony Point* (Westminster, MD: Heritage Books, 2009), pp.137–307. All information in this section is from these trial proceedings, unless otherwise stated.

200, or 250 Yards, that Precaution, I suppose, would have been taken'; but because this gun was pointed directly at the opening in the abbatis, 'the distance was so short, at which they were to fire Case Shot, it would not make a difference above five or six yards, it consequently could not have missed its Object.'

The fort had a number of heavy guns, 12-, 18- and 24-pounders, aimed at distant points. No ammunition was kept close to them, and their crews were small compared to the smaller guns used for point defence. An artilleryman explained that this was done 'upon the Idea that there would be always time enough to obtain Additionals from the Infantry.' It was common practice in America to supplement artillery crews with foot soldiers; infantrymen could provide the labour needed for serving heavy guns, leaving the more technical aspects of operating them to the trained artillerymen.[17] The court was assured that a slow match for firing guns was kept always burning, attended by a sentinel.

Lieutenant Colonel Johnson had received intelligence that an attack was possible. He ordered soldiers encamped within the fort to sleep in their clothes with their accoutrements close by. When the alarm sounded during the night, an officer went to the encampment area and found 'most of the Men paraded and standing to their Arms in front of their Tents.' The officer commanding the two companies of grenadiers in the garrison, rather than ordering the common two-rank formation, formed his companies 'one deep, in order to extend the line' which 'had several intervals between' caused by obstructions. As gunfire erupted all around in the pitch darkness, the captain commanding the grenadiers told his subordinates to keep their men low; a lieutenant testified, 'upon which I ordered them to kneel.'

When the attack came, it came suddenly. Confusion reigned in the British garrison as American troops appeared in the darkness from unexpected directions. There was not time to put up a coordinated resistance, and even though some detachments fought bravely they were quickly overwhelmed. A few defenders were killed, some managed to swim to the safety of guard ships in the river, but most surrendered to American troops who, for recognition in the darkness, had large pieces of white paper in their hats. One British officer spoke to an American officer who had checked his watch when the first shot was fired, and again at the last; the fighting was over in just 33 minutes. Only a few British artillery pieces were able to engage, but their crews fought fiercely; a 12-pounder fired 27 rounds of ammunition during the attack, and a 3-pounder fired a remarkable 69 rounds, more than two shots a minute (an officer testified that there were 70 rounds in the gun's ammunition box, and only one was not fired).

After the main fort had fallen, parties of British troops manning outer works remained at their posts, still unsure of what was happening. A corporal commanding an out picket ordered his men 'to stand to their Arms, but hearing no more firing, then Ordered my Men to sit down on their Packs, but not go to Sleep.' An artillery officer at an outer work, on hearing that the main work had surrendered, ordered a non-commissioned officer and two soldiers 'to turn their Coats and go and examine the Abbatis upon my right, and left' to look for avenues of escape. But bit by bit these small groups also surrendered rather than fight

---

17   Don N. Hagist, *Noble Volunteers: the British Soldiers who fought the American Revolution* (Yardley: Westholme, 2020), pp.75, 91–92.

against impossible odds. Captured soldiers from some of the outer works were ordered into the fort with their firelocks clubbed, others were told to leave their arms behind.

Some small but significant details are mentioned in the trial proceedings. Corporal William West of the 17th Regiment told the court that he looked at his watch when the attack started, and found it to be 12 o'clock – with no indication that a man of his rank having a watch was in any way remarkable. The court asked Captain Robert Douglass, Royal Artillery, if he overheard a conversation between two officers, but, perhaps as no surprise for an artillery officer, Douglass replied, 'Having the misfortune to be deaf, I did not hear the conversation in general, tho' I now and then catched a word.'

Lieutenant Colonel Johnson was on trial for allowing the fort and garrison to be captured. Focus fell on one important detail of the fort's defences; on the left flank (as viewed from the fort) a line of abattis extended into the water, at the end of which a gunboat was anchored to prevent wading soldiers from dismantling or circling around it; the gunboat was, in effect, a bastion guarding against approach from that side. But night-time squalls made the waters rough, and the gunboat's crew, as they often did in stormy conditions, moved their vessel farther out into the river. One witness at the trial summed up what many testified: 'Had the Gun Boat been at her station, and the People in her vigilant, I do not think it possible for a Column of Men to have waded thro' the water without being heard, notwithstanding the Darkness of the Night.' Johnson was exonerated of any wrongdoing.

Lieutenant Colonel Frederick Thomas and Lieutenant Colonel Cosmo Gordon, Springfield, 23 June 1780

In early June 1780 a large British force based on Staten Island crossed the narrow waterway to the mainland, landing at Elizabeth Town, New Jersey. They made an abortive attempt to advance westward and threaten the Continental Army encampment at Morristown. Failing in that attempt, they remained encamped around Elizabeth Town for the next two weeks. On 23 June, after receiving reinforcements, British, German and Loyalist troops again advanced westward, this time in two columns. Their objective was gap in the ridge of low mountains that lay between them and Morristown.

The righthand, northern, column included the Brigade of Guards, an organization created solely for the American War that consisted of officers and soldiers from Britain's three regiments of Foot Guards. This column took a road that passed north of the town of Springfield, while the other column headed directly through the town. Initially their advance was rapid, but as the morning wore on resistance steadily increased. The Guards stayed on the road while various corps of light infantry, jäger, cavalry and other skirmishers fended off opponents on the flanks.

Late in the morning heavy resistance came from Americans in an orchard to the left of the northern column. Flanking parties engaged, and the column halted while two companies of the Guards went into the orchard in support. Two cannons posted with the Brigade of Guards also engaged. Then the column moved forward about a half mile and crossed a bridge over the Rahway River. Once across, the Guards rapidly ascended a hill a formed line. Facing only little resistance in this advantageous position, and tired from the morning's long march, they took the opportunity to rest.

Between the time that the Guards stopped at the orchard and the time that they reached the heights – a period of between 30 and 60 minutes – Lieutenant Colonel Frederick Thomas, commander of the first company, lost contact with his superior, Lieutenant Colonel Cosmo Gordon. This lapse of communication eventually led to two general courts-martial. Later in 1780, Lieutenant Colonel Gordon charged Lieutenant Colonel Thomas with 'aspersing his Character, by accusing him of Neglect of Duty before the enemy, as Commanding Officer of the First Battalion of Guards, on the 23d of June, 1780, near Springfield, in the Jerseys.' In 1782, Thomas charged Gordon, somewhat obviously, with 'Neglect of Duty before the enemy, on the 23d of June, 1780, near Springfield, in the Jerseys.' The first trial lasted 10 days and the published proceedings filled 117 pages, the second spanned 15 days and covered 145 pages. The trial proceedings focus on just one hour of a day-long running battle, providing significant information about how the Brigade of Guards operated on that day as well as a number of other interesting details.[18]

When the Brigade of Guards was first assembled in 1776 it consisted of eight battalion companies and two flank companies. The brigade was reorganized several times during the war; several witnesses explained that, in June 1780, there were only six battalion companies. The flank companies were on the expedition to Springfield but were not operating directly with battalion companies. Two field guns, commanded by a Royal Artillery lieutenant, were attached to the Brigade of Guards.

The Guards battalion companies marched 'by divisions in column, following successively in a direct line.' Divisions typically were equivalent to companies, but no deponent in the trial stated this equivalence. Companies of the Guards consisted nominally of 100 private men each which, in the two-rank formation commonly used in America, would make for a company front too wide for most roads. Possibly the companies were much weaker in strength, but more likely the Guards officers used 'division' to describe a subset of a company, probably a half-company.

When the Guards left the road and ascended a hill, they did so in the same columnar formation used on the road. But at the top they formed a line (the arrangement of companies is not stated). And then, even though there was scattered enemy fire, officers recognized the need for a break after an exhausting march. In the words of one officer, 'he formed them facing outwards towards the enemy, and ordered them to halt, recommending to the men to lie on their arms under the shade of the bushes; it being about noon and excessively hot, and the men a good deal blown by a rapid march.' Another officer noted that the arms were 'piled,' using the common parlance for standing up muskets in groups of three in a tripod, with ramrods interlocked to keep them in place. Several witnesses described the soldiers relaxing, some sitting, some standing, some lying down.

At issue in both trials was the whereabouts of Lieutenant Colonel Gordon between the time the Brigade halted by the orchard and the time they settled on the hill. The brigade commander had left the column to seek orders; Gordon, as commander of the first battalion,

---

18   Anon., *The Trial of Lieut. Col. Thomas, of the First Regiment of Foot Guards, on a Charge exhibited by Lieut. Col. Cosmo Gordon, for aspersing his Character* ... (London: J. Ridley, 1781); Anon., *The Trial of the Hon. Col. Cosmo Gordon, of the Third Regiment of Foot-Guards, for Neglect of Duty before the Enemy* ... (London: G. Harlow, 1783). All information in this section is from these trial proceedings, unless otherwise stated.

consisting of three companies, assumed command for the time being. But after ascending the heights, Lieutenant Colonel Thomas, commanding the first company, could not find him, and had not seen him for some time, even though he and other officers expected him to be at the head of the brigade during an advance. One witness, referring to Scotsman Thomas's agitation at being unable to find Gordon, commented that Thomas 'was in a great passion, and when in that situation speaks thick.'

Gordon explained that he had gone to the rear of the column to seek orders. He met an officer of the Queen's Rangers, a Loyalist corps consisting of both infantry and cavalry; that officer related that 'Col. Gordon came up to me where I was standing, and requested the loan of a spy-glass I held in my hand. I gave him the glass, and accompanied him into an orchard on the left of the road.' Another officer mentioned that Gordon 'had flowers in his hat, which made him remarkable.' The enemy may have found this man in a flowered hat an attractive target, for 'whilst leaning there against a fence, observing the Rebels, a cannon-ball from them struck the fence, directly by his side.' Another deponent recalled, 'there was an officer of the Guards who told him he had better take the flowers out of his hat, for he (the Officer) thought the Rebels aimed at him.'

Others remembered seeing Gordon, apparently after this close call, on the near side of a hedge, and 'he appeared to be moving, almost on his hands and feet.' Another deponent saw him 'standing in a loose manner, with his hat off, wiping his face.' When the Guards ascended the hill, Gordon was in the rear, 'ascending it, on foot, and out of breath'; he was later seen 'sitting on a stone near the bottom of the hill.' This testimony even brought out an interesting personal detail about one officer; Captain Thomas Swanton of the 3rd Regiment of Foot Guards commented that 'the distance was not very great; though he himself was very near-sighted, he could distinguish Col. Gordon.'

One witness mentioned a troop of German Hussars who wore 'high, white caps,' but another disputed this, asserting that 'no part of the Cavalry with Gen. Matthew's brigade had white in their caps.' Captain Frederick Diemar's troop of cavalry, assembled from Brunswick soldiers in British service who had escaped from captivity, 'were dressed in blue, with tall black caps,' according to a deponent. Another testified that 'the Troop of Horse belonging to the Queen's Rangers, were dressed in short green coats, and high black caps,' while 'the Cavalry belonging to the Jagers were certainly dressed in long green coats, and cocked hats.'

A particularly interesting comment came from Lieutenant Augustus O'Hara of the Royal Artillery, who commanded the two guns attached to the Brigade of Guards. When these guns engaged the enemy in the orchard, Lieutenant Colonel Gordon spent some time offering recommendations on where to fire. One would think that, given Gordon's higher rank, the artillery officer would see himself as subordinate, but O'Hara testified, 'Col. Gordon gave him a great many directions; but he did not pay any attention to them, as he thought himself the best judge of the firing of his own guns.' Another comment by O'Hara implies that the guns and limbers were normally drawn by horses, but illustrates the importance of improvisation and fast movement on the battlefield; O'Hara said that 'He was obliged to draw one of his guns some hundred yards by men, which occasioned his limbers with the ammunition to be left behind; he therefore halted the guns till the ammunition could be brought up.'

A few other incidental details were mentioned by deponents in the trial. One described the road as being bordered by a 'little stone wall, with a single rail at top' which a person 'could have vaulted over … with the assistance of a stick' – although the relevance of this last observation is not apparent. Thomas Hobbs, a private soldier in the Guards, was a servant to Lieutenant Colonel Thomas. On the day of battle, 'he had the care of a horse and pair of canteens belonging to Col. Howard, and of a few things belonging to Col. Thomas.' Shortly before the action in the orchard began, Hobbs stopped 'to repair his canteens,' but the trial proceedings offer no details of the nature of these canteens or the repairs.

According to testimony, in the months after the battle Lieutenant Colonel Thomas talked disparagingly to his fellow officers about Lieutenant Colonel Gordon's apparent neglect of duty. Word got back to Gordon, who even heard rumours that officers in the brigade proposed 'sending him to Coventry,' a euphemism still in use that refers to ostracizing someone. This talk led to the trial of Lieutenant Colonel Thomas in 1780, which in turn led to the trial of Lieutenant Colonel Gordon in 1782. The court, after hearing extensive accounts from witnesses in both trials, found both of the defendants innocent of the charges.

Two trials and two acquittals should have been enough. But it was not. By June 1783 both men were back in London and their dispute continued. Gordon ultimately demanded 'satisfaction' from Thomas. They met on the morning of 6 September 1783 'at the ring at Hyde Park' and, attended by seconds, exchanged shots. Both men were wounded, but Gordon's injury was slight while Thomas's was fatal, and he soon expired. A year later Gordon was tried for murder before a civil court and was once again acquitted.[19]

Conclusion

Trial testimony does not change our broad understanding of the war's course or the outcomes of battles. What they do offer are remarkable details on army operations, material culture, and even physical attributes of individuals. They reveal much about the difficulties of discerning events as they unfolded, making decisions with incomplete and uncertain information, and communicating amid the mayhem of combat. Personality conflicts, recent illness, youthful inexperience, and even near-sightedness played small but meaningful roles in how officers behaved in battle.

Bibliography

Primary Sources
Library of Congress, Washington, DC
    A topographical chart of the bay of Narraganset in the province of New England
The National Archives, Kew, UK (TNA)
    WO 12/1246: Muster rolls, 16th Light Dragoons
    WO 12/2750: Muster rolls, 10th Regiment of Foot
    WO 25/210: Succession books, 1764-1771

---

19   Anon., *The Trial of Cosmo Gordon, Esq., Commonly Called the Honourable Cosmo Gordon, for the Wilful Murder of Frederick Thomas, Esq In a Duel in Hyde Park, on the Fourth of September, 1783: who was Tried at Justice Hall in the Old Bailey, on Friday the 17th of September, 1784* (London: E. Hodgson, 1784).

WO 65/26: 1776 printed annual army list
WO 65/30: 1780 printed annual army list
WO 71/84: Trial of Henry Evatt
WO 71/87: Trial of John Vatas
WO 71/87: Trial of Richard Blackmore
WO 71/87: Trial of Daniel McGuin
WO 71/93: Trial of Henry Johnson
University Library, University of Durham: Journal of Viscount Cantilupe

Printed Primary Sources
Anon. (ed.), *Collections of the New York Historical Society for the year 1883* (New York: New York Historical Society, 1884)
Anon., *The Trial of Cosmo Gordon, Esq., Commonly Called the Honourable Cosmo Gordon, for the Wilful Murder of Frederick Thomas, Esq In a Duel in Hyde Park, on the Fourth of September, 1783: who was Tried at Justice Hall in the Old Bailey, on Friday the 17th of September, 1784* (London: E. Hodgson, 1784)
Anon., *The Trial of Lieut. Col. Thomas, of the First Regiment of Foot Guards, on a Charge exhibited by Lieut. Col. Cosmo Gordon, for aspersing his Character ...* (London: J. Ridley, 1781)
Anon., *The Trial of the Hon. Col. Cosmo Gordon, of the Third Regiment of Foot-Guards, for Neglect of Duty before the Enemy ...* (London: G. Harlow, 1783)
Chase, Philander D. and Edward G. Lengel (eds), *The Papers of George Washington, Revolutionary War Series, vol.11, 19 August 1777–25 October 1777* (Charlottesville: University Press of Virginia, 2001)
Gruber, Ira D. (ed.), *John Peebles American War: the Diary of a Scottish Grenadier, 1776-1782* (Mechanicsburg, PA: Stackpole Books, for the Army Records Society, 1998)
Mackenzie, Frederick, *The Diary of Frederick Mackenzie* (Cambridge, MA: Harvard University Press, 1930)

Secondary Sources
Hagist, Don N., *Noble Volunteers: the British Soldiers who fought the American Revolution* (Yardley: Westholme, 2020)
Lichtenwanger, William, 'The Music of "The Star-Spangled Banner": From Ludgate Hill to Capitol Hill', *The Quarterly Journal of the Library of Congress*, vol.34, no.3 (July 1977), pp.136–170
Loprieno, Don, *The Enterprise in Contemplation: the Midnight Assault of Stony Point* (Westminster, MD: Heritage Books, 2009)
Marshall, Douglas W. and Howard H. Peckham, *Campaigns of the American Revolution: an Atlas of Battlefield Maps* (Ann Arbor, MI: The University of Michigan Press, 1976)

Index

From Reason to Revolution – Warfare 1721-1815

http://www.helion.co.uk/series/from-reason-to-revolution-1721-1815.php

The 'From Reason to Revolution' series covers the period of military history 1721–1815, an era in which fortress-based strategy and linear battles gave way to the nation-in-arms and the beginnings of total war.

This era saw the evolution and growth of light troops of all arms, and of increasingly flexible command systems to cope with the growing armies fielded by nations able to mobilise far greater proportions of their manpower than ever before. Many of these developments were fired by the great political upheavals of the era, with revolutions in America and France bringing about social change which in turn fed back into the military sphere as whole nations readied themselves for war. Only in the closing years of the period, as the reactionary powers began to regain the upper hand, did a military synthesis of the best of the old and the new become possible.

The series will examine the military and naval history of the period in a greater degree of detail than has hitherto been attempted, and has a very wide brief, with the intention of covering all aspects from the battles, campaigns, logistics, and tactics, to the personalities, armies, uniforms, and equipment.

Submissions

The publishers would be pleased to receive submissions for this series. Please contact series editor Andrew Bamford via email (andrewbamford@helion.co.uk), or in writing to Helion & Company Limited, Unit 8 Amherst Business Centre, Budbrooke Road, Warwick, CV34 5WE

Titles